"*The Ominous Parallels* offers a truly revolutionary idea. . . . The book is clear, tight, disciplined, beautifully structured, and brilliantly reasoned. Its style is clear and hard as crystal—and as sparkling. . . . As to my personal reaction, I can express it best by paraphrasing a line from *Atlas Shrugged*: 'It's so wonderful to see a great, new, crucial achievement which is not mine!' "
                                        —Ayn Rand

"Extraordinarily perceptive . . . frightening insights. . . . Everyone concerned with the collectivist trend in today's world should read this book."   —Alan Greenspan

"A fascinating weave of German history, philosophic determinism, and Objectivist polemic."   —*Chicago Tribune*

THE
OMINOUS PARALLELS

LEONARD PEIKOFF is universally recognized as the pre-eminent Rand scholar writing today. He worked closely with Ayn Rand for thirty years and was designated by her as her intellectual heir and heir to her estate. He has taught philosophy at Hunter College, Long Island University, and New York University and is now host of the national radio talk show *Philosophy: Who Needs It*.

THE OMINOUS PARALLELS
The End of
Freedom in America

by
Leonard Peikoff

Introduction by Ayn Rand

A MERIDIAN BOOK

MERIDIAN
Published by Penguin Group
Penguin Group (USA) Inc., 375 Hudson Street, New York, New York 10014, U.S.A.
Penguin Group (Canada), 90 Eglinton Avenue East, Suite 700, Toronto,
Ontario, Canada M4P 2Y3 (a division of Pearson Penguin Canada Inc.)
Penguin Books Ltd., 80 Strand, London WC2R 0RL, England
Penguin Ireland, 25 St. Stephen's Green, Dublin 2, Ireland
(a division of Penguin Books Ltd.)
Penguin Group (Australia), 250 Camberwell Road, Camberwell, Victoria 3124,
Australia (a division of Pearson Australia Group Pty. Ltd.)
Penguin Books India Pvt. Ltd., 11 Community Centre, Panchsheel Park,
New Delhi – 110 017, India
Penguin Group (NZ), 67 Apollo Drive, Rosedale, North Shore 0745, Auckland,
New Zealand (a division of Pearson New Zealand Ltd.)
Penguin Books (South Africa) (Pty.) Ltd., 24 Sturdee Avenue, Rosebank,
Johannesburg 2196, South Africa

Penguin Books Ltd., Registered Offices: 80 Strand, London WC2R 0RL, England

Published by Meridian, a member of Penguin Group (USA) Inc.
Previously published in a Mentor edition.

First Meridian Printing, July 1993
17 19 20 18

CIP data is available

Printed in the United States of America

Contents

Introduction

It gives me great pleasure to introduce the first book by an Objectivist philosopher other than myself.

Perhaps the best recommendation I can give this book—and its author, Dr. Leonard Peikoff—is to say that it and he are not of today's cultural mainstream. They will be part of tomorrow's.

It is not necessary for me to prove that something is wrong with today's world. Everybody—of any creed, color, or intellectual persuasion, old and young, rich and poor, conservative and liberal, foreign and domestic—senses that something monstrous is destroying the world. But no one knows what it is, and people keep blaming one another—with some justice.

As a symptom of today's cultural anxiety, observe the unusual interest in and the deluge of books dealing with Nazi Germany. Every sort of semi-plausible and wholly impossible theory has been offered in futile attempts to find the cause and explain the rise of Nazism. The failure of those explanations intensifies the quest: men seem to sense that the collapse of what had been a civilized country into such monstrous evil must be understood if we are to make certain that it will not be repeated. "We dare not brush aside unexplained a horror such as Nazism," states Dr. Peikoff. If we do not know its causes, how can we be sure that our own country is not traveling the same road?

Dr. Peikoff answers these questions. He identifies the cause of Nazism—and the ominous parallels between the intellectual history of Germany and of the United States. He demonstrates that there is a science which has been all but obliterated in the modern world. "Yet this science determines the destiny of nations and the course of history . . . ," he writes. "It is the science which had to be destroyed, if the catastrophes of our time were to become possible. The science is *philosophy*."

The non-modern (and non-old-fashioned) aspect of Leonard Peikoff's book is the breadth of his vision and the stunning scale of his philosophic integration. He does not share the concrete-bound, college-induced myopia of those alleged philosophers who study the various meanings of the word "but" (the contemporary empiricists)—nor does he share the foggy stumbling and the floating abstractions of their predecessors (the rationalists). He presents the history of Germany's philosophy, in telling essentials—then the history of America's philosophy and what destroyed it. (The chapter "The Nation of the Enlightenment" is the most inspired and inspiring tribute to the Founding Fathers that I have ever read.) Then he presents the practical results—the way in which philosophic ideas direct the course and shape the particular events of the history of both countries, as reflected in politics, economics, art, literature, education, etc.

This last is the cardinal achievement of Dr. Peikoff's book. While today's philosophy departments make it a loud point to proclaim that philosophy has nothing to do with practical life or with reality (which, they add, does not exist)—Dr. Peikoff shows to their mangled victims what philosophy is, what it does, and how to recognize its influence all around us. He gives a virtuoso performance of shuttling effortlessly between abstractions and concretes—keeping the first tied firmly to reality and thus illuminating the second. He shows that a nation brought up to regard the principles of duty and self-sacrifice as cardinal virtues will be helpless when confronted by a gang of thugs who demand obedience and self-sacrifice.

It is a tragic irony of our time that the two worst, bloodiest tribes in history, the Nazis of Germany and the Communists of Soviet Russia, both of whom are motivated by brute power-lust and a crudely materialistic greed for the unearned, show respect for the power of philosophy (they call it "ideology") and spend billions of their looted wealth on propaganda and indoctrination, realizing that man's mind is their most dangerous enemy and it is man's mind that they have to destroy—while the United States and the other countries of the West, who claim to believe in the superiority of the human spirit over matter, neglect philosophy, despise ideas, starve the best minds of the young, offer nothing but the stalest slogans of a materialistic altruism in the form of global giveaways, and wonder why they are losing the world to the thugs.

As an example of why the cause of Nazism should be understood (but is not), I would like to mention a recent television interview with Helmut Schmidt, Chancellor of West

Germany. Asked to name his favorite philosopher, he answered —in a changed tone of voice, a stiff, solemn, deaf-and-blind, heel-clicking tone—"Marcus Aurelius. He taught that we must do our duty above all." If he is typical of his country (and I believe he is), Germany has learned nothing.

The ineffable monster destroying the world is not an entity but a vacuum, an absence, the emptiness left by the collapse of philosophy. In that lightless emptiness, mindless men rattle frantically, bumping into one another, seeking desperately some way to exist on earth—which they cannot find without the tool they have discarded. This leads to phenomena such as Nazi Germany or Soviet Russia, as Dr. Peikoff demonstrates.

If you do not wish to be a victim of today's philosophical bankruptcy, I recommend *The Ominous Parallels* as protection and ammunition. It will protect you from supporting, unwittingly, the ideas that are destroying you and the world. It will bring order into the chaos of today's events—and show you simultaneously the enormity of the battle and the contemptible smallness of the enemy.

The Ominous Parallels offers a truly revolutionary idea in the field of the philosophy of history. The book is clear, tight, disciplined, beautifully structured, and brilliantly reasoned. Its style is clear and hard as crystal—and as sparkling. If you like my works, you will like this book.

As to my personal reaction, I can express it best by paraphrasing a line from *Atlas Shrugged:* "It's so wonderful to see a great, new, crucial achievement which is not mine!"

AYN RAND

New York
November 1980

PART ONE

THEORY

1

The Cause of Nazism

Here is the theory:

"It is thus necessary that the individual should finally come to realize that his own ego is of no importance in comparison with the existence of his nation; that the position of the individual ego is conditioned solely by the interests of the nation as a whole . . . that above all the unity of a nation's spirit and will are worth far more than the freedom of the spirit and will of an individual. . . ."

"This state of mind, which subordinates the interests of the ego to the conservation of the community, is really the first premise for every truly human culture. . . . The basic attitude from which such activity arises, we call—to distinguish it from egoism and selfishness—idealism. By this we understand only the individual's capacity to make sacrifices for the community, for his fellow men."

These statements were made in our century by the leader of a major Western nation. His countrymen regarded his viewpoint as uncontroversial. His political program implemented it faithfully.

The statements were made by Adolf Hitler. He was explaining the moral philosophy of Nazism.[1]

And here is the ultimate practice (as described by William Shirer in *The Rise and Fall of the Third Reich*):

"The gas chambers themselves [at Auschwitz] and the adjoining crematoria, viewed from a short distance, were not sinister-looking places at all; it was impossible to make them out for what they were. Over them were well-kept lawns with flower borders; the signs at the entrances merely said BATHS. The unsuspecting Jews thought they were simply being taken to the baths for the delousing which was cus-

13

tomary at all camps. And taken to the accompaniment of sweet music!

"For there was light music. An orchestra of 'young and pretty girls all dressed in white blouses and navy-blue skirts,' as one survivor remembered, had been formed from among the inmates. While the selection was being made for the gas chambers this unique musical ensemble played gay tunes from *The Merry Widow* and *Tales of Hoffmann*. Nothing solemn and somber from Beethoven. The death marches at Auschwitz were sprightly and merry tunes, straight out of Viennese and Parisian operetta.

"To such music, recalling as it did happier and more frivolous times, the men, women and children were led into the 'bath houses,' where they were told to undress preparatory to taking a 'shower.' Sometimes they were even given towels. Once they were inside the 'shower-room'—and perhaps this was the first moment that they may have suspected something was amiss, for as many as two thousand of them were packed into the chamber like sardines, making it difficult to take a bath—the massive door was slid shut, locked and hermetically sealed. Up above where the well-groomed lawn and flower beds almost concealed the mushroom-shaped lids of vents that ran up from the hall of death, orderlies stood ready to drop into them the amethyst-blue crystals of hydrogen cyanide. . . .

"Surviving prisoners watching from blocks nearby remembered how for a time the signal for the orderlies to pour the crystals down the vents was given by a Sergeant Moll. *'Na, gib ihnen schon zu fressen'* ('All right, give 'em something to chew on'), he would laugh and the crystals would be poured through the openings, which were then sealed.

"Through heavy-glass portholes the executioners could watch what happened. The naked prisoners below would be looking up at the showers from which no water spouted or perhaps at the floor wondering why there were no drains. It took some moments for the gas to have much effect. But soon the inmates became aware that it was issuing from the perforations in the vents. It was then that they usually panicked, crowding away from the pipes and finally stampeding toward the huge metal door where, as Reitlinger puts it, 'they piled up in one blue clammy blood-spattered pyramid, clawing and mauling each other even in death.' "[2]

The Nazis were not a tribe of prehistoric savages. Their crimes were the official, legal acts and policies of modern Germany—an educated, industrialized, *civilized* Western European nation, a nation renowned throughout the world for the luster of its intellectual and cultural achievements. By reason of its long line of famous artists and thinkers, Germany has been called "the land of poets and philosophers."

But its education offered the country no protection against the Sergeant Molls in its ranks. The German university students were among the earliest groups to back Hitler. The intellectuals were among his regime's most ardent supporters. Professors with distinguished academic credentials, eager to pronounce their benediction on the Führer's cause, put their scholarship to work full time; they turned out a library of admiring volumes, adorned with obscure allusions and learned references.

The Nazis did not gain power against the country's wishes. In this respect there was no gulf between the intellectuals and the people. The Nazi party was elected to office by the freely cast ballots of millions of German voters, including men on every social, economic, and educational level. In the national election of July 1932, the Nazis obtained 37 percent of the vote and a plurality of seats in the Reichstag. On January 30, 1933, in full accordance with the country's legal and constitutional principles, Hitler was appointed Chancellor. Five weeks later, in the last (and semi-free) election of the pre-totalitarian period, the Nazis obtained 17 million votes, 44 percent of the total.

The voters were aware of the Nazi ideology. Nazi literature, including statements of the Nazi plans for the future, papered the country during the last years of the Weimar Republic. *Mein Kampf* alone sold more than 200,000 copies between 1925 and 1932. The essence of the political system which Hitler intended to establish in Germany was clear.

In 1933, when Hitler did establish the system he had promised, he did not find it necessary to forbid foreign travel. Until World War II, those Germans who wished to flee the country could do so. The overwhelming majority did not. They were satisfied to remain.

The system which Hitler established—the social reality which so many Germans were so eager to embrace or so willing to endure—the politics which began in a theory and ended in Auschwitz—was: the "total state." The term, from which the adjective "totalitarian" derives, was coined by Hitler's mentor, Mussolini.

The state must have absolute power over every man and over every sphere of human activity, the Nazis declared. "The authority of the Führer is not limited by checks and controls, by special autonomous bodies or individual rights, but it is free and independent, all-inclusive and unlimited," said Ernst Huber, an official party spokesman, in 1933.

"The concept of personal liberties of the individual as opposed to the authority of the state had to disappear; it is not to be reconciled with the principle of the nationalistic Reich," said Huber to a country which listened, and nodded. "There are no personal liberties of the individual which fall outside of the realm of the state and which must be respected by the state. . . . The constitution of the nationalistic Reich is therefore not based upon a system of inborn and inalienable rights of the individual."[8]

If the term "statism" designates concentration of power in the state at the expense of individual liberty, then Nazism in politics was a form of statism. In principle, it did not represent a new approach to government; it was a continuation of the political absolutism—the absolute monarchies, the oligarchies, the theocracies, the random tyrannies—which has characterized most of human history.

In degree, however, the total state does differ from its predecessors: it represents statism pressed to its limits, in theory and in practice, devouring the last remnants of the individual. Although previous dictators (and many today; e.g., in Latin America) often preached the unlimited power of the state, they were on the whole unable to enforce such power. As a rule, citizens of such countries had a kind of partial "freedom," not a freedom-on-principle, but at least a freedom-by-default.

Even the latter was effectively absent in Nazi Germany. The efficiency of the government in dominating its subjects, the all-encompassing character of its coercion, the complete mass regimentation on a scale involving millions of men— and, one might add, the enormity of the slaughter, the planned, systematic mass slaughter, in peacetime, initiated by a government against its own citizens—these are the insignia of twentieth-century totalitarianism (Nazi *and* communist), which are without parallel in recorded history. In the totalitarian regimes, as the Germans found out after only a few months of Hitler's rule, every detail of life is prescribed, or proscribed. There is no longer any distinction between private matters and public matters. "There are to be no more private Germans," said Friedrich Sieburg, a Nazi writer; "each is to attain significance only by his service to the state, and to find complete self-fulfillment in this service." "The only person who is still a private individual in Germany," boasted Robert Ley, a member of the Nazi hierarchy, after several years of Nazi rule, "is somebody who is asleep."[4]

In place of the despised "private individuals," the Germans heard daily or hourly about a different kind of entity, a supreme entity, whose will, it was said, is what determines the course and actions of the state: the nation, the whole, the *group*. Over and over, the Germans heard the idea that underlies the advocacy of omnipotent government, the idea that totalitarians of every kind stress as the justification of their total states: *collectivism*.

Collectivism is the theory that the group (the collective) has primacy over the individual. Collectivism holds that, in human affairs, the collective—society, the community, the nation, the proletariat, the race, etc.—is *the unit of reality and the standard of value*. On this view, the individual has reality only as part of the group, and value only insofar as he serves it; on his own he has no political rights; he is to be sacrificed for the group whenever it—or its representative, the state— deems this desirable.

Fascism, said one of its leading spokesmen, Alfredo Rocco, stresses

> the necessity, for which the older doctrines make little allowance, of sacrifice, even up to the total immolation of individuals, in behalf of society. . . . For Liberalism [i.e., individualism], the individual is the end and society the means; nor is it conceivable that the individual, considered in the dignity of an ultimate finality, be lowered to mere instrumentality. For Fascism, society is the end, individuals the means, and its whole life consists in using individuals as instruments for its social ends.[5]

"[T]he higher interests involved in the life of the whole,"

said Hitler in a 1933 speech, "must here set the limits and lay down the duties of the interests of the individual." Men, echoed the Nazis, have to "realize that the State is more important than the individual, that individuals must be willing and ready to sacrifice themselves for Nation and Führer." The people, said the Nazis, "form a true organism," a "living unity," whose cells are individual persons. In reality, therefore—appearances to the contrary notwithstanding—there is no such thing as an "isolated individual" or an autonomous man.[6]

Just as the individual is to be regarded merely as a fragment of the group, the Nazis said, so his possessions are to be regarded as a fragment of the group's wealth.

> "Private property" as conceived under the liberalistic economic order was a reversal of the true concept of property [wrote Huber]. This "private property" represented the right of the individual to manage and to speculate with inherited or acquired property as he pleased, without regard for the general interests. . . . German socialism had to overcome this "private," that is, unrestrained and irresponsible view of property. All property is common property. The owner is bound by the people and the Reich to the responsible management of his goods. His legal position is only justified when he satisfies this responsibility to the community.[7]

Contrary to the Marxists, the Nazis did not advocate public ownership of the means of production. They did demand that the government oversee and run the nation's economy. The issue of legal ownership, they explained, is secondary; what counts is the issue of *control*. Private citizens, therefore, may continue to hold titles to property—so long as the state reserves to itself the unqualified right to regulate the use of their property.

If "ownership" means the right to determine the use and disposal of material goods, then Nazism endowed the state with every real prerogative of ownership. What the individual retained was merely a formal deed, a contentless deed, which conferred no rights on its holder. Under communism, there is collective ownership of property *de jure*. Under Nazism, there is the same collective ownership *de facto*.

During the Hitler years—in order to finance the party's programs, including the war expenditures—every social group in Germany was mercilessly exploited and drained. White-collar salaries and the earnings of small businessmen were deliberately held down by government controls, freezes, taxes. Big business was bled by taxes and "special contributions" of every kind, and strangled by the bureaucracy. (Amid "the Niagara of thousands of special decrees and laws," writes Shirer, "even the most astute businessman was often lost, and special lawyers had to be employed to enable a firm to function. The graft involved in finding one's way to key officials . . . became in the late thirties astronomical."[8]) At the same time the income of the farmers was held down, and there was a desperate flight to the cities—where the middle class, especially the small tradesmen, were soon in desperate straits, and where the workers were forced to labor at low wages for increasingly longer hours (up to 60 or more per week).

But the Nazis defended their policies, and the country did not rebel; it accepted the Nazi argument. Selfish individuals may be unhappy, the Nazis said, but what we have established in Germany is the ideal system, *socialism*. In its Nazi usage this term is not restricted to a theory of economics; it is to be understood in a fundamental sense. "Socialism" for the Nazis denotes the principle of collectivism as such and its corollary, statism—in every field of human action, including but not limited to economics.

"To be a socialist," says Goebbels, "is to submit the I to the thou; socialism is sacrificing the individual to the whole."[9]

By this definition, the Nazis practiced what they preached. They practiced it at home and then abroad. No one can claim that they did not sacrifice enough individuals.

The question is: why?

What could explain a system such as Nazism? What permitted it to happen?

An evil of such magnitude cannot be a product of superficial factors. In order to make it, and its German popularity, intelligible, one must penetrate to its deepest, most hidden roots. One must grasp its nature and its causes in terms of *fundamentals*.

Unfortunately, this has not been the approach of most observers. As a rule, commentators have attempted to explain

Nazism by the opposite method: by the newspaper headlines or the practical crises of the moment.

It has been said, for instance, that the Germans embraced Nazism because they lost World War I. Austria lost that war also, but this did not cause it to turn Nazi (it went under only when invaded by Hitler in 1938). Italy, on the other hand, one of the victorious powers at the Versailles Conference of 1919, went Fascist in 1922.

It has been said that the cause of· Nazism was the Great Depression. All the industrial nations suffered the ravages of the Depression. Few turned to Nazism.

It has been said that the cause of Nazism was the weakness of the non-totalitarian parties in the Weimar Republic, the pressure-group warfare which they encouraged, and the governmental paralysis that followed. This does not explain *why* or in what basic respect the non-totalitarians were weak, nor does it take into account the many countries in which social clashes and governmental drifting have *not* led to Nazism.

There is no direct causal relationship or even any approximate correlation between specific practical crises (singly or in combination) and the development of Nazism. Practical crises confront a country with the need for action. They do not determine what the action will be. In the face of military ruin, economic strangulation, or governmental collapse, men may choose to investigate the disaster's causes and to discover a more rational course of action for the future, i.e., they may choose to think. Or they may choose to hate, or to pray, or to beg, or to kill. On such matters, the crisis itself is silent.

There are other interpretations of Nazism, besides the "practical crisis" theory.

Religious writers often claim that the cause of Nazism is the secularism or the scientific spirit of the modern world. This evades the facts that the Germans at the time, especially in Prussia, were one of the most religious peoples in Western Europe; that the Weimar Republic was a hotbed of mystic cults, of which Nazism was one; and that Germany's largest and most devout religious group, the Lutherans, counted themselves among Hitler's staunchest followers.

There is the Marxist interpretation of Nazism, according to which Hitler is the inevitable result of capitalism. This evades the facts that Germany after Bismarck was the least capitalistic country of Western Europe; that the Weimar Republic from the start was a controlled economy, with the controls growing steadily; and that the word "Nazism" is an abbreviation for "National Socialism."

There are the Aryan racists in reverse, who say that the cause of Nazism is the "innate depravity" of the Germans. This evades the fact that "depravity" is a moral concept, which implies that man is not predetermined but has free choice. It also evades the fact that regimes similar to Hitler's, regimes differing only in the degree of brutality they perpetrated, have appeared in our century across the globe—not only in Italy, Japan, Argentina, and the like, but also, in the form of communism, in Russia, China, and their satellites.

Then there is the Freudian interpretation, according to which the cause of Nazism is the Germans' Oedipus complex or their death wish or their toilet training, etc. This evades the fact that arbitrary constructs, such as Freud is famous for, can be manipulated to "explain" anything, and therefore explain nothing.

We dare not brush aside unexplained a horror such as Nazism.

Many writers have noted similarities between America today and Germany before Hitler, then have shrugged off their own observations—succumbing to the notion, spread by today's intellectuals, that it is bad history to compare two different countries. This notion, itself a symptom of our current crisis, means that there are no principles governing human action, and that it is bad history to learn from history.

The similarities, however, cannot be shrugged off. Our crisis is real. The crisis is the fact that our country, the United States of America—the freest, the most productive, and the most moral country in the world—is now moving in Hitler's direction.

America is moving toward a Nazi form of totalitarianism. It has been doing this for decades. It has been doing so gradually, by default, and for the most part unknowingly, but it is doing so systematically and without significant opposition. In every cultural area—from science and education to art and religion to politics and economics—the trend is now unmistakable.

There are differences between America and the Weimar Republic. Our future, as far as one can judge, is still indeterminate. But the current trend will not be checked unless we grasp, in terms of essentials, the ominous parallels between the two countries—and, above all, the basic cause behind those parallels. If we are to avoid a fate like that of Germany, we must find out what made such a fate possible. We must find out what, at root, is required to turn a country, Germany or any other, into a Nazi dictatorship; and then we must uproot that root.

We need to look for something deeper than *practical* conditions, something that dictates men's view of what constitutes the practical.

In an advanced, civilized country, a handful of men were able to gain for their criminal schemes the enthusiastic backing of millions of decent, educated, law-abiding citizens. What is the factor that made this possible?

Criminal groups and schemes have existed throughout history, in every country. They have been able to succeed only in certain periods. The mere presence of such groups is not sufficient to account for their victory. Something made so many Germans so vulnerable to a takeover. Something armed the criminals and disarmed the country.

Observe in this connection that the Nazis, correctly, regarded the power of propaganda as an indispensable tool.

The Nazis could not have won the support of the German masses but for the systematic preaching of a complex array of theories, doctrines, opinions, notions, beliefs. And not one of their central beliefs was original. They found those beliefs, widespread and waiting, in the culture; they seized upon them and broadcast them at top volume, thrusting them with a new intensity back into the streets of Germany. And the men in the streets heard and recognized and sympathized with and embraced those beliefs, and voted for their exponents.

The Germans would not have recognized or embraced those beliefs in the nineteenth century, when the West was still being influenced by the remnants of the Age of Reason and the Enlightenment, when the doctrines of the rights of man and the autonomy of the individual were paramount. But by the twentieth century such doctrines, and the convictions on which they depended, were paramount no longer.

Germany was *ideologically* ripe for Hitler. The *intellectual* groundwork had been prepared. The country's *ideas*—a certain special category of ideas—were ready.

There is a science whose subject matter is that category of ideas.

Today, in our colleges, this science has sunk to the lowest point in its history. Its teachers have declared that it has no questions to ask, no method to follow, no answers to offer. As a result, it is disappearing—losing its identity, its intelligibility, its students, and the last vestiges of its once noble reputation. No one—among the intellectuals or the general public—would suspect any longer that this science could be relevant to human life or action.

Yet this science determines the destiny of nations and the course of history. It is the source of a nation's frame of reference and code of values, the root of a people's character and culture, the fundamental cause shaping men's choices and decisions in every crucial area of their lives. It is the science which directs men to embrace this world or to seek out some other that is said to transcend it—which directs them to reason or superstition, to the pursuit of happiness or of self-sacrifice, to production or starvation, to freedom or slavery, to life or death. It is the science which made the difference between the East and the West, between the Middle Ages and the Renaissance, between the Founding Fathers of the new continent and the Adolf Hitlers of the old. It is the science which had to be destroyed, if the catastrophes of our time were to become possible.

The science is *philosophy*.

Philosophy is the study of the nature of existence, of knowledge, and of values.

The branch of philosophy that studies existence is *metaphysics*. Metaphysics identifies the nature of the universe as a whole. It tells men what kind of world they live in, and whether there is a supernatural dimension beyond it. It tells men whether they live in a world of solid entities, natural laws, absolute facts, or in a world of illusory fragments, unpredictable miracles, and ceaseless flux. It tells men whether the things they perceive by their senses and mind form a comprehensible reality, with which they can deal, or some kind of unreal appearance, which leaves them staring and helpless.

The branch of philosophy that studies knowledge is *epistemology*. Epistemology identifies the proper means of acquiring knowledge. It tells men which mental processes to employ as methods of cognition, and which to reject as invalid or deceptive. Above all, epistemology tells men whether reason is their faculty of gaining knowledge, and if so how it works—or whether there is a means of knowledge other than reason, such as faith, or the instinct of society, or the feelings of the dictator.

The branch of philosophy that studies values is *ethics* (or morality), which rests on both the above branches—on a view of the world in which man acts, and of man's nature, including his means of knowledge. Ethics defines a code of values to guide human actions. It tells men the proper purpose of man's life, and the means of achieving it; it provides the standard by which men are to judge good and evil, right and wrong, the desirable and the undesirable. Ethics tells a man, for instance, to pursue his own fulfillment—or to sacrifice himself for the sake of something else, such as God or his neighbor.

The branch of philosophy that applies ethics to social questions is *politics*, which studies the nature of social systems and the proper functions of government. Politics is not the start, but the product of a philosophic system. By their nature, political questions cannot be raised or judged except on the basis of some view of existence, of values, and of man's proper means of knowledge.

Since men cannot live or act without some kind of basic guidance, the issues of philosophy in some form necessarily affect every man, in every social group and class. Most men, however, do not consider such issues in explicit terms. They absorb their ideas—implicitly, eclectically, and with many contradictions—from the cultural atmosphere around them, building into their souls without identifying it the various ideological vibrations emanating from school and church and arts and media and mores.

A cultural atmosphere is not a primary. It is created, ultimately, by a handful of men: by those whose lifework it is to deal with, originate, and propagate fundamental ideas. For the great majority of men the influence of philosophy is indirect and unrecognized. But it is real.

The root cause of Nazism lies in a power that most people ignore, disparage—and underestimate. The cause is not the events hailed or cursed in headlines and street rallies, but the esoteric writings of the professors who, decades or centuries earlier, laid the foundation for those events. The symbol of the cause is not the munitions plants or union halls or bank vaults of Germany, but its ivory towers. What came out of the towers in this regard is only coils of obscure, virtually indecipherable jargon. But that jargon is fatal.

"[The Nazi] death camps," notes a writer in *The New York Times*, "were conceived, built and often administered by Ph.D.'s."[10]

What had those Ph.D.'s been taught to think in their schools and universities—and *where did such ideas come from?*

2

The Totalitarian Universe

It took centuries and a brain-stopping chain of falsehoods to bring a whole people to the state of Hitler-worship. Modern German culture, including its Nazi climax, is the result of a complex development in the history of philosophy, involving dozens of figures stretching back to the beginnings of Western thought. The same figures helped to shape every Western nation; but in other countries, to varying extents, the results were mixed, because there was also an opposite influence or antidote at work. In Germany, by the turn of our century, the cultural atmosphere was unmixed; the traces of the antidote had long since disappeared, and the intellectual establishment was monolithic.

If we view the West's philosophic development in terms of essentials, three fateful turning points stand out, three major philosophers who, above all others, are responsible for generating the disease of collectivism and transmitting it to the dictators of our century.

The three are: Plato—Kant—Hegel. (The antidote to them is: Aristotle.)

Plato is the father of collectivism in the West. He is the first thinker to formulate a systematic view of reality, with a collectivist politics as its culmination. In essence, Plato's metaphysics holds that the universe consists of two opposed dimensions: true reality—a perfect, immutable, supernatural realm, nonmaterial, nonspatial, nontemporal, nonperceivable—and the material world in which we live. The material world, Plato holds, is only an imperfect appearance of true reality, a semireal reflection or projection of it. (Because Plato's metaphysics holds that reality is thus fundamentally spiritual or nonmaterial in nature, it is described technically in philosophy as "idealism.")

The content of true reality, according to Plato, is a set of universals or Forms—in effect, a set of disembodied abstractions representing that which is in common among various groups of particulars in this world. Thus for Plato abstractions are supernatural existents. They are nonmaterial entities in another dimension, independent of man's mind and of any of their material embodiments. The Forms, Plato tells us repeatedly, are what is really real. The particulars they subsume—the concretes that make up this world—are not; they have only a shadowy, dreamlike half-reality.

Momentous conclusions about man are implicit in this metaphysics (and were later made explicit by a long line of Platonists): since individual men are merely particular instances of the universal "man," they are not ultimately real. What is real about men is only the Form which they share in common and reflect. To common sense, there appear to be many separate, individual men, each independent of the others, each fully real in his own right. To Platonism, this is a deception; all the seemingly individual men are *really* the same one Form, in various reflections or manifestations. Thus, all men ultimately comprise one unity, and no earthly man is an autonomous entity—just as, if a man were reflected in a multifaceted mirror, the many reflections would not be autonomous entities.

What follows in regard to human action, according to Plato, is a life of self-sacrificial service. When men gather in society, says Plato, the unit of reality, and the standard of value, is the "community as a whole." Each man therefore must strive, as far as he can, to wipe out his individuality (his personal desires, ambitions, etc.) and merge himself into the community, becoming one with it and living only to serve its welfare. On this view, the collective is not an aggregate, but an entity. Society (the state) is regarded as a living organism (this is the so-called "organic theory of the state"), and the individual becomes merely a cell of this organism's body, with no more rights or privileges than belong to any such cell.

"The first and highest form of the state and of the government and of the law," Plato writes, is a condition

in which the private and individual is altogether banished from life, and things which are by nature private,
such as eyes and ears and hands, have become common,
and in some way see and hear and act in common, and
all men express praise and blame and feel joy and sor-
row on the same occasions, and whatever laws there are
unite the city to the utmost. ...

As for those individualistic terms "mine" and "not mine,"
"another's" and "not another's": "The best ordered state will
be the one in which the largest number of persons use these
terms in the same sense, and which accordingly most nearly
resembles a single person."[1]

The advocacy of the omnipotent state follows from the
above as a matter of course. The function and authority of
the state, according to Plato, should be unlimited. The state
should indoctrinate the citizens with government-approved
ideas in government-run schools, censor all art and literature
and philosophy, assign men their vocations as they come of
age, regulate their economic—and in certain cases even their
sexual—activities, etc. The program of government domination of the individual is thoroughly worked out. In Plato's
Republic and *Laws* one can read the details, which are the
first blueprint of the totalitarian ideal.

The blueprint includes the view that the state should be
ruled by a special elite: the philosophers. Their title to absolute power, Plato explains, is their special wisdom, a wisdom
which derives from their insight into true reality, and especially into its supreme, governing principle: the so-called
"Form of the Good." Without a grasp of this Form, according to Plato, no man can understand the universe or
know how to conduct his life.

But to grasp this crucial principle, Plato continues—and
here one can begin to see the relevance of epistemology to
politics—the mind is inadequate. The Form of the Good cannot be known by the use of reason; it cannot be reached by a
process of logic; it transcends human concepts and human
language; it cannot be defined, described, or discussed. It can
be grasped, after years of an ascetic preparation, only by an
ineffable mystic experience—a kind of sudden, incommunica-
ble revelation or intuition, which is reserved to the philosophical elite. The mass of men, by contrast, are entangled in the

personal concerns of this life. They are enslaved to the lower world revealed to them by their senses. They are incapable of achieving mystic contact with a supernatural principle. They are fit only to obey orders.

Such, in its essentials, is the view of reality, of man, and of the state which one of the most influential philosophers of all time infused into the stream of Western culture. It has served ever since as the basic theoretical foundation by reference to which aspiring and actual dictators, ancient and modern, have sought to justify their political systems.

Some of those dictators never read or even heard of Plato, but absorbed his kind of ideas indirectly, at home, in church, in the streets, or from the gutter. Some, however, did go back to the source. Plato, notes Walter Kaufmann,

> was widely read in German schools [under the Nazis], and special editions were prepared for Greek classes in the *Gymnasium*, gathering together allegedly fascist passages. . . . Instead of compiling a list of the many similar contributions to the Plato literature, it may suffice to mention that Dr. Hans F. K. Günther, from whom the Nazis admittedly received their racial theories, also devoted a whole book to Plato. . . .

As to Alfred Rosenberg, Hitler's official ideologist, he "celebrates Plato as 'one who wanted in the end to save his people on a racial basis, through a forcible constitution, dictatorial in every detail.' "[2]

If mankind has not perished from such constitutions, if it has not collapsed permanently into the swamp of statism, but has fought its way up through tortured centuries of brief rises and long-drawn-out falls—like a man fighting paralysis by the power of an inexhaustible vitality—it is because that power had been provided by a giant whose philosophic system is, on virtually every fundamental issue, the opposite of Plato's. The great spokesman for man and for this earth is *Aristotle*.

Aristotle is the champion of this world, the champion of nature, as against the supernaturalism of Plato. Denying Plato's World of Forms, Aristotle maintains that there is only one reality: the world of particulars in which we live, the world men perceive by means of their physical senses. Universals, he holds, are merely aspects of existing entities, isolated in thought by a process of selective attention; they have no existence apart from particulars. Reality is comprised, not of Platonic abstractions, but of concrete, individual entities, each with a definite nature, each obeying the laws inherent in its nature. Aristotle's universe is the universe of science. The physical world, in his view, is not a shadowy projection controlled by a divine dimension, but an autonomous, self-sufficient realm. It is an orderly, intelligible, *natural* realm, open to the mind of man.

In such a universe, knowledge cannot be acquired by special revelations from another dimension; there is no place for ineffable intuitions of the beyond. Repudiating the mystical elements in Plato's epistemology, Aristotle is the father of logic and the champion of *reason* as man's only means of knowledge. Knowledge, he holds, must be based on and derived from the data of sense experience; it must be formulated in terms of objectively defined concepts; it must be validated by a process of logic.

For Plato, the good life is essentially one of renunciation and selflessness: man should flee from the pleasures of this world in the name of fidelity to a higher dimension, just as he should negate his own individuality in the name of union with the collective. But for Aristotle, the good life is one of personal self-fulfillment. Man should enjoy the values of this world. Using his mind to the fullest, each man should work to achieve his own happiness here on earth. And in the process he should be conscious of his *own* value. Pride, writes Aristotle—a rational pride in oneself and in one's moral character—is, when it is earned, the "crown of the virtues."[8]

A proud man does not negate his own identity. He does not sink selflessly into the community. He is not a promising subject for the Platonic state.

Although Aristotle's writings do include a polemic against the more extreme features of Plato's collectivism, Aristotle himself is not a consistent advocate of political individualism. His own politics is a mixture of statist and antistatist elements. But the primary significance of Aristotle, or of any philosopher, does not lie in his politics. It lies in the fundamentals of his system: his metaphysics and epistemology.

It has been said that, in his basic attitude toward life, every man is either Platonic or Aristotelian. The same may be said of periods of Western history. The medieval period, under the sway of such philosophers as Plotinus and Augustine, was an era dominated by Platonism. During much of this period Aristotle's philosophy was almost unknown in the West. But, owing largely to the influence of Thomas Aquinas, Aristotle was rediscovered in the thirteenth century.

The Renaissance represented a rebirth of the Aristotelian spirit. The results of that spirit are written across the next two centuries, which men describe, properly, as the Age of Reason and the Age of Enlightenment. The results include the rise of modern science; the rise of an individualist political philosophy (the work of John Locke and others); the consequent spread of freedom across the civilized world; and the birth of the freest country in history, the United States of America. The great corollary of these results, the product of men who were armed with the knowledge of the scientists and who were free at last to act, was the Industrial Revolution, which turned poverty into abundance and transformed the face of the West. The Aristotelianism released by Aquinas and the Renaissance was sweeping away the dogmas and the shackles of the past. Reason, freedom, and production were replacing faith, force, and poverty. The age-old foundations of statism were being challenged and undercut.

The tragedy of the West, however, lies in the fact that the seeds of Platonism had been firmly embedded in philosophy almost from its beginning, and had been growing steadily through the post-Renaissance period. Thus, while the revolutionary achievements inspired by Aristotelianism were reshaping the life of the West, an intellectual counterrevolution was at work, gradually gathering momentum. A succession of thinkers was striving to reverse the Aristotelian trend and to resurrect the basic principles of Platonism.

The climax of this development came in the late eighteenth century. The man who consummated the successful anti-Aristotelian revolution—the man who, more than any other, put an end to the Enlightenment and opened the door to its opposite—was a German philosopher, the most influential German philosopher in history: *Immanuel Kant.*

One of Kant's major goals was to save religion (including the essence of religious morality) from the onslaughts of science. His system represents a massive effort to raise the principles of Platonism, in a somewhat altered form, once again to a position of commanding authority over Western culture.

Kant places his primary emphasis on epistemological issues. His method of attack is to wage a campaign against the human mind. Man's mind, he holds, is unable to acquire any knowledge of reality.

In any process of cognition, according to Kant, whether it be sense experience or abstract thought, the mind automatically alters and distorts the evidence confronting it. It filters or structures the material it receives from reality, in accordance with a set of innate and *subjective* processing devices, whose operation it cannot escape. The world that men perceive, therefore—the world of orderly, spatiotemporal, material entities—is essentially a creation of man's consciousness. What men perceive is not reality "as it is," but merely reality as it *appears* to man, given the special structure of the human mind. Thus for Kant, as for Plato, the universe consists of two opposed dimensions: true reality, a supersensible realm of "things in themselves" (in Kant's terminology), and a world of appearances which is not ultimately real, the material world men perceive by means of their physical senses.

Plato was more than a Platonist; despite his mysticism, he was also a pagan Greek. As such he exhibited a certain authentic respect for reason, a respect which was implicit in Greek philosophy no matter how explicitly irrational it became. The Kantian mysticism, however, suffers from no such pagan restraints. It flows forth triumphantly, sweeping the prostrate human mind before it. Since man can never escape the distorting agents inherent in the structure of his consciousness, says Kant, "things in themselves" are in principle unknowable. Reason is impotent to discover anything about reality; if it tries, it can only bog down in impenetrable contradictions. Logic is merely a subjective human device, devoid of reference to or basis in reality. Science, while useful as a means of ordering the data of the world of appearances, is limited to describing a surface world of man's own creation and says nothing about things as they really are.

Must men then resign themselves to a total skepticism? No, says Kant, there is one means of piercing the barrier between man and existence. Since reason, logic, and science are denied access to reality, the door is now open for men to approach reality by a different, *nonrational* method. The door is now open to *faith*. Taking their cue from their needs, men can properly *believe* (for instance, in God and in an afterlife), even though they cannot prove the truth of their beliefs. And no matter how powerful the rational argument against their faith, that argument can always be dismissed out-of-hand: one need merely remind its advocate that rational knowledge and rational concepts are applicable only to the world of appearances, not to reality.

In a word, reason having been silenced, the way is cleared once more for an orgy of mystic fantasy. (The name of this orgy, the philosophic term for the nineteenth-century intellectuals' revolt against reason and the Enlightenment, is: romanticism.) "I have," writes Kant, "therefore found it necessary to deny *knowledge*, in order to make room for *faith*."[4]

Kant also found it necessary to deny *happiness*, in order to make room for *duty*. The essence of moral virtue, he says, is selflessness—selfless, lifelong obedience to duty, without any expectation of reward, and regardless of how much it might make one suffer.

Kant's attack on reason, this world, and man's happiness was the decisive turning point. As the main line of modern philosophy rapidly absorbed his basic tenets, the last elements of the Aristotelian approach were abandoned, particularly in Germany. Philosophers turned as a group to variants of Platonism, this time an extreme, militant Platonism, a Platonism shorn of its last vestiges of respect for reason.

It is Kant who made possible the sudden mushrooming of the Platonic collectivism in the modern world, and especially in Germany. Kant is not a full-fledged statist, but a philosopher's political views, to the extent that they contradict the essentials of his system, have little historical significance. Kant accepts certain elements of individualism, not because of his basic approach, but in spite of it, as a legacy of the Enlightenment period in which he lived. This merely suggests that Kant did not grasp the political implications of his own metaphysics and epistemology.

His heirs, however, did. A line of German romanticist philosophers followed Kant in the nineteenth century, each claiming to be his true follower, each avid for a reality beyond this world and a means of knowledge beyond reason, each contributing his share to the growth of an impassioned collectivism that poisoned the intellectual atmosphere of Germany. The most famous of these men, the most influential, the ruling figure of nineteenth-century philosophy, was *Hegel*.

Hegel is a post-Kantian Platonist. Taking full advantage of the anti-Aristotelianism sanctioned by Kant, Hegel launches an attack on the root principles of Aristotle's philosophy: on the principles of Aristotelian logic (which even Kant had not dared to challenge directly). Reality, declares Hegel, is inherently contradictory; it is a systematic progression of colliding contradictions organized in triads of thesis, antithesis, synthesis—and men must think accordingly. They should not strive for old-fashioned, "static" consistency. They should not be "limited" by the "one-sided" Aristotelian view that every existent has a specific identity, that things are what they are, that A is A. On the contrary, they owe their ultimate allegiance to a higher principle: the principle of the "identity of opposites," the principle that things are *not* what they are, that A is *non*-A.

Hegel describes the above as a new conception of "reason," and as a new, "dialectic" logic.

On its basis he proceeds to erect his own version of Platonism. Like Plato and Kant, he is an idealist in metaphysics. True reality, he holds, is a nonmaterial dimension, beyond time and space and human sense-perception. In Hegel's version, reality is a dynamic cosmic mind or thought-process, which in various contexts is referred to as the Absolute, the Spirit, the World-Reason, God, etc. According to Hegel, it is in the essential nature of this entity to undergo a constant process of evolution or development, unfolding itself in various stages. In one of these stages, the Absolute "externalizes" itself, assuming the form of a material world. Continuing its career, it takes on the appearance of a multiplicity of human beings, each seemingly distinct from the others, each seemingly an autonomous individual with his own personal thoughts and desires.

The appearance of such separate individuals represents, however, merely a comparatively low stage in the Absolute's career. It is not the final truth about reality. It does not represent the culmination of the Absolute's development. At that stage, i.e., at the apex or climax of reality, it turns out, in Hegel's view, that distinctions of any kind, including the distinctions between mind and matter and between one man

and another, are unreal (opposites are identical, A is non-A).
It turns out that everything is one, and that the things of this
world—which appear to us to be individual, self-contained
entities, each real in its own right—are merely so many partial aspects of one all-inclusive, all-consuming whole: the Absolute, which alone has full reality.

The ethics and politics which Hegel derives from his fundamental philosophy can be indicated by two sentences from
his *Philosophy of Right*: "A single person, I need hardly say,
is something subordinate, and as such he must dedicate himself to the ethical whole. Hence if the state claims life, the individual must surrender it."[5]

Hegel's collectivism and state-worship are more explicit
than anything to be found in Plato's writings. Since everything is ultimately one, the group, he holds, has primacy over
the individual. If each man learns to suppress his identity and
coalesce with his fellows, the resulting collective entity, the
state, will be a truer reflection of reality, a higher manifestation of the Absolute. The state in this view is not an association of autonomous individuals. It is itself an individual, a
mystic "person" that swallows up the citizens and transcends
them, an independent, self-sustaining organism, made of human beings, with a will and purpose of its own. "[A]ll the
worth which the human being possesses," writes Hegel, "all
spiritual reality, he possesses only through the State."[6]

The state-organism is no mere secular entity. As a
manifestation of the Absolute, it is a creature of God, and
thus demands not merely obedience from its citizens but rev-
erential worship. "The State is the Divine Idea as it exists on
earth." "The march of God in the world, that is what the
state is." The purpose of the state, therefore, is not the protection of its citizens. The state is not a means to any human
end. As an entity with supernatural credentials, it is "an absolute unmoved end in itself," and it "has supreme right against
the individual, whose supreme duty is to be a member of the
state."[7]

The above are the kinds of political ideas which Hegel,
more than any other man, injected into the mind of early
nineteenth-century Germany. Perpetuated in a variety of
forms by a long chain of secondary figures and derivative influences, these ideas gradually became commonplaces in Germany and in other countries, including Italy. The aspiring

dictators of the twentieth century and their intellectual defenders moved with alacrity to embrace such commonplaces and to cash in on them.

Both the Fascists and the Nazis were in the forefront of this trend.

In the Fascist literature the influence of Hegel is generally acknowledged. Prominent neo-Hegelian philosophers, such as Mario Palmieri and Giovanni Gentile, upheld Fascism on a Hegelian foundation and earned a formal endorsement from Mussolini. "The world seen through Fascism," writes Mussolini,

> is not this material world which appears on the surface, in which man is an individual separated from all others and standing by himself. . . . The man of Fascism is an individual who is nation and fatherland, which is a moral law, binding together individuals and the generations into a tradition and a mission, suppressing the instinct for a life enclosed within the brief round of pleasure in order to restore within duty a higher life free from the limits of time and space. . . .[8]

The Nazi literature is not so overtly Hegelian in its formulations. Posing as the spokesmen for a higher *biological* truth, the Nazis generally dropped the idealistic metaphysics of Hegel and even attacked him. Admittedly or not, however, the Nazis, like the Fascists, rely on the ideas of Hegel—not only for their basic collectivist approach but for many of the more specific political theories necessary to implement it in practice.

Hegel, for instance, seeks to undercut any individualist opponents, by proclaiming that statism represents a passion for human liberty.

A man is free, Hegel explains, when he acts as he himself wills to act. But since "the state is the true self of the individual," what a man *really* wills, even though he may not know it, is what the state wills. Liberty, therefore, is obedience to the orders of the government. Such obedience guarantees true freedom for the real self, even if the illusory self is being sent to Auschwitz.[9]

The masses of men, notes Hegel, do not understand the above viewpoint. The people, therefore, "does *not* know what it wills. To know what one wills, and still more to know what the absolute will, Reason, wills, is the fruit of profound apprehension and insight, precisely the things which are *not* popular."[10] Hence Hegel (like Plato) is opposed to the theory of popularly elected, representative government. Instead, he calls for an authoritarian state resembling a Prussian monarchy. The monarch's decrees, we are told, embody the *true* will of the people.

"And if liberty is to be the attribute of the real man," says Mussolini, "and not of the scarecrow invented by the individualistic Liberalism, then Fascism is for liberty. It is for the only kind of liberty that is serious—the liberty of the State. . . ." "There is no freedom of the individual," says the Nazi Otto Dietrich. "There is only freedom of peoples, nations or races; for these are the only material and historical realities through which the life of the individual exists." "The Führer-Reich of the people," says Huber, "is founded on the recognition that the true will of the people cannot be disclosed through parliamentary votes and plebiscites but that the will of the people in its pure and uncorrupted form can only be expressed through the Führer."[11]

In his defense of monarchy, Hegel stops short of advocating complete dictatorship. In his theory of "heroes," however, he makes little effort to conceal that this is his viewpoint. A few superior beings throughout the ages, he holds—e.g., Alexander, Caesar, Napoleon—have functioned as "agents of the World-Spirit." These men have been endowed with a special mission: to advance the evolution of Spirit (carry out the will of God) in their era. Guided by Providence, the "world-historical hero" seizes the initiative and takes direct action; through him the Spirit, "impinging on the outer world as on a shell, bursts it in pieces. . . ." Such individuals, Hegel concedes, often leave a trail of corpses in their wake. Nevertheless, they are exempt from moral judgment:

> For the History of the World occupies a higher ground than that on which morality has properly its position. . . . [M]oral claims that are irrelevant must not be brought into collision with world-historical deeds and their accomplishment. The Litany of private virtues . . . must not be raised against them.[12]

Here, sanctioned by an intricate metaphysical system, is a call for a militaristic dictator to throw aside morality and "burst the world in pieces" in accordance with his concept of destiny. Issued by the most prestigious German philosopher of the nineteenth century, it is an invitation for a Führer to step forward. Philosophers cannot issue such invitations with impunity. One way or another the next representative of the Absolute is going to get the message.

"However weak the individual may be when compared with the omnipotence and will of Providence," said Hitler in a 1937 speech,

> yet at the moment when he acts as Providence would have him act he becomes immeasurably strong. Then there streams down upon him that force which has marked all greatness in the world's history. And when I look back only on the five years which lie behind us, then I feel that I am justified in saying: That has not been the work of man alone.[18]

Just as there are world-historical heroes, according to Hegel, so there are world-historical *peoples*. In any given era, he holds, *one* nation is the special vehicle of the World Spirit in its process of self-unfolding. That nation, he says, has "absolute right" over all the others, which are "without rights" and "count no longer in world history." "Absolute right" includes the right to launch war.[14]

War among nations, in Hegel's view, is an inevitable, and desirable, expression of the evolution of Spirit. And, since the history of the world faithfully expresses this evolution, the nation that wins the wars of a given era is obviously the one backed by the Spirit. Justice, therefore, must always be on the side of the winner. Might makes right—stripped of its jargon, this is the meaning of Hegel's doctrine.

Hegel's form of collectivism is *nationalism*. The nation, he holds—not mankind as a whole, or the majority, or the race, or the proletariat—is the favored group, the one which is to be the standard of value and the collector of men's sacrifices. And of all the world's nations, he reports, Germany is the culmination to date. It is currently the representative of the Spirit.

Religions have often divided men into the chosen and the

damned, and then interpreted history as the struggle of the chosen to carry out the divine plan. Hegel's philosophy of history amounts to this viewpoint. Hegel's distinctiveness, however, lies in his definition of the chosen. The messianic group on his theory is not men of a particular religion or sect, but men of a particular nationality.

The initiators of German nationalism in the nineteenth century were not the Junkers, the military men, big business, or the middle classes. "All these groups," notes Ludwig von Mises,

> were at first strongly opposed to the aspirations of Pan-Germanism. But their resistance was vain because it lacked an ideological backing. There were no longer any liberal [individualistic] authors in Germany. Thus the nationalist writers and professors easily conquered. Very soon the youth came back from the universities and lower schools convinced Pan-Germans.[15]

On this issue, the leading teacher of the teachers of the youth was Hegel.

The Nazis accept Hegel's theory, with certain adaptations.

The Nazis agree that a cosmic agency has divided men into antithetic groups, the chosen and the damned, whose actions and destiny are predetermined and outside of any individual's choice or control. They agree that the chosen have "absolute right" to smash the rest of mankind. They agree that might, being the expression of destiny, makes right. But, since they mix a certain element of biology into this framework, they often provide a different answer to the question: who chooses the chosen? It is not the World Spirit that does it, Hitler often suggests, but *nature*, using the mechanism of the "survival of the fittest." The chosen are catapulted to a position of world dominance, and their recourse to brutality is justified, not by the Hegelian process of evolution, but by the *Darwinian*.

Although the catch phrases of the Social Darwinists, in the above form, are all over *Mein Kampf*, they never attained the status of official party doctrine. Other Nazi writers remained free to denounce Darwin and Darwinism as incompatible with Nazism—as irreligious, "mechanistic," "internationalistic." On the whole, Nazism never decided this question. Nature and God, the Nazis sometimes say, are merely different forms in which the same reality manifests itself; so there is really no difference, after all, between natural and divine selection.

The Nazis' predilection for biology-plus-religion culminates in their biological version of the chosen-damned dichotomy. The people chosen by God/nature, they hold, are not confined to a single nation. They are spread across the globe, marked off by a distinctive physical appearance (they are tall, long-headed, blond, etc.) and a special, innate "race soul" (which makes them truthful, energetic, persistent, the "founder of all higher humanity," etc.). These men are the Aryans (or the Nordics)—the master race. The damned are all the other breeds, especially the Jews. The Jew, claims Hitler, is by his nature alien and cunning, a communist subversive and a capitalist exploiter; he is "the personification of the devil" and "the symbol of all evil."[16]

The Nazi collectivism, technically, is a form of racism rather than of nationalism. But the Nazis were able to combine the two doctrines easily, by the device of holding that Germany contains the purest Aryan blood.

The direct source of the Nazi racial ideas was the theoreticians of racism (e.g., Count de Gobineau and H. S. Chamberlain), a group who rose to sudden prominence in Europe in the latter half of the nineteenth century. These men accepted wholeheartedly the collectivist sentiment of the period's intellectuals, and then sought to gain for that sentiment the appearance of scientific support—by translating collectivism into the language of the favorite science of the time, biology. The result was a mounting torrent on the following order (from Vacher de Lapouge, a nineteenth-century French Aryan-glorifier): "The blood which one has in one's veins at birth one keeps all one's life. The individual is stifled by his race and is nothing. The race, the nation, is all."[17] No amount of passion for biology (or for Darwin) could produce such an utterance. A dose of Hegel, however, could.

What the theoreticians of racism did was to *secularize* the Hegelian approach, as Karl Popper explains eloquently. Marx, he observes,

> replaced Hegel's 'Spirit' by matter, and by material and economic interests. In the same way, racialism sub-

stitutes for Hegel's 'Spirit' something material, the quasi-biological conception of Blood or Race. Instead of 'Spirit,' Blood is the self-developing essence; instead of 'Spirit,' Blood is the Sovereign of the world, and displays itself on the Stage of History; and instead of its 'Spirit,' the Blood of a nation determines its essential destiny.

The transubstantiation of Hegelianism into racialism or of Spirit into Blood does not greatly alter the main tendency of Hegelianism. It only gives it a tinge of biology and of modern evolutionism.[18]

Every central doctrine of the Nazi politics, racism included, is an expression or variant of the theory of collectivism. Such doctrines cannot rise to the ascendancy, neither among the intellectuals nor in the mind of the public, except in a culture already saturated with a mystical-collectivist philosophy.

In the case of Germany, this means: saturated with the ideas of Hegel.

●   ●   ●

No philosopher could produce a cataclysm such as Nazism single-handed. A complex series of other intellectual influences—both leading to and proceeding from Hegel—was involved in preparing the climate for the rise of the Nazis. The sum of these accessory influences determined the specific form of Hegelian statism prevalent in modern Germany and picked up by the Nazis. The theoreticians of racism were merely one such influence.

There was also Martin Luther, regarded by the Nazis as a major hero, who was the greatest single power in the development of German religion and, through this means, an influence on the philosophies of both Kant and Hegel. Luther is anti-reason ("Whoever wants to be a Christian should tear the eyes out of his reason"), intensely pro-German, and crudely anti-Semitic ("[F]ie on you wherever you be, you damned Jews, who dare to clasp this earnest, glorious, consoling Word of God to your maggoty, mortal, miserly belly, and are not ashamed to display your greed so openly"). He formally enlists God on the side of the state. Unconditional obedience to the government's edicts, he holds, is a Christian virtue.

[I]n a like manner we must endure the authority of the prince. If he misuse or abuse his authority, we are not to entertain a grudge, seek revenge or punishment. Obedience is to be rendered for God's sake, for the ruler is God's representative. However they may tax or exact, we must obey and endure patiently.[19]

There was J.G. Fichte, another Nazi hero, who was an early post-Kantian idealist and an important influence on subsequent German thought (including Hegel's). Politically, Fichte, like Hegel, anticipates all the central tenets of the Nazis. He is a champion of the organic theory of the state, and an authoritarian who yearns for an elite of scholar-dictators to rule the ignorant masses. Because of his advocacy of state control of the economy, he is often regarded as the father of modern socialism. "[T]he individual life has no real existence," he writes, "since it has no value of itself, but must and *should* sink to nothing; while, on the contrary, the Race alone exists, since it alone *ought to be* looked upon as really living." Fichte is also one of the principal sources of the theory, and delusions, of German nationalism. "[T]o have character and to be German," he remarks, "undoubtedly mean the same. . . ."[20]

There was Karl Marx, the creator of modern communism and an archvillain and competitor in the Nazi eyes, who nevertheless helped pave the way for Nazism by popularizing all the fundamental principles of Hegel, including his rejection of Aristotelian logic. Marx pioneered the technique, later adapted by the racists, of secularizing Hegel's ideas; he substitutes economic forces for the Absolute as the determiner of history, and thus replaces Hegel's warring nations by the class struggle, and Hegel's monarchy by the dictatorship of the proletariat. It is wrong, Marx writes, to "postulate an abstract—*isolated*—human individual." "*My own existence* is a social activity. For this reason, what I myself produce I produce for society, and with the consciousness of acting as a social being." In the classless society, he predicts, men will shed all concern for personal prerogatives, individual rights, private property. They will want only to blend with the whole. Then at last "the narrow horizon of bourgeois right [can] be fully left behind. . . ."[21]

There was Friedrich Nietzsche, the prophet of the super-

man and of the will to power, who was acclaimed by Hitler
as one of his precursors. The extent of Nietzsche's actual influence in regard to the rise of Nazism is debatable. He is antistatist, antiracist, and in many respects a defender of the
individual. Nevertheless, he is a fervid romanticist, who revels
in the post-Kantian anti-reason orgy, and there is much in his
disjointed, aphoristic writings that the Nazis were able to
quote with relish. A view of the universe as a realm of clashing wills, ceaseless strife, and violent conflict; a glorification
of cruelty and conquest, of "the magnificent *blond brute,* avidly rampant for spoil and victory";[22] the view that a few su-
perbeings, "beyond good and evil," have the right to enslave
the inferior masses for their own higher purposes—this is part
of the Nietzschean legacy, as interpreted (with some justification) by the Nazis.

And there were many other such voices in Germany, ranging from dreamy apostles of otherworldly mysticism to
mindless champions of this-worldly nationalism (many German intellectuals were both). Those best-known for the
former attitude include Meister Eckhart, a medieval neo-Pla-
tonist often called the father of German mysticism; Arthur
Schopenhauer, an Orientalist doom-preacher who was a major influence on men such as Nietzsche and Freud; and
Friedrich Schleiermacher, a leading romanticist theologian.
Those best-known for the latter attitude include Heinrich von
Treitschke, an historian of the Prussian school, who helped to
spread Hegel's ideas ("The grandeur of war lies in the utter
annihilation of puny man in the great conception of the
State. . . ."); Richard Wagner, a fiercely racist disciple of
Schopenhauer ("[We must] be brave enough to deny our intellect"); and Arthur Moeller van den Bruck, a literary critic
and youth mentor in the Weimar Republic, who coined the
term "the Third Reich" ("We have to be strong enough to
live in contradictions").[23]

All of these men and movements contributed the notes, the
chords, or the screeches that fused into the Horst Wessel
song. And they are merely some of the obvious voices in
Germany from a chorus sustained across hundreds of years
and gradually rising in volume. If the brutes finally rose from
the gutters and stamped a swastika across the doctrines of the
centuries; if, plucking the naked essence of those doctrines
from the atmosphere, they began to preach the worship of

the all-powerful, collectivist, militarist state, ruled by a master Führer in the name of a master race; and if, finding an avid following, they proceeded to drench the world in blood—one need not ask what made it possible.

In one respect, Hegel's share of the responsibility has been widely recognized: the similarity between his politics and that of Hitler is hard to escape. But Hegel's politics is not a primary. It is an expression of his fundamental philosophy, which is the culmination of a long historical development.

Hegel would not have been possible but for Kant, who would not have been possible but for Plato. These three, more than any others, are the intellectual builders of Auschwitz.

3

Hitler's War Against Reason

Statism and the advocacy of reason are philosophical opposites. They cannot coexist—neither in a philosophic system nor in a nation.

If men uphold reason, they will be led, ultimately, to conclude that men should deal with one another as free agents, settling their disputes by an appeal to the mind, i.e., by a process of voluntary, rational persuasion. If men reject reason, they will be led, ultimately, to conclude the opposite: that men have no way to deal with one another at all—no way except physical force, wielded by an elite endowed with an allegedly superior, mystic means of cognition.

The branch of philosophy that deals with the powers of reason as a cognitive instrument is epistemology, and this issue is the key to its relationship to politics. It is not an accident that Plato, Kant, Hegel, Marx, and the whole tradition of German nationalism from Luther on, advocated a variety of anti-senses, anti-logic, anti-intellect doctrines. The statism all these figures upheld or fostered is a result; the root lies in their view of knowledge, i.e., of man's mind.

The aspiring dictator may not be able to identify in philosophic terms the clash between reason and his particular schemes. But he, too, is aware of it. In some (usually unverbalized) form, he knows that he cannot demand unthinking obedience from men, or gain their consent to the permanent rule of brutality, until he has first persuaded his future subjects to ditch their brains and their independent, self-assertive judgment. He knows that he can succeed only with a populace conditioned to seek neither evidence nor argument, a populace which, having shrugged aside the demands of logic, will agree with, and then endure, anything. Hence the specta-

45

cle of statists, of every variety and throughout history, both
before and during their period in power, systematically attacking the mind. In some terms, these men have grasped
that their political goals cannot be achieved until the proper
epistemological base is established.

Hitler grasped it, too.

In one sense it is incongruous to speak of a "Nazi epistemology." The leading Nazis were not philosophers; they
presented no systematic theory of knowledge and were ignorant of most of the specific issues in the field. Nevertheless,
there *is* a Nazi epistemology, in the sense of an unequivocal,
consistent, and passionately urged position on the subject's
fundamental issue.

"We are now at the end of the Age of Reason," Hitler declared to Hermann Rauschning. "The intellect has grown au-
tocratic, and has become a disease of life."

"The life of a race and of a people is . . . a mystical synthesis," writes Rosenberg, "a manifestation of the soul, which
cannot be explained by the logic of reason nor by causal
analysis."

"Even the most profound, the most learned of intellects
touches the surface of things only," writes Gottfried Neesse, a
young Nazi intellectual.

> Everything of which we are conscious, all that is think-
> able and understandable, is but thin snow on the high
> mountains of the unconscious, snow that will quickly
> melt under the storms of fate, of some intoxication, of
> the trembling of the soul. Life would rather hide its ulti-
> mate secrets in a small folksong heard in the village
> night than in fat and scholarly books. It is vain to try to
> plumb the depths. We will never, by ourselves, be able
> to learn the essential. All we can do is be moved by it.[1]

What should men appeal to for guidance once the intellect
has been rejected? "We must distrust the intelligence and the
conscience," states Hitler, "and must place our trust in our
instincts." "Trust your instincts, your feelings, or whatever
you like to call them," says Hitler. The last clause indicates
the latitude permitted to the Nazis on this question. They
were free to advocate—and did advocate, privately and publicly—every *non*rational source of alleged knowledge that

men have ever invented, including revelation, intuition, trances, magic, and astrology (the latter was a special favorite of Goebbels). What they could not advocate and were urged not to practice was a single cognitive method, the one Hitler grasped to be incompatible with Nazism: "At a mass meeting," said Hitler to Rauschning,

> thought is eliminated. And because this is the state of mind I require, because it secures to me the best sounding-board for my speeches, I order everyone to attend the meetings, where they become part of the mass whether they like it or not, 'intellectuals' and *bourgeois* as well as workers. I mingle the people. I speak to them only as the mass.

"The masses are like an animal that obeys its instincts. They do not reach conclusions by reasoning."[2]

Reason is the faculty that identifies, in conceptual terms, the material provided by man's senses. "Irrationalism" is the doctrine that reason is not a valid means of knowledge or a proper guide to action. "Mysticism" is the doctrine that man has a *non*sensory, *non*rational means of knowledge. Irrationalism and mysticism together constitute the essence of the Nazi epistemology.

The politics of Nazism—with its racist obsessions, its anti-Semitic demonology, its gesticulating Führer transmitting directives from Providence, and its all-obliterating appeal to the power of brute force—is unprecedented in the West, not for its collectivism but for its *undisguised* irrationality. The brazenness of this revelation is matched (and made possible) only by the brazenness of the Nazi epistemology. Its distinctive feature is self-proclaimed barbarianism, i.e., undisguised, boastfully trumpeted defiance of reason.

In the Nazi leadership's view, Rauschning (a onetime friend of Hitler's) reports, "the more inconsistent and irrational is their doctrine, the better. . . . [E]verything that might have gone to the making up of a systematic, logically conceived doctrine is dismissed as a trifle, with sovereign contempt." "To all doubts and questions," said Rosenberg, "the new man of the first German empire has only one answer: Nevertheless, I will!" "When I hear the word 'culture,'" said Hanns Johst (President of the Reich Theater Chamber), in an immortal line, "I slip back the safety-catch of my revolver."[3]

"People set us down as enemies of the intelligence," declared Hitler. "We are. But in a much deeper sense than these conceited dolts of *bourgeois* scientists ever dream of."[4]

The enmity extends across the board, to all the central forms and expressions of human reason—from its first, groping appearance in the life of the young child, to its major existential product in the modern world, the Industrial Revolution. The former is to be defeated by teaching children to despise their brains; the latter, by teaching the country to return to nature.

Childhood education, Hitler holds, must concentrate on "the breeding of absolutely healthy bodies," and on the development of "instincts" or "character," i.e., the particular emotions the Nazis wished to inculcate—while systematically downgrading any intellectual element and de-emphasizing the process of cognition. "We don't intend to educate our children into becoming miniature scholars," said Hans Schemm, a leading Nazi educator. "The real values resting in the German child are not awakened by stuffing a great mass of knowledge into him. . . . Therefore, I say: Let us have, rather, ten pounds less knowledge and ten calories more character!" In one of his utterances, Hitler leaves no doubt about the nature of such "character": "A violently active, dominating, intrepid, brutal youth—that is what I am after. . . . I will have no intellectual training. Knowledge is ruin to my young men."[5]

So is the product of knowledge. Nazi literature heaps abuse on wealth, cities, machinery, and Germany's preoccupation, in Hitler's words, with "an industrialization as boundless as it was harmful." The credo of modern society, writes the Nazi Werner Sombart in a bitter denunciation, is: "More motors, more currency, more goods! More rapid production, more rapid travel, livelier enjoyment! Prosperity! Progress! Without end, without end!"[6] The antonym of such progress is indicated by the second part of the Nazi slogan: "Blood and Soil." "Soil" in this context means the life of the humble, unthinking peasant, or of state-run, racially pure agricultural communes, as against the life of the "cunning," "mongrelized" city dweller. It means the selfless martial discipline of Germany's Middle Ages, as against the modern desire for economic comfort and well-being. It means a mystical merging with primitive nature, as against an atmosphere of insatiable, profit-seeking production and "cold," calculating mechanization.

Most Nazis, concerned with the need for armaments, do not urge the dismantling of industry. What they do demand is its subservience to the right kind of men, the ones whose allegiance is not to science or business but to instinct and raw nature. Such subservience, in the words of one observer, is what takes "the sting" out of industrialism for the Nazis.[7] The "sting," at root, is the fact that modern industry is a product of man's mind.

In summoning the Germans so openly to a life of muscles and mindlessness, Hitler was counting on a widespread antireason attitude, an attitude that no political party by itself could have created or sustained. In the field of epistemology, the Nazis were merely repeating and cashing in on the slogans of a nineteenth-century intellectual movement, one which pervaded every country of Europe, but which had its center and greatest influence in Germany. This movement— the defiant rejection of the Enlightenment spirit—is called *romanticism*.*

Progressively abandoning their Aristotelian heritage, the philosophers of the Enlightenment had reached a state of formal bankruptcy in the skepticism of David Hume. Hume claimed that neither the senses nor reason can yield reliable knowledge. He concluded that man is a helpless creature caught in an unintelligible universe. Meanwhile a variety of lesser figures (such as Rousseau, the admirer of the "noble savage") were foreshadowing the era to come. They were suggesting that reason had had its chance but had failed, and that something else, something opposite, holds the key to reality and the future.

The two figures who created the new era and made this viewpoint the norm in the West—the two who welded the mystic stirrings of the late eighteenth century into a powerful, self-conscious, *intellectually respectable* voice, and who placed that voice at the base of all later philosophy—were

---

*The term "romanticism" is also used in esthetics, to designate an art school opposed to classicism and later to naturalism. This usage must be firmly distinguished from the broad, philosophic sense of the term explained in the text.

Kant and Hegel. Kant is the father of the romanticist movement. It is he who claimed to have proved for the first time
that existence is in principle unknowable to man's mind.
Thereafter, Hegel, Kant's chief heir, most powerfully articulated the new movement's central ideas, in every branch of
philosophy.

But neither Kant nor Hegel is a full romanticist. Kant
opened the door to the movement, but hesitated to walk
firmly through. Hegel did walk through, but paid vigorous lip
service to reason all the way. There were many, however,
who did not hesitate and who did little to mask their views.
In Germany the most influential of these men were J.G. Her-
der (another hero of the Nazis), Fichte, Friedrich Schlegel,
Schelling, Schleiermacher, Schopenhauer, and Nietzsche. The
product of this main romanticist line was an army of lesser
intellectuals and fellow travelers (generally cruder and more
open than their mentors), who helped to spread the new approach to every corner of Germany.

The romanticists held (following Kant) that reason is a
faculty restricted to a surface world of appearances and incapable of penetrating to true reality. Man's true source of
knowledge, they declared (drawing explicitly the conclusion
Kant had implied), is: feeling—or passion, or intuition, or
faith, etc. Man in this view is not a rational being; he is in
essence an emotional being, and he must seek the truth and
live his life accordingly.

Although most of the romanticists advocated some form of
religion, religion is not an essential component of this philosophy. On the whole, the romanticists were more modern
than that. They offered a somewhat secularized version of the
earlier religious approach, stressing instinct more than revelation, the voice of the subconscious more than of the supernatural. But they never forgot their philosophic ancestors and
brothers-in-spirit. While condemning the civilization of the
Enlightenment, they passionately admired two cultures: the
medieval and the Oriental.

Hostile to the "cold" objectivity of the scientific method,
the romanticists turned to avowedly subjective fantasies, prid-
ing themselves on their absorption in an inner world of in-
tense feeling. Scornful of the "shallowness" of Aristotelian
logic, they flaunted the fact that the universes *they* construct-
ed were brimming with "depth," i.e., with contradictions, A's

endlessly blending into non-A's and vice versa. Contemptuous of the "static" world of the Enlightenment thinkers—a world of stable, enduring *entities*—the romanticists denied the very existence of entities. Their "dynamic" universe was a resurrection of the ancient theory of Heraclitus: reality is a stream of change without entities or of action without anything that acts; it is a wild, chaotic flux, which the orderly "Enlightenment mind" cannot grasp.

Opposed most of all to *analysis,* to the "dissection" of reality performed by man's conceptual faculty, to the distinctions made by man's intellect, the romanticists praised *wholes,* so-called "organic" wholes. (The source of this particular notion is Kant's *Critique of Judgment.*) The whole, they declared, is not the sum of its parts; it is a thing which consumes and transcends its constituents, obliterating their separate identities in the process.

The master "organic" whole, these men commonly held, is reality itself, variously called the Absolute, God, etc. Typically, it was construed as a kind of cosmic craving, an all-encompassing impulse or process of striving, called simply the "Will." (This theory developed from Kant's idea that the demands of the will are the key to the universe.) The advocates of such a view are known as "voluntarists," because of their claim that will is the essence of reality, and that the physical world is merely will's superficial manifestation.

Voluntarism is a frontal assault on reason. The theory implies that reality as such—and man, too, as part of it—is inherently irrational and even insane. In Schopenhauer's version, for instance, the World-Will is described as blind, insatiable, and absolutely senseless. As a result, its offshoot, the world of appearances in which we live, is a nightmare universe condemning man to ceaseless agony. The only escape, Schopenhauer says, is the denial of one's will to live, followed by the oblivion of Nirvana. In Nietzsche's version, what rules man (and, he suggests, reality) is an equally blind and senseless will, the "will to power"—which is, Nietzsche says, not to be denied but exultantly affirmed. To affirm it, he holds, one must reject the mind and act instead on the spontaneous, drunken outpourings of the orgiastic "Dionysian" element in man (raw passion). "Why? You ask, why?" declares Zarathustra, in a remark that encapsulates the romanticism in Nietzsche and the unreason in romanticism. "I am not one of those whom one may ask about their why."[8]

The philosophers' flight into a world of Will, or of the past, or of the East, did not prevent their followers, especially in the latter part of the nineteenth century, from applying the romanticist viewpoint to the issues and concerns of life on earth.

An education stressing the intellect, such men charged, places too great a burden on the child and thwarts his emotional development. An education teaching facts and objectivity improperly emphasizes external factors at the expense of the child's "inner experience." What Germany needs, they concluded, is a new kind of institution: not cold, cognition-centered "learning-schools," but feeling-centered "Lebensschulen" (life-schools). Encouraged by liberal progressives and conservative nationalists alike, the romanticist educators proceeded gradually to supply this need—first in the empire, then in the Republic. (Thus the schools were ready for the Nazi educators, when their time came.)

Modern science and its product, the Industrial Revolution—the advocates of romanticism charged—thwart the emotional development of everyone, whether child or adult. Individualism, they said, is "atomistic," capitalism is "materialistic," urban life is artificial, factories are ugly, labor-saving machinery is soulless and a source of misery. By contrast, medieval peasants, in one commentator's words, "were supposed to have been happy, natural, uncitified, and uncultured, literally in contact with the earth (a supposedly most beneficial tie). . . ." "I will destroy [the present] order of things, which wastes man's powers in service of dead matter . . . ," concluded Wagner.[9]

Like Hegel, and generally under his influence, the romanticists concerned with politics characteristically found an "organic" *social* whole to exalt: Germany. Selfless service to the Volk (the people), most of them said, is the essence of virtue. Such service, they usually added, requires obedience to a dictator soon to appear in Germany, a "hero" who can divine the will of the Volk and mercilessly smash any nation or group (such as the Jews) that stands in its way.

A well-known German historian has remarked that the romanticist element in German thought would appear to Western eyes as "a *queer mixture of mysticism and brutal-*

ity."[10] The formulation errs only in the adjective "queer." The mixture's two ingredients have a magnetic affinity for each other: the first makes possible and leads to the second (and not only in Germany).

By the time of the Weimar Republic, Germany's intellectuals—Protestants, Catholics, and Jews alike—had reached a philosophical consensus. If we are to solve our country's problems, they said to one another and to the public, we must follow the right approach to knowledge. The right approach, as they conceived it, was eloquently described by Walther Rathenau, who was not a fulminating nationalist or racist, but an admired liberal commentator, a practical man (government minister, diplomat, industrialist), and a Jew.

> The most profound error of the social thought of our day is found in the belief that one can demand of scientific knowledge impulses to will and ideal goals. Understanding will never be able to tell us what to believe, what to hope for, what to live for, and what to offer up sacrifices for. Instinct and feeling, illumination and intuitive vision—these are the things that lead us into the realm of forces that determine the meaning of our existence.[11]

Rathenau and his colleagues did not know the full nature of the "realm of forces" into which they were delivering the country. They did not know who ruled that kind of realm. They did not foresee the consequences of the "instinct and feeling" they were begging for. They found out.

In 1922, the "instinct and feeling" confronted Rathenau in practical reality. He was assassinated by a gang of anti-Semitic nationalists. A decade later the same fate befell the Weimar Republic.

* * *

Pervaded by attacks on every idea and method essential to the function of the reasoning mind, the cultural atmosphere of the Weimar Republic was an invaluable asset to the Nazis. They made full use of it, taking from their surroundings whatever epistemological doctrines they needed in order to implement their irrationalist approach, assured in advance of a receptive mass audience.

Of these doctrines, two in particular were emphasized by the Nazis, the combination becoming a characteristic leitmotif of theirs. One of the doctrines is age-old; the other is an offshoot of romanticism. The first is *dogmatism* (the advocacy of faith in immutable revelations); the second is *pragmatism*.

The concept of faith does not pertain to the content of a man's ideas, but to the method by which they are to be accepted. "Faith" designates blind acceptance of a certain ideational content, acceptance induced by feeling in the absence of evidence or proof. It is obvious, therefore, why Nazi (and Fascist) leaders insist on faith from their followers. "Faith," writes Hitler,

> is harder to shake than knowledge, love succumbs less to change than respect, hate is more enduring than aversion, and the impetus to the mightiest upheavals on this earth has at all times consisted less in a scientific knowledge dominating the masses than in a fanaticism which inspired them and sometimes in a hysteria which drove them forward.[12]

In the West, the stronghold of the demand for faith, the institution which issues that demand in the most sophisticated manner, is the Catholic Church. Hitler, accordingly, admired the Church. He admired not its teachings but its methods— "its knowledge of human nature," its hierarchical organization, its discipline, "its uncommonly clever tactics." One of its cleverest tactics, he believed, is its unyielding dogmatism.

Faith, he explains in *Mein Kampf*, must be "unconditional." It cannot in any essential way be made dependent on arguments, proofs, reasons. Its content must be offered to the masses in the form of rigid dogmas, "dogmas as such." Once a doctrine has been announced publicly, therefore, there can be no changes in it, no debates, no discussion. "For how shall we fill people with blind faith in the correctness of a doctrine, if we ourselves spread uncertainty and doubt by constant changes in its outward structure?"

"I have followed [the Church]," Hitler told Rauschning,

> in giving our party program the character of unalterable finality, like the Creed. The Church has never al-

lowed the Creed to be interfered with. It is fifteen hundred years since it was formulated, but every suggestion for its amendment, every logical criticism or attack on it, has been rejected. The Church has realized that anything and everything can be built up on a document of that sort, no matter how contradictory or irreconcilable with it. The faithful will swallow it whole, so long as logical reasoning is never allowed to be brought to bear on it.[13]

Dogma, whether Nazi or otherwise, requires an authority able to give it the stamp of an official imprimatur. The Nazi authority is obvious. "Just as the Roman Catholic considers the Pope infallible in all matters concerning religion and morals," writes Goering,

> so do we National Socialists believe with the same inner conviction that for us the Leader is in all political and other matters concerning the national and social interests of the people simply infallible. [Hitler's authority derives from] something mystical, inexpressible, almost incomprehensible which this unique man possesses, and he who cannot feel it instinctively will not be able to grasp it at all.[14]

Given their commitment to the method of faith (and their tendency to imitate the Catholic Church), it is not astonishing that some Nazis went all the way in this issue. A tendency never given the status of official ideology yet fairly prominent in the movement was voiced in a demand made by several of its leading figures (though Hitler himself regarded it as impractical until the Nazis won the war): the demand that Nazism itself be turned into a full-fledged religion. These voices urged a state religion supplanting the older creeds, with its own symbols, its own rituals, and its own zealots avid to convert Christians into fanatic Hitler-believers, as, once, ancient missionaries had converted pagans into fanatic Christians. "Adolf Hitler," exclaimed one such believer (the Nazi Minister for Church Affairs), "is the true Holy Ghost!"[15]

The Nazis did not survive long enough to complete this development. To the end, they could not decide whether to retain Christianity, construing Nazism merely as its latest, truest version ("positive Christianity," this wing often called it)—or to concoct a distinctively Nazi creed out of a hodge-podge of elements drawn from pagan Teutonic mythology and romanticist metaphysics. In either case, however, whether advanced as a form of or successor to Christianity, what Nazism did unfailingly demand of its followers was the essence of the religious mentality: an attitude of awed, submissive, faithful adoration. "We believe on this earth *solely* in Adolf Hitler . . . ," intoned Dr. Robert Ley to a reverent audience of 15,000 Hitler Youths. "We believe that God has sent us Adolf Hitler."[16]

Seventeen centuries earlier, Tertullian, one of the Church Fathers, had explained that religion by its nature requires the subversion of reason, the belief in the irrational *because* it is irrational. He had delivered a ringing anti-reason manifesto, declaring, in regard to the dogma of God's self-sacrifice on the cross: "It is believable, because it is absurd; it is certain, because it is impossible."

If Tertullian's is the correct view of religion, the Nazis were evidently qualified to enter the field. The absurdity of their dogma matched anything offered by the medievals.

The other half of the Nazis' epistemological leitmotif, the concomitant of the Nazi dogmatism, is the Nazi pragmatism. To grasp the relationship between these two halves, one must first grasp the nature of pragmatism, including its philosophic roots.

Those who regard the intellect as cut off from reality tend to regard the man of intellect as an impractical theoretician, who is impotent to act or achieve goals in the real world. According to this viewpoint, a fundamental dichotomy cuts through human life: thought versus action, intelligence versus achievement, knowing versus doing. "The know-it-alls," states Hitler, "are the enemies of action."[17]

In elaborating this idea the Nazis repeat most of the voluntarist commonplaces of the later romanticists. The essence of human nature, they say, is "will," which they regard as man's means of access to reality and as the ultimate source of human action. "Will" in this context means a set of blind, irrational (and allegedly innate) drives that crave an outlet—and Nazism means giving them one. It means (according to a party slogan) "the triumph of the will," through a life of blind, irrational action, action unmediated and untouched by the operation of intelligence.

The voluntarist worship of mindless action may be designated by the term "activism." Activism is the form of irrationalism which extols direct physical action, based on will or instinct or faith, while repudiating the intellect and its products, such as abstractions, theory, programs, philosophy. In a very literal sense, activism is irrationalism—in action. "We approach the realities of the world only in strong emotion and in action . . . ," says Hitler.

> Men misuse their intelligence. It is not the seat of a special dignity of mankind, but merely an instrument in the struggle for life. Man is here to act. Only as a being in action does he fulfill his natural vocation. Contemplative natures, retrospective like all intellectuals, are dead persons who miss the meaning of life.

Professor L.G. Tirala, a philosophically trained Nazi ideologist, sees beyond the obvious romanticist sources of this attitude. He traces the Nazi activism to the two-world philosophy of Kant (which in turn he ascribes to Kant's "Aryan" nature). Kant's view, he writes, is:

> "The essence of the world is richer and deeper than the world of appearance." The world of activity and action is subject to different laws from the world of appearance. . . . [T]his primacy of action, of the world of action—in the case of Kant, especially the world of ethical action—arises from a primary predisposition of the Aryan race which does not derive from the quibbling, hairsplitting intellect ["klüglerischen Verstand"]. All Teutonic men of science have acknowledged this truth more or less consciously in a primacy of action over pure thinking. *The deed is all, the thought nothing!*[18]

Unreservedly accepting such a viewpoint, Nazis and Fascists alike frequently state that it is a matter of indifference whether the doctrines fed to the masses are true or false, right or wrong, sane or absurd. Leaders in both movements are content, even proud, publicly to describe their own ideologies as "myths" (a term popularized by the French romanticist Georges Sorel). A "myth," in the Sorelian-Fascist-Nazi sense, is not a deliberate falsehood; it is an ideology concocted for purposes of action, without reference to such issues as truth or falsehood. It is addressed not to man's capacity for reason, but to a mob's lust for faith, not to the fact-seeking intellect, but to the feeling-ridden, action-craving "will." "We have created our myth," states Mussolini. "The myth is a faith, it is a passion. . . . Our myth is the Nation, our myth is the greatness of the Nation!" Ours, writes Rosenberg in his best-known book, *The Myth of the Twentieth Century*, is "the myth of the blood, the belief that it is by the blood that the divine mission of man is to be defended. . . ."[19]

The advocacy of "myth" is one form of a more general epistemological position that had come to dominate much of the philosophic world by the latter part of the nineteenth century. Thinkers for decades had been saturated with the Kantian view that facts "in themselves" are unknowable, and with the voluntarist view that action has primacy over thought. As a result, a growing chorus—helped along by Schopenhauer, Marx, and Nietzsche, among others—began to suggest that men should dispense with any concern for facts or reality. Ideas, it was increasingly claimed, *all* ideas, are merely subjective tools designed to serve human purposes; if, therefore, an idea leads in action to desirable consequences, i.e., to the sorts of consequences desired by its advocates, it should be accepted as true on that ground alone, without reference to the (unknowable) facts of reality.

This new approach reached its climax and found its enduring name in America, in the writings of William James. James called it: *pragmatism*. "Truth independent; truth that we *find* merely; truth no longer malleable to human need"—this, says James, is what the pragmatist dispenses with. " 'The true,' to put it very briefly, is only the expedient in the way of our thinking, just as 'the right' is only the expedient in the way of our behaving."[20]

Both Fascist and Nazi leaders embraced the new approach to truth eagerly—in their advocacy of "myth," and in other, even more explicit forms.[21]

The standard by which ideas are to be judged, Hitler says repeatedly, is not "abstract" considerations of logic or fidelity to fact. The standard is: usefulness to the Volk. "Every thought and every idea, every doctrine and all knowledge," he writes in *Mein Kampf*, "must serve this purpose ["the existence and reproduction of our race and our people"]. And everything must be examined from this point of view and used or rejected according to its utility. Then no theory will stiffen into a dead doctrine. . . ."[22]

What of the non-pragmatist concern for the truth, the *objective* truth, of an idea? "[M]any apparent [Nazi] absurdities, exaggerations or eccentricities," writes one student of the movement,

> must be ascribed neither to ignorance nor stupidity or even vindictiveness; they arise from a primary and more or less conscious disregard of objective truth. For the only function of cognition in political, and even philosophical matters as they see it is to equip the fighting nation and the leaders who mould it with the most effective weapons possible.

"There is no such thing as truth," explains Hitler, "either in the moral or in the scientific sense." Or as Goebbels puts the point: "Important is not what is right but what wins."[23]

The corollary of such an attitude is unceasing intellectual flux; pragmatism leads to *relativism*. An idea, the pragmatist holds, must be judged as true or false according to its utility in a particular situation. What works today, in one situation, need not work tomorrow, in another. Thus truth is mutable. There are no "rigid" principles, not in any field. There are no absolutes.

"The needs of a state," says Hitler, ". . . are the sole determining factor. What may be necessary today need not be so tomorrow. This is not a question of theoretical suppositions, but of practical decisions dictated by existing circumstances. Therefore, I may—nay, must—change or repudiate under changed conditions tomorrow what I consider correct today."

The masses, Hitler told Rauschning, are ignorant; they have succumbed to the illusion that some ideas are absolutes. "The initiates know that there is nothing fixed, that everything is continually changing." (This is the Heraclitean doctrine, widely promulgated by the romanticists.)

"I tell you," declared Goering, dismissing a criticism of

Hitler's economic policies, "if the Führer wishes it then two times two are five."[24]

It is instructive to note that Goering's statement can be taken interchangeably as an expression of pragmatism or of dogmatism.

In their *dogmatist* capacity, the Nazis demand blind faith in a creed allegedly revealed to the Führer by God. In their *pragmatist* capacity, they stress action, expediency, and change more than God and faith. Not infrequently, these two epistemological elements come into clashing contradiction in the Nazi formulations. Nazism is the revealed truth—there is no truth. Nazi pronouncements are immutable—there are no absolutes. The creed is sacred—it is a convenient myth for practical purposes. And so on.

Observe that the Nazis give no evidence of being disturbed by this clash.

One of the reasons is that the clash was somewhat concealed, since the two elements were to an extent addressed to different audiences. The first was aimed primarily at the mass public, the second at the inner elite. "The masses," Hitler explained to Rauschning, "need something for the imagination, they need fixed, permanent doctrines."[25] This, however, is not a full explanation, inasmuch as the Nazis propagated large doses of each element side by side, both publicly and privately.

A deeper reason is that the Nazis boastfully rejected Aristotelian logic, with its demand for intellectual consistency, and were therefore untroubled by any contradictions.

But the overriding reason lies in the fact that the clash is trivial: in fundamental terms, dogmatism and pragmatism are philosophically interchangeable. They are two variants of the same irrationalism, conducting the same assault on the human mind and on reality.

The dogmatist rejects the intellect in the name of revelations from another dimension. The pragmatist rejects the intellect in the name of a flux of expedient myths. The dogmatist rejects reality, the reality men live in and perceive, avowing instead his allegiance to God. The pragmatist agrees, merely replacing God by "the people" (or the state, or the party). In both cases and in both respects, it is only the rejection that is essential—in fact, in philosophy, or to the Nazis.

What the Nazi leaders primarily sought to achieve by

means of their philosophy was obedience, the blind obedience of their followers and countrymen to the Führer. Judged by this criterion, the theory of dogmatism and the theory of pragmatism—singly or in combination—are unbeatable.

One cannot seriously oppose a doctrine, or an order, except by reference to facts that one has observed and grasped. Qua dogmatist, the Nazi is eager to brush aside such facts in favor of faith in the supernatural—as revealed to and by the Führer. Qua pragmatist, the Nazi denies facts, any facts, on principle, substituting "social utility" as his guide to truth—such utility to be determined by the embodiment and voice of society: the Führer. In both capacities, the Nazi is philosophically primed to hear, and heed, the same message, the one message the party leadership addressed urgently to every mind within range, the message expressed by Goebbels as follows: "Hear nothing that we do not wish you to hear. See nothing that we do not wish you to see. Believe nothing that we do not wish you to believe. Think nothing that we do not wish you to think."[26]

In essence, it made no difference to the Nazi leaders whether a man obeyed them for dogmatist or for pragmatist reasons, because of his commitment to God in Heaven or to the Volk on earth. What mattered was *that he obeyed*. But the Nazis preferred a man to obey for both reasons together. Dogmatism gave the Führer's words the aura of supernatural authority; pragmatism gave him all the "flexibility" he could want. The combination made it possible to claim that, when the Führer speaks, his statement is a holy truth to be revered—until he contradicts it, whereupon his new statement is to be revered; etc. Thus the Führer unites the infallibility of God's representative with the nihilism of a Machiavellian skeptic, and a new phenomenon, new at least in its brazen openness, enters the world scene: the absolute of the moment, or the immutable which never stands still, issued by an omniscience that ceaselessly changes its mind.

After many centuries of religion and one century of romanticism, most Germans were sufficiently trained in unreason. They were ready to accept the above kind of combination or at minimum one of its elements. These men were epistemologically ripe. They were willing or eager to regard Hitler, not reality, as their fundamental frame of reference. Dr. Hans Frank, Nazi Minister of Justice and President of the German Bar Association, speaks eloquently for this mentality. "Formerly, we were in the habit of saying: *this is right or wrong;* to-day, we must put the question accordingly: *What would the 'Führer' say?"*

Do abstract epistemological theories play a role in human life? What happens to men who learn, in church and in school, from early childhood on up, *not* to say "this is right or wrong"? During the war Hans Frank was Governor General of occupied Poland. He was personally responsible for the massacre of thousands of Polish intellectuals and participated in the slaughter of three and a half million Polish Jews. When a Nazi leader in Czechoslovakia hung posters proclaiming the execution of seven Czechs, Dr. Frank declared boastfully: "If I wished to order that one should hang up posters about every seven Poles shot, there would not be enough forests in Poland with which to make the paper for these posters."[27]

*   *   *

Implicit in dogmatism and in pragmatism is a third theory—part metaphysical, part epistemological—that is fundamental to the Nazi viewpoint: *subjectivism.*

In metaphysics, "subjectivism" is the view that reality (the "object") is dependent on human consciousness (the "subject"). In epistemology, as a result, subjectivists hold that a man need not concern himself with the facts of reality; instead, to arrive at knowledge or truth, he need merely turn his attention inward, consulting the appropriate contents of consciousness, the ones with the power to make reality conform to their dictates. According to the most widespread form of subjectivism, the elements which possess this power are *feelings.*

In essence, subjectivism is the doctrine that feelings are the creator of facts, and therefore men's primary tool of cognition. If men feel it, declares the subjectivist, that makes it so.[28]

The alternative to subjectivism is the advocacy of objectivity—an attitude which rests on the view that reality exists independent of human consciousness; that the role of the subject is not to create the object, but to perceive it; and that knowledge of reality can be acquired only by directing one's attention outward to the facts.

Objectivity, according to the Nazis, is a crime. It is the antonym of "instinct," and therefore a crime against the Fatherland. What Germany requires of its citizens, Hitler says repeatedly, and what Nazism offers is not dispassionate thought or even-handed judgment of fact, but unbridled nationalist emotion, emotion based on will and clinging to faith (dogmatism) or "myth" (pragmatism)—emotion that concedes nothing to any antagonist, no matter what the caliber of his arguments. "Anyone who wants to win the broad masses must know the key that opens the door to their heart," writes Hitler. "Its name is not objectivity (read weakness), but will and power." "As for me," states Goering, "I am *subjective*, I commit myself to *my people* and acknowledge nothing else on earth. I thank my Maker for having created me without what they call a 'sense of objectivity.'" "We are not objective," says Hans Schemm, the Nazi educator, "we are German."[29]

Western leaders could hardly have conceived of such statements in the eighteenth century. In our era, they utter them boastfully. The difference is the romanticist movement.

Although the theory of subjectivism was accepted in part by every important post-Renaissance philosopher, it did not achieve a successful sweep of the philosophic world until the appearance of the *Critique of Pure Reason*. "Things-in-themselves," said Kant, exist, but are unknowable; the world men perceive and deal with, the "phenomenal world," is a human creation, a product of fundamental mechanisms inherent in the structure of human consciousness. On this view, it is the essence of the subject to create the object; and objectivity, as defined above, is impossible to man. It is impossible in principle, by the very nature of the human mind.[30] If so, the romanticists concluded, we must reject the attempt to practice it. Objectivity, they said, like reason itself, is futile—and harmful. The would-be objective man, they said, is "detached," "bloodless," and the like, whereas man should instead be "warm," "committed," "vital." He should live and function under the guidance of a flow of "spontaneous" passion, uninhibited by facts, logic, or concern for external reality.

There are two different kinds of subjectivism, distinguished by their answers to the question: *whose* consciousness creates reality? Kant rejected the older of these two, which was the view that each man's feelings create a private universe for him. Instead, Kant ushered in the era of *social* subjectivism—the view that it is not the consciousness of individuals, but of *groups*, that creates reality. In Kant's system, mankind as a whole is the decisive group; what creates the phenomenal world is not the idiosyncrasies of particular individuals, but the mental structure common to all men.

Later philosophers accepted Kant's fundamental approach, but carried it a step further. If, many claimed, the mind's structure is a brute given, which cannot be explained—as Kant had said—then there is no reason why all men should have the same mental structure. There is no reason why mankind should not be splintered into *competing* groups, each defined by its own distinctive type of consciousness, each vying with the others to capture and control reality.

The first world movement thus to pluralize the Kantian position was Marxism, which propounded a social subjectivism in terms of competing economic classes. On this issue, as on many others, the Nazis follow the Marxists, but substitute race for class.

Racial subjectivism holds that a man's inborn racial constitution determines his mental processes, his intellectual outlook, his thought patterns, his feelings, his conclusions—and that these conclusions, however well established, are valid only for members of a given race, who share the same underlying constitution. "Knowledge and truth," one Nazi explains, "are peculiarities originating in definite forms of consciousness, and hence attuned exclusively to the specific essence of their mother-consciousness." On this view, each race creates its own truth (and, in effect, its own universe). There is no such thing as "*the* truth" in any issue, the truth which corresponds to the facts. There is only truth relative to a group— truth "for us" versus truth "for them," German truth versus British truth, "Nordic science" versus "the Liberal-Jewish science," etc.[31]

Men of different races, therefore, are separated by an unbridgeable gulf, an epistemological gulf, which makes it impossible for them to communicate or to resolve disputes peacefully. "An alien may be as critical as he wants to be," states Carl Schmitt, "he may be intelligent in his endeavor, he may read books and write them, but he thinks and understands things differently because he belongs to a *different kind,* and he remains within the existential conditions of his own kind in every decisive thought." (Schmitt was an influential political scientist and onetime communist, who ended as a leading Nazi theorist.)[82]

It is useless, the Nazis add, for men of "different kind" to turn to logic to resolve their disagreements, because there is not only a different truth for each race, but also a different logic. There is not one correct method of reasoning binding on all men, they say, but many opposite methods, *many logics*—Aryan, British, Jewish, etc.—each deriving from the mental structure of a particular group, each valid for its own group and invalid for the others. This is the Nazi doctrine (also adapted from the Marxists) of *polylogism.*

"[T]hinkers of the same races and predispositions will again and again ask the same questions and seek solutions in the same direction," writes the philosopher Tirala, one of the most sophisticated of the Nazi polylogists.

> And, therefore, even in the field of logic, as the foundation of all sciences, differences must be acknowledged which force thinkers and men of science to take a definite position, not only to think in this or that way, but to work differently even in the realm of the purely formal.[83]

In presenting this theory, Professor Tirala gives no indication of the nature of Aryan logical principles (nor does any other Nazi). His concern is to denounce, not to define. What he denounces is Aristotelian logic.

Subjectivism, in any version or application, is incompatible with Aristotle's laws of logic. According to Aristotle, everything is something, it is what it is independent of men's opinions or feelings about it, A is A (the Law of Identity). According to the subjectivist, A does not have to be A, it can be whatever consciousness ordains; it can be A "for one" and non-A "for another"; it can be both A and non-A, or neither, or both-and-neither simultaneously, if that is how men feel. To the philosophical defender of subjectivism, accordingly, the basic ideological enemy is far removed from the antagonists of the moment; the enemy is Aristotle.

Aristotle, Tirala writes, is emphatically not an Aryan. Aristotle was physically (according to reports) and spiritually (on the basis of his writings) to be judged a representative of the race which is not capable of producing science: his Western soul is conformable to the magical world-picture. This soul cannot understand the questioning of the Aryan spirit.[34]

Aristotle, the father of logic, regarded it as man's method of reaching conclusions objectively, by deriving them without contradiction from the facts of reality—ultimately, from the evidence provided by the senses. The polylogist sweeps this view aside and turns logic into its antithesis. By rejecting the Law of Identity, he repudiates all cognitive standards, claiming the right, based on *his* "logic," to endorse any contradiction he feels like, whenever he feels like it. Logic thus becomes a subjective device to "justify" anything anyone wishes. Logic, "Aryan logic," becomes a Nazi weapon: in the beginning was the Führer, who created the principles of inference.

In the Nazis' attack on logic, all the major elements of their irrationalist epistemology—dogmatism, activism, pragmatism, relativism, subjectivism—blend and unite. Qua dogmatist, the Nazi holds faith to be superior to logic. Qua activist, he dismisses logic in favor of action. Qua pragmatist, he is free to endorse contradictions, provided they "work." Qua relativist, he rejects the absolutism of the Law of Identity. And, qua subjectivist, the Nazi simply wipes out logic by giving its name to his random, "Aryan" feelings. These theories may differ somewhat. The conclusion to which they lead does not.

Nor do these theories differ in their practical results.

To the dogmatist who cannot persuade others to buy his revelations, there is a decisive method of silencing unbelievers: force. To the activist, the action to be taken is clear: murder. To the pragmatist, the thing that "works," if it is massive enough, is: destruction. To the relativist, peace may have been a good thing yesterday, but there are no absolutes. To the subjectivists and racializers and polylogists, a bullet in the back is valid "for you."

On their own, the Nazis could not have begun to achieve what the intellectuals accomplished for them. On their own, the Nazis could not supply the thinking needed to undercut a country, not even the thinking that told men not to think. They could not supply the philosophy, not even the philosophy that told men to despise philosophy. All of this had to be originated, formulated, and spread by intellectuals—ultimately, by philosophers.

But finding a country ready for them, the Nazis knew what to do with it. They knew how to add death-laden goose-steppers to the theory of unreason—and even what to call the combination, which was their version of the zeitgeist. Goebbels and Rosenberg called it: *steel romanticism.*

These are "times when not the mind but the fist decides," declared Hitler in *Mein Kampf.* The philosophers had eliminated the mind and provided him with the times he needed.

"I need men who will not stop to think if they're ordered to knock someone down!" Hitler told Rauschning. He had no trouble finding them.[35]

Epistemology had done its work.

4

The Ethics of Evil

In essence, there are two opposite approaches to morality: the pro-self approach versus the anti-self approach, or the ethics of *egoism* versus the ethics of *self-sacrifice*.

Egoists hold that a man's primary moral obligation is to achieve his own welfare (egoists do not necessarily agree on the nature of man's welfare). Advocates of self-sacrifice hold that a man's primary obligation is to serve some entity outside of himself. The first school holds that virtue consists of actions which benefit a man, which bring him a personal reward, a profit, a gain of some kind. The second holds that the essence of virtue is unrewarded duty, the renunciation of gain, self-denial. The first esteems the self and advocates selfishness, maintaining that each man should be the beneficiary of his own actions. The second regards selfishness in any form as evil.

"[T]he wishes and the selfishness of the individual must appear as nothing and submit," declares Hitler in *Mein Kampf*; a man must "renounce putting forward his personal opinion and interests and sacrifice both. . . ."

Morality, writes Edgar Jung, a contemporary German rightist with the same viewpoint, consists in the "self-abandonment of the Ego for the sake of higher values." Such an attitude, he notes, is the ethical base of collectivism, which demands of each man a life of "subservience to the Whole." Individualism, by contrast—since it grants man the right to pursue his own happiness—rests on the opposite attitude: "Every form of individualism sets up the Ego as the highest value, thus stunting morality. . . ."[1]

The political implementation of "subservience to the Whole," according to the Nazis, is subservience to the state—which requires of every German the opposite of self-

68

assertion. Hence the ruling principle of Nazism, as defined by a group of Nazi youth leaders. The principle is: "We will." "And, if anyone were still to ask: '*What* do we will?'—the answer is given by the basic idea of National Socialism: 'Sacrifice!' "[2]

Since the proper beneficiary of man's sacrifices, according to Nazism, is the group (the race or nation), the essence of virtue or idealism is easy to define. It is expressed in the slogan "Gemeinnutz geht vor Eigennutz" ("The common good comes before private good"). "This self-sacrificing will to give one's personal labor and if necessary one's own life for others," writes Hitler,

> is most strongly developed in the Aryan. The Aryan is not greatest in his mental qualities as such, but in the extent of his willingness to put all his abilities in the service of the community. In him the instinct of self-preservation has reached the noblest form, since he willingly subordinates his own ego to the life of the community and, if the hour demands, even sacrifices it.[3]

"Du bist nichts; dein Volk ist alles" ("You are nothing; your people is everything"), states another Nazi slogan, summarizing the essence of the Nazi moral viewpoint.

(Because Hitler demands sacrifice in behalf of the German nation rather than for the world as a whole, some commentators have described Nazism as a form of egoism, so-called "national egoism." This phrase is a contradiction in terms; the concept of egoism is not applicable to collectives, whether national or international. "Egoism" designates an ethical theory, and ethics defines values to guide an individual's choices and actions. When a theory demands that the individual wipe himself out of existence, when it denies him the moral right to exhibit any personal motivation or to pursue any private goal, it makes no difference what beneficiary, collective or supernatural, the theory then goes on to sponsor. Such a theory is the opposite of egoism.)

It has been said that men are selfish by nature and that they will not obey the demand for self-sacrifice. The Germans obeyed it.

The Nazi party did attract a great many thugs, crooks, and drifters into its ranks. But such men are an inconsequential minority in any country; they were not the reason for Hitler's rise. The reason was the millions of *non*-thugs in the land of poets and philosophers, the decent, law-abiding Germans who found hope and inspiration in Hitler, the legions of unhappy, abstemious, duty-bound men and women who condemned what they saw as the selfishness of the Weimar Republic, and who were eager to take part in the new moral crusade that Hitler promised to lead. The reason was the "good Germans"—above all, their concept of "the good."

"[H]ow little the masses were driven by the famous instinct of self-preservation," observes Hannah Arendt, a lifelong student of the totalitarian phenomenon, noting the modern Europeans' passive, unprotesting acceptance of disaster, their "indifference in the face of death or other personal catastrophes. . . ." "Compared with their nonmaterialism, a Christian monk looks like a man absorbed in worldly affairs." "The fanaticism of members of totalitarian movements," she adds, "so clearly different in quality from the greatest loyalty of members of ordinary parties, is produced by the lack of self-interest of masses who are quite prepared to sacrifice themselves."[4]

"[I]f the party and the NKVD now require me to confess to such things [crimes he did not commit] they must have good reasons for what they are doing," said a former agent of the Russian secret police. "My duty as a loyal Soviet citizen is not to withhold the confession required of me." "Do you know what I am hoping?" a girl in a Nazi breeding home told an American interviewer, her eyes shining. "I am hoping that I will have pain, much pain when my child is born. I want to feel that I am going through a real ordeal— for the Führer!" In behalf of the Nazi cause, said Adolph Eichmann, he would have sacrificed everything and everybody, even his own father; he said it proudly, to the Israeli police, "to show what an 'idealist' he had always been."[5]

The totalitarian kind of "idealism," on which Hitler and Stalin counted, was virtually unknown during the Enlightenment or in the "bourgeois" nineteenth century. In our era, it became a cultural force, gaining armies of active defenders and millions of passive admirers, not only in Germany and Russia but around the world.

As in metaphysics and epistemology, so in ethics, which is their expression: something prepared the Germans *morally* for Hitler, and the figure at the root of modern developments is Kant. The primary force behind him in this case is not Plato, but the ethics of Christianity, which Kant carried to its climax.

The major Greek philosophers did not urge self-sacrifice on men, but self-realization. Socrates, Aristotle, even Plato to some extent, taught that man is a value; that his purpose in life should be the achievement of his own well-being; and that this requires among other conditions the fullest exercise of his intellect. Since reason is the "most authoritative element" in man, writes Aristotle—the most eloquent exponent of the Greek egoism—"therefore the man who loves [reason] and gratifies it is most of all a lover of self. . . . In this sense, then, as has been said, a man should be a lover of self. . . ."[6]

Man is "sordid," retorts Augustine, the leading Christian thinker before Aquinas; he is a "deformed and squalid" creature, "tainted with ulcers and sores." Without God's grace, man's self is rotted, his mind is helpless, his body is lust-ridden, his life is hell. For such a creature, Augustine says, the moral imperative is renunciation. Man must give up the pagan reliance on reason and turn for truth to revelation—which is the virtue of faith. He must give up the prideful quest for a sense of self-value and admit his innate unworthiness, which is the virtue of humility. He must give up earthly pleasures in order to serve the Lord (and, secondarily, the needy), which is the virtue of love. Men must offer themselves to God "in sacrifice," writes Augustine. God "did not leave any part of life which should be free and find itself room to desire the enjoyment of something else."[7]

"And all that you [God] asked of me was to deny my own will and accept yours," said Augustine, and the centuries of churchmen thereafter. Deny your will, echoes the German mystic Meister Eckhart, in a voice which carried to Luther and to Kant among many others. Practice the "virtue above all virtues," obedience. "You will never hear an obedient person saying: 'I want it so and so; I must have this or that.' You will hear only of utter denial of self. . . . Begin, therefore, first with self and forget yourself!"[8]

Christianity prepared the ground. It paved the way for modern totalitarianism by entrenching three fundamentals in the Western mind: in metaphysics, the worship of the supernatural; in epistemology, the reliance on faith; as a consequence, in ethics, the reverence for self-sacrifice.

But the Christian code, thanks to the Greeks' influence, is more than an ethics of self-sacrifice. Christianity holds out to man a personal incentive, an infinite reward which each can hope to gain as recompense for his sacrifices: the salvation of his soul, his *own* soul, in blissful union with God. Like the Greeks before him, the virtuous Christian should be consumed by the desire for happiness—not for the this-worldly variety, but for an eternity of joy after death. And like the Greeks he should, at least to some extent, value himself—not his arrogant reason or lustful body, but the image of God in him, his true self: his spirit. The medieval moralist was caught in a contradiction. He urged man to forget his self—in order to save his (true) self; to do his duty, scorning personal happiness—in order to experience the latter forever; to despise his own person, mind and body—yet love his neighbor as himself.

When the medieval era drew to a close (owing to the rediscovery of Aristotle) and men turned once again to life in this world, thinkers began consciously to emulate the Greek approach to virtues and values. They began to advocate self-respect, self-realization, the cultivation of reason, the pursuit of happiness, success on earth. But just as the seeds of mysticism were firmly embedded in modern epistemology from the outset, so was their counterpart in modern ethics. The Christian passion for self-sacrifice had pervaded the Western soul, penetrating to the root of the philosophers' sense of good and evil.

In one respect, however, the moderns reinterpreted the Christian viewpoint. Jesus had commanded man first to love God and then as a consequence to love his neighbor. In accordance with the secular spirit of their era, modern philosophers inverted this hierarchy. Hesitantly, then confidently, then routinely, they downplayed the supernatural element in Christianity and emphasized the virtue of service to society. As God waned in the eyes of the moralists of sacrifice, the neighbor waxed.

How were men to combine the nascent Greek egoism with the ethics of sacrifice? They were advised by most thinkers to reach some kind of compromise or "harmony" between the two. The dominant idea of a proper harmony is eloquently indicated by Adam Smith, the Christian champion of laissez-faire, who was also one of the Enlightenment's leading moralists.

It is not true, Smith writes, "that a regard to the welfare of society should be the sole virtuous motive of action, but only that in any competition it ought to cast the balance against all other motives."

Assuming that a man is honest and industrious, says Smith, his pursuit of his self-interest "is regarded as a most respectable and even, in some degree, as an amiable and agreeable quality. . . ." Nevertheless, Smith goes on, "it never is considered as one either of the most endearing or of the most ennobling of the virtues. It commands a certain cold esteem, but seems not entitled to any very ardent love or admiration."

What *is* entitled to "ardent love"?

> The wise and virtuous man is at all times willing that his own private interest should be sacrificed to the public interest of his own particular order or society. He is at all times willing, too, that the interest of this order or society should be sacrificed to the greater interest of the state or sovereignty of which it is only a subordinate part: he should, therefore, be equally willing that all those inferior interests should be sacrificed to the greater interest of the universe, to the interest of that great society of all sensible and intelligent beings of which God himself is the immediate administrator and director.[9]

In their deepest hearts, whatever their intellectual attempts at "harmony," the Enlightenment moralists (deists included) remain Christians, not medieval saints urging self-mortification, but modern "moderates" who are content to tolerate the self—and eager to extol its piecemeal abnegation. Man's ego, in their eyes, is not a demon to be exorcised, but a homely stepchild to be dutifully awarded "a certain cold esteem," before one proceeds to the realm of "ardent love or admiration," the truly moral realm: self-sacrifice. It is as if the philosophers of the period render reluctantly unto Aristotle the things that are Aristotle's, but joyously unto Augustine the things that are Augustine's—and the things of Augustine are everything of importance.

An age of moral moderates is always a period of historical transition, a prelude to an age of moral extremism, as the dominant element in the compromise progressively gains ascendancy. The collapse of the Enlightenment moralists' precarious structure waited only for the extremist to appear.

The moralist who would not permit them to have man's ego and eat it, too, was Kant. Kant put an end to the Enlightenment in ethics as he had done in epistemology. His method was to unleash the code of self-sacrifice in its pure form, purged of the last remnants of the Greek influence.

The motor behind Hitler was not men's immorality or amorality; it was the Germans' obedience to *morality*—as defined by their nation's leading moral philosopher.

Morality, according to Kant, possesses an *intrinsic* dignity; moral action is an end in itself, not a means to an end. As far as morality is concerned, the consequences of an action are irrelevant. Thus virtue has nothing to do with the pursuit of rewards of any kind. The good-will heeds the laws of morality, Kant writes, "without any end or advantage to be gained by it. . . ."

For this reason, the worst corrupters of morality are those philosophers who offer "boasting eulogies . . . of the advantages of happiness," and hold that morality is a means to its achievement. Many false ethical theories have been advanced, in Kant's view, but "the principle of one's own happiness is the most objectionable of all. This is not merely because it is false. . . . Rather, it is because this principle supports morality with incentives which undermine it and destroy all its sublimity. . . ."[10]

Most of Kant's predecessors had assumed that men are motivated by the desire for happiness. Kant concedes this assumption. All men, he holds, "crave happiness first and unconditionally," and do so "by a necessity of nature." Nevertheless, he insists, morality has nothing to do with nature. The ground of moral obligation "must not be sought in the nature of man or in the circumstances in which he is placed. . . ." Regardless of nature, therefore, the "real end" of a creature such as man is not "its preservation, its welfare—in a word, its happiness. . . ."

This does not mean that morality is based on divine decree. Philosophy, writes Kant, must "show its purity as the

absolute sustainer" of moral laws, "even though it is supported by nothing in either heaven or earth."[11]

Moral laws, according to Kant, are a set of orders issued
to man by a nonheavenly, nonearthly entity (which I shall
discuss shortly), a set of unconditional commandments or
"categorical imperatives"—to be sharply contrasted with mere
"counsels of prudence." The latter are rules advising one how
best to achieve one's own welfare; such rules have for Kant
no moral significance. By contrast, a categorical imperative
pronounces an action "as good in itself," no matter what the
result, and thus "commands absolutely and without any
incentives. . . ."

Unconditional obedience to such imperatives, "the submission of my will to a law without the intervention of other influences on my mind," is man's noblest virtue, the "far more
worthy purpose of [men's] existence . . . the supreme condition to which the private purposes of men must for the most
part defer."

The name for such obedience is *duty*. "[T]he necessity of
my actions from pure respect for the practical [i.e., moral]
law constitutes duty. To duty every other motive must give
place. . . ."[12]

Kant draws a fundamental distinction between actions motivated by incentive or desire, actions which a man personally
wants to perform to attain some end—these he calls actions
from "inclination"—and actions motivated by reverence for
duty. The former, he holds, are by their nature devoid of
moral worth, which belongs exclusively to the latter. It is not
enough that a man *do* the right thing, that his acts be "in accord with" duty; the moral man must act *from* duty; he must
do his duty simply *because* it is his duty.

In theory, Kant states, a man deserves moral credit for an
action done from duty, even if his inclinations also favor
it—but only insofar as the latter are incidental and play no
role in his motivation. But in practice, Kant maintains, whenever the two coincide no one can *know* that he has escaped
the influence of inclination. For all practical purposes, therefore, a moral man must have no private stake in the outcome
of his actions, no personal motive, no expectation of profit or
gain of any kind.

Even then, however, he cannot be sure that no fragment of
desire is "secretly" moving him. The far clearer case, the one

case in which a man can at least come close to knowing that he is moral, occurs when the man's desires *clash* with his duty and he acts in defiance of his desires. Kant illustrates:

> [I]t is a duty to preserve one's life, and moreover everyone has a direct inclination to do so. But for that reason the often anxious care which most men take of it has no intrinsic worth, and the maxim of doing so has no moral import. They preserve their lives according to duty, but not from duty. But if adversities and hopeless sorrow completely take away the relish for life, if an unfortunate man, strong in soul, is indignant rather than despondent or dejected over his fate and wishes for death, and yet preserves his life without loving it and from neither inclination nor fear but from duty—then his maxim has a moral import.[13]

This is the sort of motivation that should govern a man in telling the truth, keeping his promises, developing his talents, etc. It should also govern him in the performance of another virtue: service to others. The latter is not a fundamental virtue, in Kant's view, merely one among many of equal importance. It is, however, one of man's duties and should be performed as such. There are, Kant says, "many persons so sympathetically constituted that without any motive of vanity or selfishness they find an inner satisfaction in spreading joy. . . ." In Kant's opinion, however,

> that kind of action has no true moral worth. . . . But assume that the mind of that friend to mankind was clouded by a sorrow of his own which extinguished all sympathy with the lot of others. . . . And now suppose him to tear himself, unsolicited by inclination, out of this dead insensibility and to perform this action only from duty and without any inclination—then for the first time his action has genuine moral worth.[14]

Kant acknowledges that the dutiful actions he counsels are "actions whose feasibility might be seriously doubted by those who base everything on experience. . . ."[15] For him, however, this is not a problem.

Experience, according to Kant, acquaints human beings

only with the phenomenal realm, the world of things as they appear to man given the distorting structure of his cognitive faculties. It does not reveal reality, the noumenal realm, the world of things in themselves, which is unknowable. In developing this dichotomy, Kant is more consistent than any of his skeptical predecessors. He applies it not only to the object of cognition, but also to the subject. A man's self, he maintains, like everything else, is a part of reality—it, too, is something in itself—and if reality is unknowable, then *so is a man's self*. A man is able, Kant concludes, to know only his phenomenal ego, his self as it appears to him (in introspection); he cannot know his noumenal ego, his "ego as it is in itself."

Man is, therefore, a creature in metaphysical conflict. He is so to speak a metaphysical biped, with one (unreal) foot in the phenomenal world and one (unknowable) foot in the noumenal world.

It is the noumenal foot that is the source of morality, the creator of man's duties, the entity which issues categorical imperatives and demands unconditional obedience. Man's earthly reason, Kant explains, is unable to provide a basis for morality; man's earthly will is ruled by the law of the pursuit of happiness. But when, in thought, we "transport ourselves" into "an order of things altogether different," we find the solution to these problems. We find that man can be "subject to certain laws," yet can be "independent as a thing or a being in itself." We find that man's true reason is replete with moral commandments, and that his true will is free, free to acknowledge the supreme authority of those commandments and to obey them.

Thus man on earth is obligated to heed the categorical imperatives of morality. He is obligated, whatever the resistance of his desires, because he himself—his real self, himself in itself—is their author. "[T]he intelligible [noumenal] world is (and must be conceived as) directly legislative for my will, which belongs wholly to the intelligible world. . . . Therefore I must regard the laws of the intelligible world as imperatives for me, and actions in accord with this principle as duties."[16]

It must be remembered that the noumenal world, including the noumenal self, is unknowable to man in Kant's view—and that the category of causality is inapplicable to it. The question, therefore, arises: how can man be influenced in any way. by the dictates of the noumenal self, to which he has neither cognitive nor causal relation? In other words, how is it possible for man on earth to take any interest in morality (as construed by Kant)? "But to make this conceivable," states Kant, "is precisely the problem we cannot solve." Kant does not regard this as a flaw in his system; rather, it is "a reproach which we must make to human reason generally. . . ."[17]

Although he is an avowed innovator in epistemology, Kant observes that in the field of morality he is not teaching "anything new," but merely developing "the universally received concept of morals. . . ."[18] In regard to the fundamentals of his ethics, this is true. Kant is the heir and perpetuator of the centuries of Christianity, which had urged on man a continuous struggle against "temptation" in the name of obedience to duty. (Kant himself was raised in a moral atmosphere of this sort carried to an extreme by a sect of puritanical Protestants.)

But Kant is not merely the child of his predecessors. There is a sense in which he *is* an innovator in ethics.

Kant is the first philosopher of self-sacrifice to advance this ethics as a matter of philosophic *principle*, explicit, self-conscious, uncompromised—essentially uncontradicted by any remnants of the Greek, pro-self viewpoint.

Thus, although he believed that the dutiful man would be rewarded with happiness after death (and that this is proper), Kant holds that the man who is motivated by such a consideration is nonmoral (since he is still acting from inclination, albeit a supernaturally oriented one). Nor will Kant permit the dutiful man to be motivated even by the desire to feel a sense of moral self-approval. "An action done merely for the sake of this feeling would be a self-centred action without moral worth," writes one British Kantian (H.J. Paton). "[I]t is always a denial of morality," Paton explains, "to bid men pursue it for what they will get out of it. . . ."[19]

The main line of pre-Kantian moralists had urged man to perform certain actions in order to reach a goal of some kind. They had urged man to love the object which is the good (however it was conceived) and strive to gain it, even if most transferred the quest to the next life. They had asked man to practice a code of virtues as a means to the attainment of *values*. Kant dissociates virtue from the pursuit of any goal. He dissociates it from man's love of or even interest in any object. Which means: *he dissociates morality from values, any values, values as such.* In "volition from duty," he writes, "the renunciation of all interest is the specific mark of the categorical imperative. . . ." This, Kant declares, is what distinguishes him from his predecessors, who failed to discover morality: they "never arrived at duty but only at the necessity of action from a certain interest."[20]

For the same reason, they never arrived at a proper concept of moral perfection, either. A perfect (or divine) will, Kant maintains, requires moral principles to guide it, though not the constraint of imperatives and duties because, by its nature, it obeys the moral law without any distracting inclinations. Such a will is free from conflict not because it is moved by a consuming passion for morality, but because it is not moved by passion or love of any kind, not even love for the good. Its perfection is precisely that it is untainted by any interest in anything. "An interest," writes Kant, "is present only in a dependent will which is not of itself always in accord with reason; in the divine will we cannot conceive of an interest."[21]

This is Kant's concept of moral perfection: perfection as subjection to law in the absence of any love or desire, perfection as not merely disinterested but *uninterested* subjection to law, perfection as selflessness, selflessness in the most profound and all-encompassing sense. This is the concept that underlies Kant's approach to man and to the concerns of human life. Moral imperatives and duties, Kant states, exist only for a "will not absolutely good," i.e., for a "being who is subject to wants and inclinations," i.e., for *a being with the capacity to hold personal values.* It is personal values that Kant condemns, not as evil, but as a "subjective imperfection" of man's lower, phenomenal nature—not as loathsome, but as meriting disdain and even "contempt." A desire, Kant holds—any desire, no matter what its object—is unworthy of the distinctively *moral* emotion: respect. I can approve of a given inclination, remarks Kant, but "I can have no respect for any inclination whatsoever, whether my own or that of another. . . ."[22]

The opposite of perfection (in Kant's view)—the opposite of non-interest, non-desire, non-value—is *self-love.* Christian moralists had always opposed self-love, but no one before

Kant ever reached his thoroughness in this regard. The fundamental ethical alternative, according to Kant, can be stated succinctly: it is the law of morality *versus* the principle of self-love. The first derives from man's noumenal character, the second from his "natural predisposition." The first gives rise to categorical imperatives, the second to counsels of prudence. The first, "stripped of all admixture of sensuous things," has "a worth which thwarts my self-love." The second "is the source of an incalculably great antagonism to morality," "the very source of evil."[23]

This does not mean that self-love in and by itself is evil, according to Kant; it is merely amoral. Evil consists in *loving* self-love; evil consists in giving self-love priority over morality in one's heart.

> Consequently man (even the best) is evil only in that he reverses the moral order. . . . He adopts, indeed, the moral law along with the law of self-love; yet when he becomes aware that they cannot remain on a par with each other . . . he makes the incentive of self-love and its inclinations the condition of obedience to the moral law; whereas, on the contrary, the latter, as the *supreme condition* of the satisfaction of the former, ought to have been adopted . . . as the sole incentive.

It is of no avail that such a man's *actions* may be unimpeachable. "The empirical character is then good, but the intelligible [noumenal] character is still evil."[24]

According to Kant, this capitulation to self-love, this "*wickedness* (the wickedness of the human heart), which secretly undermines the [moral] disposition with soul-destroying principles," taints every man.

> Out of love for humanity I am willing to admit that most of our actions are in accordance with duty; but, if we look more closely at our thoughts and aspirations, we everywhere come upon the dear self, which is always there, and it is this instead of the stern command of duty (which would often require self-denial) which supports our plans.[25]

It follows that men—"men in general, even to the best of

them"—are evil. We can, says Kant, "call it a *radical* innate *evil* in human nature"—an "innate corruption of man which unfits him for all good." (This is Kant's version of Original Sin.)

The genesis of man's evil, says Kant, is beyond comprehension. It cannot derive from man's noumenal being, which in itself predisposes man to good, or from the fact of man's inclinations (man cannot be held responsible for their existence, Kant believes). Evil, Kant holds, is by its nature *volitional,* and therefore man's evil must consist in a "perversion of our will"—a perversion that is innate, yet produced by men's free choices; a perversion *"inextirpable* by human powers," "yet none the less brought upon us by ourselves"; in short, something "inscrutable."[26]

"How it is possible," states Kant, "for a naturally evil man to make himself a good man wholly surpasses our comprehension; for how can a bad tree bring forth good fruit?"[27] Nevertheless, he insists, it *is* possible. It is man's obligation to overcome his innate evil and regenerate himself morally—a thing just as mysterious as, but no more mysterious than, the origin of man's evil.

Kant's prescription for man's moral rebirth reveals still another respect in which his ethics outdoes anything characteristic of his predecessors.

The path to moral rebirth does not lie in the obliteration of self-love and its inclinations. Kant is not an Oriental mystic; he does not advocate the cessation of feeling. Man, he holds, is partly a phenomenal being; as such, man must *and should* experience desire for the things of this world. Man's wickedness is not that he desires, but that he does not sacrifice his desires when duty demands it. His wickedness is not that he has needs, whose fulfillment "alone can make life worth desiring," but that he does not frustrate his needs, that he proceeds to *make* life worth desiring, i.e., to "cater to their satisfaction . . . in opposition to the law. . . ." Man's inclinations do present a certain problem: they "make difficult the *execution* of the good maxim which opposes them . . ."; but "genuine evil consists in this, that a man does not *will* to withstand those inclinations when they tempt him to transgress. . . ."[28]

Since men's inclinations reflect the natural craving for happiness, i.e., the inescapable law of self-love, men experience such temptation chronically and acutely. Yet in Kant's opinion this is no bar to men's spiritual regeneration; on the contrary, it can be a positive help. "[M]an can frame to himself no concept of the degree and strength of a force like that of a moral disposition except by picturing it as encompassed by obstacles, and yet, in the face of the fiercest onslaughts, victorious."[29]

It is not inner peace that Kant holds out to man, not otherworldly serenity or ethereal tranquillity, but war, a bloody, unremitting war against passionate, indomitable temptation. It is the lot of the moral man to struggle against undutiful feelings inherent in his nature, and the more intensely he feels and the more desperately he struggles, the greater his claim to virtue. It is the lot of the moral man to burn with desire and then, on principle—the principle of duty—to thwart it. The hallmark of the moral man is to suffer.

Kant makes no attempt to minimize this aspect of his viewpoint. The ideal man, he writes, is "a person who would be willing not merely to discharge all human duties himself . . . but even, though tempted by the greatest allurements, to take upon himself every affliction, up to the most ignominious death. . . ." Christianity, Kant observes, pictured the redemption of humanity as occurring once and for all through the suffering of humanity's representative, Jesus. In Kant's opinion, this is but a symbolic representation of the truth. The truth is that *every* moral man must endure suffering, "the suffering which the new [moral] man, in becoming dead to the *old*, must accept *throughout life*. . . ." (Last emphasis added.)[30]

Should the new man object that his suffering is unjust, given his sincere conversion to virtue, he may read the following: "Man, on the contrary, who is never free from guilt even though he has taken on the very same disposition [as Jesus], can regard as truly merited the sufferings that may overtake him, by whatever road they come. . . ." Should the new man cry that he cannot understand how it is possible for him, without reward of any kind, to persevere in his battle against the onslaughts of personal desire, he may read that "the very incomprehensibility of this" should be an inspiration to him. The incomprehensibility, "which announces a divine origin, acts perforce upon the spirit even to the point

of exaltation, and strengthens it for whatever sacrifice a
man's respect for his duty may demand of him."[31] (It must be
remembered that the new man endures such an existence in
order to obey a moral code, any man's interest in which, by
Kant's statement, is also incomprehensible.)

" 'Sacrifice' "—I am quoting the antipode of Kant, Ayn
Rand, in *Atlas Shrugged*—

> is the surrender of that which you value in favor of
> that which you don't. . . . It is not a sacrifice to
> renounce the unwanted. It is not a sacrifice to give your
> life for others, if death is your personal desire. To
> achieve the virtue of sacrifice, you must want to live,
> you must love it, you must burn with passion for this
> earth and for all the splendor it can give you—you must
> feel the twist of every knife as it slashes your desires
> away from your reach and drains your love out of your
> body. It is not mere death that the morality of sacrifice
> holds out to you as an ideal, but death by slow torture.[32]

In this exact sense of the term, it is sacrifice—sacrifice as
against apathy or indifference, sacrifice continual and sear-
ing—which is the essence of Kant's moral counsel to living
men.

If men lived the sort of life Kant demands, who or what
would gain from it? Nothing and no one. The concept of
"gain" has been expunged from morality. For Kant, it is the
dutiful sacrifice as such that constitutes a man's claim to virtue; the welfare of any recipient is morally incidental. Virtue,
for Kant, is not the service of an interest—neither of the self
nor of God nor of others. (A man can claim moral credit for
service to others in this view, not because *they* benefit, but
only insofar as *he* loses.)

Here is the essence and climax of the ethics of self-sacrifice, finally, after two thousand years, come to full, philosophic expression in the Western world: your interests—of
whatever kind, including the interest in being moral—are a
mark of moral imperfection *because* they are interests. Your
desires, regardless of their content, deserve no respect *because*
they are desires. Do your duty, which is yours *because* you
have desires, and which is sublime *because*, unadulterated by
the stigma of any gain, it shines forth unsullied, in loss, pain,

conflict, torture. Sacrifice the thing you want, without beneficiaries, supernatural or social; sacrifice your values, your
self-interest, your happiness, your self, *because* they are your
values, your self-interest, your happiness, your self; sacrifice
them to morality, i.e., to the noumenal dimension, i.e., to
nothing knowable or conceivable to man, i.e., as far as man
living on this earth is concerned, to *nothing*.

The moral commandment is: thou shalt sacrifice, sacrifice
everything, sacrifice for the sake of sacrifice, *as an end in itself*.

Here, to use the rightist Jung's phrase, is a morality which
advocates the "self-abandonment of the Ego," in a manner
that surpasses anything in the previous history of the West.

The consistency of Kant's ethics reflects the consistency of
his epistemology. The Greeks had affirmed both the power of
man's intellect and the value of his happiness. The Christians
had denied reason the role of arbiter of truth, but had
granted it some validity as an aid in the pursuit of
knowledge, and they had, correspondingly, granted some validity to men's pursuit of personal desires. Kant goes all the
way in both fields: if a man's senses or reason is involved in
the cognition of an object, the object he grasps is, by that
fact, nonreal; if a man's desires are involved in the motivation of an action, the action is, to that extent, nonmoral.
Thus man's mind and his self are struck down together—and
knocked out of the field of philosophy.

Kant did not preach Nazism. But, on a fundamental level
and for the first time, he flung at Western man its precondition: "Du bist nichts" ("You are nothing").

"Dein Volk ist alles" ("Your people is everything") soon
followed. Most nineteenth-century philosophers accepted every essential of Kant's philosophy and morality, except the
idea of an unknowable dimension. They proceeded to name a
surrogate for the noumenal self, an ego-swallowing, duty-im-
posing, sacrifice-demanding power to replace it. Following the
trend of the Christian development since the Renaissance, the
power they named was: the neighbor (or society, or mankind).

The result was a new moral creed, which swept the romanticist circles of Europe from the time of the first post-Kantians, and which continues to rule Western intellectuals to the

present day. The man who named the creed is the philosopher Auguste Comte. The name he coined is *altruism*.

The medieval adoration of God, says Comte, must now be transmuted into the adoration of a new divinity, the "goddess" Humanity. Sacrifice for the sake of the Lord is outdated; it must give way fully to sacrifice for the sake of others. And this time, Comte says, man must really be selfless; he must renounce not only the element of egoism approved by the Enlightenment, but also the "exorbitant selfishness" that characterized the medieval pursuit of salvation.[33] The new creed, in short, is Christianity secularized—and, thanks to Kant, with the Greek element removed.

"Altruism" is the view that man must place others above self as the fundamental rule of life, and that his greatest virtue is self-sacrifice in their behalf. (Altruists do not necessarily agree on *which* others, whether mankind as a whole or only part of it.) "Altruism" does not mean kindness, benevolence, sympathy, or the like, all of which are possible to egoists; the term means "otherism"; it means that the welfare of others must become the highest value and ruling purpose of every man's existence.

In Germany, the center of Kant's power, this idea reached its most passionate expression. In place of the earlier timid or grudging approval of self-interest, the following is what the country's philosophers, for a full century, hammered into every German ear, mind, school, and conscience.

He who "desires any life or being, or any joy of life, except *in* the Race and *for* the Race, with whatever vesture of good deeds he may seek to hide his deformity, is nevertheless, at bottom, only a mean, base, and therefore unhappy man." (Fichte)

"The noble type of consciousness . . . assumes a negative attitude toward its own special purposes, its particular content and individual existence, and lets them disappear. This type of mind is the heroism of Service. . . . [Its self-sacrifice is that] it gives itself up as completely as in the case of death. . . ." (Hegel)

A man must not desire "any reward for his works," whether it be "direct or indirect, near or remote," even if what he desires is "to work out [his] own perfection"—because morality excludes "*self-interest* in the widest sense of the term. . . . The absence of all egoistic motivation

is, therefore, *the criterion of an action of moral worth.*"
(Schopenhauer)

Someday, "need and enjoyment" will have "lost their *egoistic* character"—after we have swept aside the mentalities created by private property, who drown every human tradition "in the icy water of egotistical calculation," leaving "no other bond between man and man than naked self-interest, than callous 'cash payment.' " (Marx) [84]

The German thinkers fought among themselves on many issues, but not on fundamentals. They could not conceive a non-Kantian approach to philosophy or a non-altruist approach to morality, and they shaped the German mind accordingly. [85]

When the Germans of our century heard the following, therefore, they were ready to listen respectfully.

Christian ethics is an "ethic of self-salvation, i.e., of egoism. . . . Christian ethics place the Ego in the centre of thinking. 'A German *Volkisch* ethic educates men to make the People the centre of their thought.' " (Professor Ernst Bergmann, a Nazi intellectual)

"The Third Reich has not inscribed happiness on its banners, but virtue." (Kurt Gauger)

"Education to the heroic life is education to the fulfillment of duty"—which is what makes "the difference between this [Nazi] world of heroic self-sacrifice and the liberalistic world of barter." (Friedrich Beck)

"[I]n the chase after their own happiness men fall from heaven into a real hell. Yes, even posterity forgets the men who have only served their own advantage and praises the heroes who have renounced their own happiness. . . . Our own German language possesses a word which magnificently designates this kind of activity: *Pflichterfüllung* (fulfillment of duty); it means not to be self-sufficient but to serve the community." (*Mein Kampf*) [86]

During the Weimar years, there were many opponents of Hitler eager to pit their version of the country's ethics against his, men who demanded sacrifice not for the sake of the race, but of some other group. None of them challenged the basic premise of the German ethics: the duty of men to live for others, the right of those others to be lived for. From the outset, therefore, the opponents of Nazism were disarmed: since they equated selflessness with virtue, they could not avoid conceding that Nazism, however misguided, was a form of moral idealism.

The view that he was misguided did not cost Hitler many votes; it signaled merely a political dispute. The view that he was an idealist helped win him the country; it was a moral sanction which, in a different kind of era, he could never have hoped for.

Of all the Weimar groups invoking morality, the Nazis were the most fervent. Nazism, observes historian Koppel Pinson,

> was, as a matter of fact, the only large political movement in Germany that gave evidence of genuine idealistic, even though perversely misguided, sacrifice. . . . All the idealistic will to sacrifice seemed to be concentrated on the Right. This not only gave the movement internal strength but also served to attract a wider and larger following.

"National Socialism," writes Pinson, "with all its moral nihilism, also knew how to appeal to the idealistic impulse for sacrifice." So it did.[37]

*　　*　　*

The Nazis do not merely issue generalized exhortations to self-sacrifice. They also accept every significant consequence or expression of the altruist ethics advanced by modern philosophers.

One such expression is the elevation of the group to the position of moral lawgiver, a doctrine whose primary source is Hegel.

Kant and Fichte had said that a man can discover the content of good and evil by his own judgment, independent of the views of society. Hegel rejects this approach as too individualistic. The principles of morality, he claims, are to be determined not by an individual's mind but by his "real self," the community or the state—whose traditions and laws, in Hegel's opinion, constitute the real standard of good and evil. In the ethical man, Hegel tells us, the last vestiges of selfishness have disappeared: "the self-will of the individual has vanished together with his private conscience which had claimed independence. . . ."[38]

Modern altruists took over from the medievals the principle of self-sacrifice, then dislodged God from the position of supreme collector, replacing him with "other men." Hegel's approach pushes this trend a step further, demanding not only service to others, but also obedience to them. Others (the group) become at once the highest value and the source of values, the recipient of the individual's sacrifices and the definer of his duties, the ultimate beneficiary and the unchallengeable moral authority together, thus taking over fully the ethical role once reserved to the divine.

There had always been thinkers who advocated social conformity with a cynical or tired shrug, on the grounds that moral principles are impractical or unknowable. Only in the era of modern altruism, however, did philosophers begin to preach conformity with righteous fire—not because morality is unknowable, but because society is its source, not as a counsel of expediency, but as the virtue of self-subordination to others.

Since men do not agree in their moral feelings, according to Hegel, each group (each nation) properly legislates its own moral code, to which its own members must be obedient though that code is not binding on alien groups. This is the doctrine of social subjectivism applied to ethics. In the pre-Kantian era, ethical subjectivism was restricted to occasional skeptics; since Kant it has dominated the field of philosophy. The deepest roots of this modern shift are twofold: in epistemology, the romanticist advocacy of feeling as superior to reason; in ethics, the altruist advocacy of others as superior to self. The result is a view of morality in which the ruling standard is: the feelings of others.

On both grounds, the Nazis accept the modern view wholeheartedly, in a racialized version. Morality, they hold, is a product of racial instinct or national character: "[M]orals vary according to peoples, and so the national idea prevails in the domain of morals." Ethical ideas, like all others, are devoid of objectivity; there is no such thing as "*the* truth" in ethics, they say, but only "our truth," i.e., truth for a given race. The individual, therefore, cannot judge moral issues on his own; he must find out what his country's "race soul" approves and then act accordingly. "Right," declares Rosenberg, "is that which Aryan people find right; wrong is that which they reject."[39]

By the same token, no "alien" can criticize any German action or submit it to the judgment of an impartial, universally applicable code of morality. Anything is right, right for Germans, if the Volk decrees it. As the source of right, the Volk antecedes moral principles and is not to be limited by them.

Nor is it to be limited by its own previous moral declarations. The main line of Greek and of Christian philosophy had held that basic moral principles are immutable. The post-Kantians generally swept any such viewpoint aside: society is eminently mutable—and a mutable authority cannot generate an immutable code. If it is the decrees of society that create morality, thinkers concluded, then morality is subject to continual change. There can be no moral principles outside the prerogative of society to modify, repeal, or replace.

The Nazis agree. They, too, repudiate any unchanging code of values, any fixed theory of the nature of good and evil, virtue and vice. No ethical principles, they hold, their own included, are permanently valid. There are no moral absolutes. As in everything else, so in ethics: truth is flexible, adaptable, relative.

The Nazis' relativism in ethics is reinforced by another aspect of their ideology: their pragmatism.

According to pragmatism, the standard of truth, in morality as in science, is expediency. Ethical ideas, like all others, are to be accepted only so long as they continue to "work." Thus "Thou shalt not kill [or commit mass murder]" has the same status as "Twice two makes four": both are valid only so long as they are useful. Ethics, therefore, is mutable; virtue and vice, like truth and falsehood, are not "rigid" but relative; what counts is not abstract principles but "results." Again, by a somewhat different route, there are no moral absolutes.

The Nazis accept the social version of pragmatism. The right, they hold, is that which "works" not for an individual but for society, that which achieves public purposes, not private ones, that which promotes the welfare of the community. In this interpretation, it is the duty of the pragmatic individual to subordinate his personal desires in order to serve his fellows; i.e., it is his duty to live just as altruist theory would have him live.

In its social version, pragmatism in ethics is a *form of altruism*—an avowedly relativist, "practical" form. Qua altruists, the Nazis declare: sacrifice yourself to serve the Volk. Qua pragmatists, they declare: the right is whatever works to achieve the ends of the Volk. Both viewpoints enjoin the same basic code of conduct, and the Nazi slogan, "Right is what is good for the German people," can be taken interchangeably as a statement of either.

The man who determines what is good for the German people (and what their race soul decrees) is the man who is their embodiment and leader. For Nazism, therefore, the right and the true are to be gauged by the same ultimate standard. "*I have no conscience*," said Goering, discussing he Reichstag fire with Himmler, Frick, and others. "*My conscience is Adolf Hitler.*"[40]

As to the men who do have a conscience, the men who refuse to carry out Hitler's commands, there is, according to the Nazis, only one proper method by which to deal with them, whether they be German or non-German, anti-Nazi or uncommitted or apolitical. The advocacy of this method as a formal ethical theory is the capstone of the Nazi morality, the last of its central tenets, the most obvious (and least understood) expression of the Nazi ethical mentality.

The method is: compulsion, violence, ravishment, i.e., *physical force*, in any of its degrees from fist-backed threat to wholesale extermination.

When the Nazis glorify the Aryan as the exponent of "strength" or "power," which they never tire of doing, they do not refer to intellectual strength or unyielding integrity (these are antisocial evils in their view); they mean literal, brute strength—the power of destruction, of muscles, armies, and guns—the power effectively to wield physical force, massive force against masses of men. "Only force rules," said Hitler in 1926. "[O]n earth and in the universe force alone is decisive," he said in 1928. "Whatever goal man has reached is due to his originality plus his brutality."[41]

As his practice testified, Hitler meant this kind of utterance; it did not express a temporary mood or a fluctuating policy, but a permanent view of human life. The roots of this view lie in the Nazi epistemology and ethics.

There are only two fundamental methods by which men can deal with one another: by reason or by force, by intellectual persuasion or by physical coercion, by directing to an opponent's brain an argument—or a bullet. Since the Nazis dismiss reason out of hand, their only recourse is to embrace the second of these methods. The Nazi ethics completes the job of brute-worship: altruism gives to the use of force a *moral sanction*, making it not only an unavoidable practical recourse, but also a positive virtue, an expression of militant righteousness.

A man is morally the property of others—of those others it is his duty to serve—argue Fichte, Hegel, and the rest, explicitly or by implication. As such, a man has no moral right to refuse to make the requisite sacrifices for others. If he attempts it, he is depriving men of what is properly theirs, he is violating men's rights, their right to his service—and it is, therefore, an assertion of morality if others intervene forcibly and compel him to fulfill his obligations. "Social justice" in this view not only allows but *demands* the use of force against the non-sacrificial individual; it demands that others put a stop to his evil. Thus has moral fervor been joined to the rule of physical force, raising it from a criminal tactic to a governing principle of human relationships. (The religious advocates of self-sacrifice accept the same viewpoint, but name God, not the group, as the entity whose wishes must be enforced.)

At root, it is a dual Nazi advocacy: of unreason and of human sacrifice, which unleashes the rule of brutality. It unleashes brutality at home and abroad, in dictatorship domestically and in war internationally.

The pattern is not distinctive to the Nazis. The same cause has produced the same effect throughout Western history, no matter how varied the forms of each—whether men call their particular brand of unreason "ecstatic union with the Good" or "Divine revelation" or "dialectic logic" or "Aryan instinct"; whether they demand sacrifice in the name of the Forms or of God or of the economic class or of the master nation; whether the tyrannized subjects submit to a philosopher king or a medieval inquisitor or the dictatorship of the proletariat or the gauleiters and the Gestapo; whether the subjects are commanded to emulate the militarist conditions of Sparta, or are commanded to launch a Crusade against the infidel, or the next war of "people's liberation," or the next war for lebensraum and racial purification.

Most of these men and movements claim that their advocacy of force is temporary. Violence, they say, is necessary now, but in another dimension—in a nonmaterial reality, in the millennium, at infinity, in the classless society—men will live freely, in harmonious peace, and coercion will wither away. None, however, explains how (apart from death) his Utopia is to be reached, or how its harmony will be possible, given the premises of unreason and human sacrifice which all endorse as a permanent (not temporary) feature of their philosophies. On this issue the Nazis are more explicit than the rest: they do not apologize for preaching openly what the others practice but attempt to evade, extenuate, or minimize. The Nazis take the skeleton in the closet of centuries and rattle it boastfully. Force, they declare, will *always* be necessary, since it is in the nature of human life (which is true, if one accepts their concept of human life).

If a man is moral, says Hitler, he will submit of his own choice to the edicts of those exponents of "strength" to whom he owes his service. Idealism, he writes, "alone leads men to voluntary recognition of the privilege of force and strength, and thus makes them into a dust particle of that order which shapes and forms the whole universe." But when men, or nations, do not choose freely to become such dust particles, then: "what is refused to amicable methods, it is up to the fist to take."[42]

It has been said that the essence of the Nazi ethical mentality is difficult to define. Some commentators, observing the intensity of the Nazi altruism, conclude that the Nazis are essentially a party of burning moral idealists, that they are fanatic apostles of duty to the community. Others, however, disagree; observing the subjectivist-pragmatist-relativist aspects of the Nazi ethics and its open reliance on force, they conclude that the Nazis are essentially a gang of ethical "realists," i.e., of cynical, Machiavellian amoralists, who live by the gospel of unprincipled expediency and who are contemptuous of ideals or moral law.

This debate is artificial. In essential terms, *both* these views are correct—because these two elements of the Nazi ethics are not antithetical. They are distinguishable but harmonious aspects of one unified creed: the worship of the group.

In their Nazi form, the difference between the two is a matter of emphasis, in the nature of a division of labor. The altruist element lays down the basic approach of the Nazi ethics. It establishes the ultimate end: the welfare of a specific group; and the primary virtue: sacrifice in that group's behalf. The principle of altruism is not, however, a complete code of ethics. It does not state what constitutes the welfare of the group, or by what criteria this is to be gauged, or by what kinds of sacrifices on what kinds of occasions it is to be achieved; i.e., the altruist element, considered by itself, leaves open the specific means by which it is to be put into practice.

At this point the various derivatives of altruism take over and declare: the welfare of the group is anything it decrees, anything that satisfies its desires (subjectivism); what it decrees at present it may revoke in the future (relativism); the sacrifices that work today may fail tomorrow (pragmatism); no options may ever be foreclosed, anything goes (including brutality). In essence: altruism sets the end, and the rest gives a blank check to any means to that end. The one injects the note of fervent commitment to duty—the other, the note of unprincipled, Machiavellian realpolitik.

In the one capacity, the Nazi exudes the aura of an "idealist"—in the other, of an amoralist. But the truth is that the Nazis appeal to the particular nature of their end to derive and justify the means they use. The truth, the full truth about the Nazi ethical mentality, is the union of the two: the "idealism" defines the good abstractly, as the Nazis conceive it; the amoralism makes it possible to translate the abstraction into specific courses of action. The "idealism" validates the amoralism; the amoralism administers the "idealism."

In their formulations of the two elements, the Nazis characteristically utter clashing contradictions: sacrifice is an absolute duty—there are no absolutes; Nazism stands for social justice—justice is a myth, might makes right; the Nazi is the only virtuous man—down with conscience, the party must be practical; etc. But, as in a similar situation in their epistemology, so in ethics: this sort of clash is entirely on the surface. The clash amounts to the following. The Nazi "idealism" declares: there are no moral principles to protect the individual; we can sacrifice anyone we choose—because we are acting in the name of the only real moral principle, the welfare of the group. The Nazi amoralism declares: there are no moral principles to protect the individual; we can sacrifice anyone we choose—because the group we represent is above moral principles. The actions in both cases are the same. So is the essential, operative moral philosophy.

In epistemology, there is no fundamental contradiction between dogmatism and pragmatism; similarly, in ethics, there is no fundamental contradiction between altruism and amoralism. In epistemology, the combination enables the Führer to unite infallibility and "flexibility"; in ethics, it does an equivalent: it enables him to unite righteousness and nihilism.

In epistemology, the ultimate practical purpose of each element is the same. The purpose in ethics is the same, too: to wipe out the possibility of intellectual independence and thus ensure obedience to the Führer.

On what *moral* grounds, even in the privacy of his own mind, could a man, accepting the Nazi ethics, object to or resist any decree, no matter how brutal or monstrous, issued to him by the spokesman and embodiment of the Volk? On the grounds that the decree destroys his personal values—his goals, ambitions, happiness, life? Qua altruist, he has been trained to the view that *he* must learn to sacrifice for the sake of others. On the grounds that the decree visits suffering, expropriation, and death upon other men, who are innocent? Qua altruist, he has been trained to the view that *they* must learn to sacrifice for the sake of others. On the grounds that the decree violates his conscience, his independent moral judgment? Qua social subjectivist, he has been trained to the view that moral judgment is not his prerogative, but society's. On the grounds that the decree violates his principles? Qua pragmatist, he has been trained to the view that whatever works, as judged by the Führer, is right. On the grounds that the decree commands an absolute evil, which must be fought to the end? Qua relativist, he has been trained to the view that there are no absolutes.

The true Nazi, the man who has been philosophically prepared by all these doctrines, understands his function. He is not to express himself, but to do his duty; not to uphold his desires, but to sacrifice them; not to raise moral questions, but to accept the answers given by others; not to cling to moral principles, but to adapt himself to the ever changing voice of the collective as it determines the purpose of his life and every means to that purpose. In the field of morality, the Nazi's primary obligation is to renounce, to renounce his *self*, in the full, literal sense of the term: his values, in the name of society; his judgment, in the name of authority; his convictions, in the name of flexibility.

The Nazi metaphysics and epistemology preach *mind*-sacrifice, thereby removing facts and thought (reality and reason) from the Führer's path. The Nazi ethics completes the job: by preaching *self*-sacrifice, it removes morality from his path. The result is the destruction on every level of the possibility of individual self-assertion. The graduate of the Nazi epistemology asks: "Who am I to know?" His counterpart in ethics asks: "Who am I to know what is right?" Both give the same answer, the one absolute of their anti-absolutist mentality: "No man is an island. The Volk, or the Führer, knows best."

SS Captain Josef Kramer, the Beast of Belsen, was asked at the Nuremberg trials what his feelings were on a certain day in August 1943, when he had personally stripped and then gassed eighty women at the Natzweiler camp. He replied: "I had no feelings in carrying out these things because I had received an order to kill the eighty inmates in the way I already told you. *That, by the way, was the way I was trained.*"[40]

If one fully understands this answer of Josef Kramer, in a manner that Kramer himself perhaps did not, if one understands "the way he was trained"—trained on the deepest of all levels, at the core of his person, i.e., trained *philosophically*—one need look no further for the explanation of Nazism. What other practical result could anyone expect from a man or a culture shaped to the roots by every imaginable variant of the soul-killing ideas of a century of mind-killing, *ego*-killing philosophy?

Most men, encountering Kant's philosophy—and particularly his ethics—for the first time, regard it as inconceivable, as a perverted theory that no one could mean, live by, or ever attempt to translate into action. These same men usually regard Nazism—the actual practice of Nazism in Germany, in Poland, in the world—as inconceivable.

But in grammar, two negatives make a positive; and in a culture, in this case, two "inconceivables," if seen in relation to each other, make luminous clarity.

The Nazis took the inconceivable in theory and applied it to men's actual existence in the only way it could be done. They took the perversion in the realm of ideas and turned it into sacrificial furnaces in the realm of reality. Nothing else can explain the Nazi ideology. Nothing less can explain the Nazi practice.

He was a faithful Kantian, Adolph Eichmann told his Israeli judges. In all his bloody career, he said, he had helped some Jews only twice, and he apologized for these exceptions. "This uncompromising attitude toward the performance of his murderous duties," writes Hannah Arendt,

> damned him in the eyes of the judges more than anything else, which was comprehensible, but in his own eyes it was precisely what justified him, as it had once silenced whatever conscience he might have had left. No exceptions—this was the proof that he had always acted against his 'inclinations,' whether they were sentimental or inspired by interest, that he had always done his 'duty.'

Most Germans, Miss Arendt observes, "must have been tempted *not* to murder, *not* to rob, *not* to let their neighbors go off to their doom. . . . But, God knows, they had learned how to resist temptation."[44]

A nation taught, in the name of morality, to reject the pursuit of values can reach no other end-of-trail. Men without values are zombies or puppets—or Nazis.

*   *   *

The ranks of the Nazi movement were filled with mindless activists and nonideological brawlers, but, unknown to themselves, they acted and brawled in the service of a philosophy, the one to which the party leaders always remained faithful.

The leaders, too, were anti-intellectual. They said (in private) that Nazi ideology was merely an instrument for the control of the masses, but they never relinquished the instrument or changed its nature in any essential way. In regard to ideas, they were "pragmatic," eclectic, whim-ridden—and single-minded. Guided in part by explicit understanding of the issues, and in larger part by unidentified emotional feel, they were prepared to switch everything about their creed, except its fundamentals.

The Nazi leaders kept rewriting the theory of Aryan racism, even, during the war, going so far as to make room beside the master race for the yellow-skinned Japanese. But they never tampered with the heart of the racist theory: the worship of the group; nor did they ever make room for that which would not fit into any of the theory's variants: the independent individual. They presented themselves to the Germans as monarchists or, when more convenient, as radicals, as conservatives or as revolutionaries—but always as advocates of power, state power, *more* state power. They were theists or skeptics, idealists or materialists, dogmatists or pragmatists, but in every version they were avowed enemies of reason. They demanded self-sacrifice for the sake of the Führer or the race or the poor or the unwed mothers in the winter snow, but they demanded self-sacrifice.

"Providence," said Hitler to Rauschning,

has ordained that I should be the greatest liberator of humanity. I am freeing men from the restraints of an intelligence that has taken charge; from the dirty and degrading self-mortifications of a chimera called conscience and morality, and from the demands of a freedom and personal independence which only a very few can bear.[45]

Here he offers, if not the proper evaluation, then at least the correct order and the essential content of the Nazi philosophy, in epistemology, in ethics, in politics.

To liberate humanity from intelligence, Hitler counted on the doctrines of *irrationalism*. To rid men of conscience, he counted on the morality of *altruism*. To free the world of freedom, he counted on the idea of *collectivism*.

These three theories together constitute the essence of the Nazi philosophy, which never changed from the start of the movement to its end.

It has been said that Nazism is not a philosophy but a passion for destruction. Destruction, however, cannot be achieved with the Nazi consistency or on the Nazi scale, except by means of a certain philosophy and as an expression of it. It has been said that the Nazis are not ideologists but power-lusters. In fact, they are power-lusters whose power depends on a specific ideology. It has been said that the Nazis are not thinkers but criminals. The truth is that they are criminals spawned by thinkers, i.e., philosophically produced criminals—which is what gave them the kind of world-historical role denied to any plain criminal.

The intellectuals of the West today (as at the time of Hitler) are a product of the same philosophical trend. Most of them, still reflecting some remnant of a better past, condemn the actions of Hitler, while advocating the same basic ideas that he did (though in different variants). Such men are helpless to understand Nazism or to explain its emergence or to fight it. They purport to find the roots of Nazism in anything—in any practical crisis or any crackpot ideologue buried in the interstices of German history—in anything except fundamental philosophic ideas, the ones openly championed all around us, the ones they themselves share. Then they are forced to admit that by their account the rise of Nazism is inexplicable.

One such scholar, after presenting Nazism as an outlandish version of a narrow nineteenth-century political theory (Social Darwinism), concludes as follows: "But that such a collection of ideas could capture the allegiance of millions of rational men and women will perhaps always remain something of a mystery."[46] If his account of the Nazi ideology were true, the success of Nazism would be more than "something of a mystery"; it would be wholly unintelligible.

No weird cultural aberration produced Nazism. No intellectual lunatic fringe miraculously overwhelmed a civilized country. It is modern philosophy—not some peripheral aspect of it, but the most central of its mainstreams—which turned the Germans into a nation of killers.

The land of poets and philosophers was brought down by its poets and philosophers.

Twice in our century Germany fought to rule and impose its culture on the rest of the world. It lost both wars. But on a deeper level it is achieving its goal nevertheless. It is on the verge of winning the *philosophical* war against the West, with everything this implies.

The ideas of German philosophy have long since jumped national borders and become the trend of the West. Half the countries of Europe are already enslaved by such ideas. The rest of the continent, under similar guidance, is on the point of collapse.

There is only one country which, though paralyzed at present, is still able to resist the German takeover. In all history, it is the least likely candidate for such a takeover, if it can regain its own ideas and its self-esteem in time.

The last battle of the war of the century is now taking place—in the last of the great, unconquered nations left on earth.

5

The Nation of the Enlightenment

Since the golden age of Greece, there has been only one era of reason in twenty-three centuries of Western philosophy. During the final decades of that era, the United States of America was created as an independent nation. This is the key to the country—to its nature, its development, and its uniqueness: the United States is *the nation of the Enlightenment*.

Thomas Aquinas's reintroduction of Aristotelianism was the beginning—the beginning of the end of the medieval period, the beginning of the beginning of the era of reason.

The Renaissance carried Aquinas's achievement further. The fading of the power of religion; the revolt against the authority of the church; the breakup of the feudal caste system; the widespread assimilation of the thought of pagan antiquity; the brilliant outpouring of inventions, of explorations, of man-glorifying art; the first momentous steps of modern science—all of it meant that men had finally rediscovered the reality and the promise of this earth, of man, of man's *mind*.

The seventeenth century carried the advance still further, by means of two major achievements: in science, the discoveries that culminated in the Newtonian triumph; in philosophy, the creation (by Descartes, Locke, and others) of the first modern systems, the first attempts to provide Western man with a comprehensive world view incorporating the discoveries of the new science. Whatever their contradictions, these systems are united in proclaiming one crucial programmatic manifesto: let us sweep aside the errors of the past and make a fresh start; the universe is intelligible; there is nothing outside man's power to know, if he uses the proper method of knowledge; the method is reason.

The development from Aquinas through Locke and Newton represents more than four hundred years of stumbling,
tortuous, prodigious effort to secularize the Western mind,
i.e., to liberate man from the medieval shackles. It was the
buildup toward a climax: the eighteenth century, the *Age of
Enlightenment*. For the first time in modern history, an authentic respect for reason became the mark of an entire culture; the trend that had been implicit in the centuries-long
crusade of a handful of innovators now swept the West explicitly, reaching and inspiring educated men in every field.
Reason, for so long the wave of the future, had become the
animating force of the present. The desperate battle, it
seemed at the time, had finally been won: science had won;
ignorance, superstition, faith—i.e., religion—had lost. The
promise of the earlier centuries, it seemed, had now been ful-
filled. The philosophers and scientists had delivered on that
promise, and men were intoxicated not merely by a program
and a potential, but by the proven power and actual achievements of man's mind.

Once again, as in the high point of classical civilization,
the thinkers of the West regarded the acceptance of reason as
uncontroversial. They regarded the exercise of man's intellect
not as a sin to be proscribed, or as a handmaiden to be tolerated, or even as a breathtaking discovery to be treated
gingerly, but as *virtue*, as the norm, the to-be-expected.

It was only a brief span of decades. It did not last.

Because the systems of seventeenth-century philosophy
were profoundly flawed in every fundamental branch and issue, the very thinkers who took the lead in championing reason were also (unwittingly) preparing the way for its
eventual banishment from the philosophic scene. They were
committing all the disastrous errors of omission and commission that would shortly open the door to Hume, and then to
Kant, and then to the post-Kantian revolt against the faculty
of thought. In the graph of modern man's ascent from stag-
nant mindlessness, the Enlightenment is the high point and
the final entry. Major existential and cultural expressions of
the Enlightenment mind continued to develop into the nineteenth century and even thereafter—in science, in the rise of
romantic art, in the Industrial Revolution; but as a pervasive
philosophic force, the West's commitment to reason ended
with the eighteenth century.

Betrayed and abandoned at its height, the Enlightenment was a fleeting, precarious reprieve for the West, a brief respite from the reign of mysticism, a fragile oasis of man's liberated intellect bounded on one side by the desert of the Dark and Middle Ages (and the mixed, transitional centuries leading out of them), and on the other by the jungle of post-Kantian irrationalism.

The oasis has long since disappeared, but there is still one nation to stand as its monument: the United States of America.

Almost without exception the countries of the world owe their origins to nonideological factors: to the accidents of war, the meaningless warfare of clashing tribes, or of geography, language, custom, etc. The United States is the first nation in history to be created on the basis of *ideas*. Its Founding Fathers were not tribal chiefs or power-lusting conquerors or a revelation-encrusted priesthood; they were thinkers, thinkers of the Enlightenment—educated, articulate, thoroughly imbued with the ideas of the period. Jeered at by traditionalists on both sides of the Atlantic, these men proposed to create a nation whose institutions would be without precedent, and to do it on the basis of a theory, an abstract theory of the nature of man and of the universe. The United States, they decided, would be the first country in history to stand for something. It would be the first nation to have an avowed *philosophic* meaning.

Just as men have always been influenced by some form of philosophy, yet historians properly ascribe the birth of the science—its origin as an explicit discipline—to the ancient Greeks, so with nations: they have always been influenced by some form of philosophy, yet it was not until the United States that philosophy, as an explicit system of ideas, generated the birth of a country. The Greeks discovered philosophy. The Americans were the first to build a nation on that discovery.

Although the Enlightenment spread across Europe, introducing a liberalizing influence wherever its ideas were taken seriously (notably in England and France), there was no European country in which these ideas penetrated to the root. In Europe, the Enlightenment was in the nature of an intellectual fashion superimposed on antithetic and deeply entrenched sociopolitical structures. But the United States was a new country, a new country in a new world, and there was no such established structure to contend with. For the first and only time, the ideas of the Enlightenment became the root, the actual foundation of a nation's political institutions.

This is the great, historic feat of the United States, the source of the uniquely American character, the cause of the country's spectacular, unprecedented achievements.

But this is also the key to the tragedy of the United States. A nation based on a philosophy cannot permanently survive the collapse of that philosophy. When the European Enlightenment collapsed, there were no American thinkers of consequence to sustain or defend its principles.

Although it is the country created by philosophy, America has never produced a major philosopher. The Founding Fathers were thinkers but not philosophic innovators. They took their basic ideas from European intellectuals, they assumed with the rest of their age that these ideas were now incontestable and even self-evident, and they turned their attention to the urgent task of implementing these ideas in the realm of practical affairs.

This has always been the American pattern: from its colonial beginnings to the present day, American philosophy has been nothing but a reflection of European philosophy. Judged in terms of essentials, American thought has been a wholly derivative phenomenon, a passive, faithful handmaiden to the trends and fashions of Europe.

When Europe's ideas changed, therefore, the nation of the Enlightenment was helpless. It was left defenseless, without the philosophic resources necessary to withstand the protracted Kantian battering. From the beginning of the nineteenth century, American intellectuals, succumbing docilely to the European lead, turned increasingly against every one of America's founding ideas and ideals. While the people, taking the American system for granted, were working to build a magnificent industrial structure, the intellectuals were working to undermine the system, to discredit its root premises, to sap its self-confidence, to erode its institutions, to remake the United States in the image of the successive waves of European irrationalism.

The result is America today: a nation with the remnants of its distinctive meaning and institutions buried under more than a century and a half of intellectual wreckage; a nation which has kept some imperishable part of its original soul, but surrendered its mind to the alien ideas of the *anti*-Enlightenment; a country intellectually prostrate, haunted by a pervasive, undefined sense of uneasiness, of ominous foreboding, of national self-betrayal; a country torn by a profound conflict, without guidance or coherent direction, unable to follow its Founding Fathers or to renounce them.

*   *   *

Philosophically, the new country-to-be did not have an auspicious beginning. For a century the dominant intellectual influence in the colonies of the new world was the worst of the ideas of the old world: the devout Calvinism best articulated by *the Puritans*.

God as the vindictive sovereign of the universe; faith as the primary means of knowledge; life as a pilgrimage through an alien realm; man as a "nothing-creature" defiled by Original Sin; salvation as a miracle inexplicably granted or denied according to a rigid scheme of predestination; morality as a yoke from which man dare not pluck his neck; pleasure as a distraction, pride as the cardinal vice, human strength or efficacy as a miserable delusion; virtue as self-sacrifice, "a Surrender of our Spirits and our Bodies unto God" (and "a world of self-denial" in behalf of the neighbor)—these are the central themes of the religion that the most influential settlers from Europe brought with them to the Atlantic seaboard.[1]

The mentality of Augustinianism had been transplanted to a virgin continent. It was the period of America's Middle Ages.

Since man is innately depraved, the Puritans argued, a dictatorship ruled by the elect is required to curb his vicious impulses and enforce the Lord's commandments. Since wealth, like all values, is a gift from Heaven, men of property are not owners of their wealth, but stewards charged with a divine trust; such men are properly subject to whatever economic controls the elect deem it necessary to impose. God, in short, rules nature; his agents, therefore, rule men.

It has been said—mostly by illiterates and conservatives—that the belief in God is at the base of the American system, and that the United States is a product of Christian piety. In fact, the religious mentality was not the source of this country's distinctive institutions, but the fundamental obstacle to their emergence. So long as men took the idea of God *seriously*, the idea of America, the America conceived by the Founding Fathers, was not possible.

The transition out of the Puritan era was mediated in part by the Puritans themselves, owing to their dual heritage. As a late-sixteenth-century development, the Puritan outlook everywhere bears the mark not only of the medieval mind, but also, though less prominently, of the early modern struggle to live again in this world.

Having finally rediscovered this earth, men (including the Puritans) were eager to exploit their discovery, and it did not take long for them to grasp that this required intellectual training, personal initiative, productive enterprise (as against superstition, passivity, poverty, and the like). The former were new values in the modern world, admired to some extent throughout Europe, wherever men were animated by the Renaissance spirit. In America, these values took root more profoundly than in Europe, as a matter primarily of practical necessity. In the Puritan settlements, the requirements of existence coincided with the spirit of the Renaissance: in a wilderness, it is the values of human thought and action—or barbarism or death.

To identify the admiration of productive enterprise as the "Puritan ethic" is a misnomer, if it implies that such admiration is a religiously inspired phenomenon. What the Puritans (and their equivalents during the period) contributed to the new value-orientation was not its essential content, but its entrapment in the leftover meshes of medievalism. The claim that the pursuit of worldly success is a duty decreed by a wrathful God; the conversion of men's eager desire to exploit nature, into a grimly fearful struggle for salvation; the insistence that work must be performed selflessly, to serve God and the neighbor—all of it is medievalism reaching out to embrace and to tame an antithetic spirit.

Puritanism in America is religion trying to make terms with life on earth. It is an unstable compromise, made of two opposite philosophic approaches. In due course each was to be developed further.

The first element to be developed was the Renaissance approach. In the early decades of the eighteenth century the European Enlightenment came to America.

In every area of thought, the American Enlightenment represents a profound reversal of the Puritans' philosophic priorities. Confidence in the power of man replaced dependence on the grace of God—and that rare intellectual orientation emerged, the key to the Enlightenment approach in every branch of philosophy: *secularism without skepticism.*

In metaphysics, this meant a fundamental change in emphasis: from God to this world, the world of particulars in which men live, the realm of *nature.* For centuries of medievalism, nature had been regarded as a shadowy reflection of a transcendent dimension representing true reality. Now, whatever the vestigial concessions to the earlier mentality, men's operative conviction was that nature is an autonomous realm—solid, eternal, *real* in its own right. For centuries, nature had been regarded as a realm of miracles manipulated by a personal deity, a realm whose significance lay in the clues it offered to the purposes of its author. Now the operative conviction was that nature is a realm governed by scientific laws, which permit no miracles and which are intelligible without reference to the supernatural. Now, when men looked at nature, they saw not erratic intervention from beyond (nor inexplicable chance), but order, stability, "eternal and immutable" principles, i.e., the reign of absolute, impersonal cause and effect.

In such a universe, the fundamental epistemological principle was the sovereignty of human reason. For centuries men had sought primary truth in revelation, submitting docilely to the alleged deliverances of supernatural authority, or—later—had sought a compromise between the domain of the secular intellect and the domain of faith. Now the animating conviction was that the rational mind is man's *only* means of knowledge. Faith, revelation, mystic insight, along with the whole apparatus of Christian dogmas, mysteries, sacraments —all these the spokesmen of the Enlightenment swept aside as the futile legacy of a primitive past. *Reason the Only Oracle of Man,* Ethan Allen titled his work, expressing the widespread viewpoint. "Fix reason firmly in her seat," writes Jefferson to a nephew, "and call to her tribunal every fact, every opinion. Question with boldness even the existence of a God; because, if there is one, he must more approve of the homage of reason, than that of blindfolded fear."[2]

Reason—according to the characteristic Enlightenment

conception—is a faculty which acquires knowledge on the basis of the evidence of the senses; there are no divinely inspired, innate ideas. It is a faculty which, properly employed, can discover explanatory principles in every field and achieve certainty in regard to them. Since these principles, thinkers held, are absolute truths stating facts of reality, they are binding on every man, whatever his feelings or nationality; i.e., knowledge is *objective*. It was not heavenly illumination or skeptical doubt or subjective emotion that the Enlightenment mind extolled ("enthusiasm," i.e., irrational passion, was regarded as the cardinal epistemological sin); it was the exercise of the fact-seeking *intellect*—logical, deliberate, dispassionate, potent.

The consequence of this viewpoint was the legendary epistemological self-confidence of the period—the conviction that there are no limits to the triumphant advance of science, of human knowledge, of human progress. "The strength of the human understanding is incalculable, its keenness of discernment would ultimately penetrate into every part of nature, were it permitted to operate with uncontrolled and unqualified freedom," writes Elihu Palmer, a militant American spokesman of the period. "[I]t has hitherto been deemed a crime to think . . . ," he says; but at last men have escaped from the "long and doleful night" of Christian rule, with its "frenzy," its "religious fanaticism," its "mad enthusiasm." At last men have grasped "the unlimited power of human reason"—"Reason, which every kind of supernatural Theology abhors—Reason, which is the glory of our nature. . . ." Now, "a full scope must be given to the operation of intellectual powers, and man must feel an unqualified confidence in his own energies."[8]

A being who has discovered "the glory of his nature" cannot regard himself as a chunk of depravity whose duty is self-abasing obedience to supernatural commandments. After centuries of medieval wallowing in Original Sin and the ethics of unthinking submissiveness, a widespread wave of *moral* self-confidence now swept the West, reflecting and complementing man's new epistemological self-confidence. Just as there are no limits to man's knowledge, many thinkers held, so there are no limits to man's moral improvement. If man is not yet perfect, they held, he is at least perfectible. Just as there are objective, natural laws in science, so there are objective, natural laws in ethics; and man is capable of discovering such laws and of acting in accordance with them. He is capable not only of developing his intellect, but also of *living* by its guidance. (This, at least, was the Enlightenment's ethical program and promise.)

Whatever the vacillations or doubts of particular thinkers, the dominant trend represented a new vision and estimate of man: man as a self-sufficient, rational being and, therefore, man as basically good, as potentially noble, as a *value*.

For centuries the dominant moralists had said that man must not seek his ultimate fulfillment on earth; that he must renounce the pleasures of this life, whether as a flesh-mortifying ascetic or as an abstemious toiler, for the sake of God, salvation, and the life to come. With the new view of reality and of man, this could no longer be taken seriously. Now a new concept of the good moved insistently to the forefront of men's mind. The purpose of life, it was held, is to live, to live in this world and to enjoy it. Men refused to wait any longer. They wanted to achieve *happiness*—now, here, and as an end in itself.

For centuries, whatever their concern with the individual soul, the medievals had derogated or failed to discover the *individual man*. In philosophy, the Platonists had denied his reality; in practice, the feudal system had (by implication) treated the group—the caste, the guild, etc.—as the operative social unit. Then, in post-medieval Europe, a dawning appreciation of the individual had appeared in two different forms, in the Renaissance and the Reformation movements. Now, particularly in America, that generalized appreciation became a specific, ruling conviction.

Since reality is this world of particulars, thinkers held, the individual is fully real; the potency and value of man the rational being means the potency and value of the individual who exercises his reason. Thus when the Enlightenment upheld the pursuit of happiness, the meaning (Christian contradictions aside for the moment) was: the pursuit by each man of his own happiness, to be gained by his own independent efforts—by self-reliance and self-development leading to self-respect and self-made worldly success.

The leaders of the American Enlightenment did not reject the idea of the supernatural completely. Characteristically, they were deists, who believed that God exists as nature's remote, impersonal creator and as the original source of natural law. But, they held, having performed these functions, God thereafter retires into the role of a passive, disinterested spectator. This view (along with the continuing belief in an afterlife) is a remnant of medievalism, in process of fading out. It is in the nature of a vestigial afterthought, whose actual influence on the period is minimal. The threat to "Divine religion," observed one concerned preacher at the time, is the "indifference which prevails" and the "ridicule." Mankind, he noted, is in "great danger of being laughed out of religion. . . ."[4]

The result of the Enlightenment ideas, from every branch of philosophy, was a surging sense of liberation. "We have it in our power to begin the world over again," says Thomas Paine. "A situation, similar to the present, hath not happened since the days of Noah until now. The birthday of a new world is at hand. . . ."[5]

The father of this new world was a single philosopher: Aristotle. On countless issues Aristotle's views differ from those of the Enlightenment. But, in terms of broad fundamentals, the philosophy of Aristotle *is* the philosophy of the Enlightenment. The primacy of this world; the lawfulness and intelligibility of nature; the reality of particulars and therefore of individuals; the sovereign power of man's secular reason; the rejection of innate ideas; the nonsupernaturalist affirmation of certainty, objectivity, absolutes; the uplifted view of man and of the human potential; the value placed on intellectual development as a means to self-fulfillment and personal happiness on earth—the sum of it is Aristotelian, specifically Aristotelian, as against the mysticism of the Platonic tradition and the self-proclaimed bankruptcy of the skeptical tradition. If the key to the Enlightenment is secularism without skepticism, this means: the key is Aristotle.

In the deepest philosophic sense, it is Aristotle who laid the foundation of the United States of America. The nation of the Enlightenment is the nation of Aristotelianism.

Aristotle provided the foundation, but he did not know how to implement it politically. In the modern world, under the influence of the pervasive new climate, a succession of thinkers developed a new conception of the nature of government. The most important of these men and the one with the greatest influence on America was John Locke. The political philosophy Locke bequeathed to the Founding Fathers is what gave rise to the new nation's distinctive institutions. That political philosophy is the social implementation of the Aristotelian spirit.

Throughout history the state had been regarded, implicitly or explicitly, as the ruler of the individual—as a sovereign authority (with or without supernatural mandate), an authority logically antecedent to the citizen and to which he must submit. The Founding Fathers challenged this primordial notion. They started with the premise of the *primacy and sovereignty of the individual.* The individual, they held, logically precedes the group or the institution of government. Whether or not any social organization exists, each man possesses certain *individual rights.* And "among these are Life, Liberty and the pursuit of Happiness"—or, in the words of a New Hampshire state document, "among which are the enjoying and defending life and liberty; acquiring, possessing, and protecting property; and in a word, of seeking and obtaining happiness."[6]

These rights were regarded not as a disparate collection, but as a unity expressing a single fundamental right. Man's rights, declares Samuel Adams, often termed the father of the American Revolution, "are evident branches of, rather than deductions from, the duty of self-preservation, commonly called the first law of nature." Man's rights are *natural,* i.e., their warrant is the laws of reality, not any arbitrary human decision; and they are *inalienable,* i.e., absolutes not subject to renunciation, revocation, or infringement by any person or group. Rights, affirms John Dickinson, "are not annexed to us by parchments and seals. . . . They are born with us; exist with us; and cannot be taken from us by any human power without taking our lives. In short, they are founded on the immutable maxims of reason and justice."[7]

And "to secure these rights, Governments are instituted among Men, deriving their just powers from the consent of the governed. . . ." The powers of government are, therefore, *limited,* not merely de facto or by default, but on principle: government is forbidden to infringe man's rights. It is forbidden because, in Adams's words, "the grand end of civil government, from the very nature of its institution, is for the support, protection, and defence of those very rights. . . ."[8]

In this view, the state is the servant of the individual. It is not a sovereign possessing primary authority, but an agent possessing only delegated authority, charged by men with a specific practical function, and subject to dissolution and reconstruction if it trespasses outside its assigned purview. Far from being the ruler of man, the state, in the American conception, exists to *prevent* the division of men into rulers and ruled, It exists to enable the individual, in Locke's words, "to be free from any superior power on earth, and not to be under the will or legislative authority of man, but to have only the law of nature for his rule."[9]

"I have sworn upon the altar of God, eternal hostility against every form of tyranny over the mind of man."

Jefferson—and the other Founding Fathers—meant it. They did not confine their efforts to the battle against theocracy and monarchy. They fought, on the same grounds, invoking the same principle of individual rights, against *democracy*, i.e., the system of unlimited majority rule. They recognized that the cause of freedom is not advanced by the multiplication of despots, and they did not propose to substitute the tyranny of a mob for that of a handful of autocrats.

We must bear in mind, says Jefferson, that the will of the majority "to be rightful, must be reasonable; that the minority possess their equal rights, which equal laws must protect, and to violate which would be oppression." In a pure democracy, writes Madison in a famous passage,

> there is nothing to check the inducements to sacrifice the weaker party or an obnoxious individual. Hence it is that such democracies have ever been spectacles of turbulence and contention; have ever been found incompatible with personal security or the rights of property; and have in general been as short in their lives as they have been violent in their deaths.[10]

When the framers of the American republic spoke of "the people," they did not mean a collectivist organism one part of which was authorized to consume the rest. They meant a sum of individuals, each of whom—whether strong or weak, rich or poor—retains his inviolate guarantee of individual rights. "It is agreed," says John Adams,

> that "the end of all government is the good and ease

of the people, in a secure enjoyment of their rights, without oppression"; but it must be remembered, that the rich are *people* as well as the poor; that they have rights as well as others; that they have as clear and as sacred a right to their large property as others have to theirs which is smaller; that oppression to them is as possible and as wicked as to others.[11]

The genius of the Founding Fathers was their ability not only to grasp the revolutionary ideas of the period, but to devise a means of implementing those ideas in practice, a means of translating them from the realm of philosophic abstraction into that of sociopolitical reality. By defining in detail the division of powers within the government and the ruling procedures, including the brilliant mechanism of checks and balances, they established a system whose operation and integrity were independent, so far as possible, of the moral character of any of its temporary officials—a system impervious, so far as possible, to subversion by an aspiring dictator or by the public mood of the moment.

The heroism of the Founding Fathers was that they recognized an unprecedented opportunity, the chance to create a country of individual liberty for the first time in history—and that they staked everything on their judgment: the new nation and their own "lives, fortunes, and sacred honor." If liberty requires the principled recognition and practical implementation of man's individual rights, then Lord Acton, the famous student of liberty, spoke the truth when he said that liberty is "that which *was not*, until the last quarter of the eighteenth century in Pennsylvania."[12]

The American approach to liberty, however, rested on the philosophy of the Enlightenment—primarily, on its view of *reason* and its view of *values*, i.e., on its epistemology and its ethics. And in regard to philosophy the Americans of the revolutionary era were counting on Europe.

There was no American attempt to give systematic statement to the ideas of the Enlightenment mind, and little concern with the technical issues involved in their defense. The American thinkers functioned within an intellectual atmosphere largely taken for granted, made of generalized tendencies absorbed from Europe and invoked when necessary, in no particular order, in the course of letters, pamphlets, essays, and the like. It was an era dominated by men of action, philosophically minded but eager to apply to politics the abstract principles they had learned; men who assumed, insofar as they raised the question at all, that the philosophic base of their principles had already been established beyond challenge by the thinkers of Europe.

The Americans were counting on what did not exist. There was no such base in Europe. In every fundamental area, the thought of the European Enlightenment was filled with unanswered questions, torn by contradictions, and eminently vulnerable to challenge.

In epistemology, the European champions of the intellect had been unable to formulate a tenable view of the nature of reason or, therefore, to validate their proclaimed confidence in its power. As a result, from the beginning of the eighteenth century (and even earlier), the philosophy advocating reason was in the process of gradual, but accelerating, disintegration.

John Locke—regarded during the Enlightenment as Europe's leading philosopher, taken as the definitive spokesman for reason and the new science—is a representative case in point. The philosophy of this spokesman is a contradictory mixture, part Aristotelian, part Christian, part Cartesian, part skeptic; in short, it is an eclectic shambles all but openly inviting any Berkeley or Hume in the vicinity to rip it into shreds. The philosopher taken as the defender of nature could not establish its reality. The philosopher taken as the defender of scientific law could not validate the concept of causality, held that basic causes are outside man's power to grasp, and stated explicitly that a "science of bodies" (i.e., a science of material entities) is impossible. The philosopher taken as the champion of the senses was promulgating every doctrine necessary to invalidate them. The philosopher taken as the spokesman for the unlimited power of the human mind was proclaiming (in effect) that the field open to human cognition is a precarious island surrounded by a sea of the uncertain, the subjective, the unintelligible, the unknowable.

When the men of the Enlightenment counted on Locke (and his equivalents) as their intellectual defender, they were counting on a philosophy of reason so profoundly undercut as to be in process of self-destructing.

The same destruction was occurring in Europe in the field of ethics. Although Locke and others had held out the promise of a rational, demonstrative science of ethics, none of them delivered on this promise; none could define such an ethics. Meanwhile, European voices, rising and growing louder, were declaring that the principles of ethics are based ultimately not on reason, but on *feeling*.

James Wilson, one of the most distinguished legal philosophers of the American Enlightenment, a man who signed both the Declaration of Independence and the Constitution, expresses this view clearly. Reflecting the influence of Hume (and others), Wilson declares: "The *ultimate* ends of human actions, can never, in any case, be accounted for by reason. They recommend themselves entirely to the sentiments and affections of men, without dependence on the intellectual faculties." Morality, he states, derives from man's "moral sense" or "instincts" or "conscience." As to the validation of this faculty's pronouncements, "I can only say, I *feel* that such is my duty. Here investigation must stop. . . ."[18] Jefferson, among others, held similar views. But, regardless of who formally agreed or disagreed with Wilson on this issue, the fact is that he spoke for all of them: no American did identify the basis of a rational, scientific ethics; all, admittedly or not, were relying for ethical guidance on what they *felt* to be moral.

And what they felt is the Enlightenment mixture, which they inherited from their European mentors: the mixture endorsing Aristotelian self-assertion and self-denying, Christian love; with moral superiority awarded to the latter.

In America, the egoist element went deeper than in Europe. It was embedded implicitly in the foundations of the country. It was presupposed by the new, individualist system, which stressed the right of each man to the preservation of his own life and the pursuit of his own happiness. But the Americans did not identify the ethical issue in such terms. The general tenor of their (unsystematic) ethical statements, the dominant sentiment voiced during the period, is captured in a few brief extracts from Jefferson.

The philosophers of the ancient world, he writes, were "really great" in defining "precepts related chiefly to ourselves . . . [but in] developing our duties to others, they were short and defective." They did not advocate "charity and love to our fellow men" or "benevolence [to] the whole family of mankind." It was Jesus who left man the principles of "the most perfect and sublime" ethics—the ethics of "universal philanthropy, not only to kindred and friends, to neighbors and countrymen, but to all mankind"; the ethics which recognizes that there is "implanted in our breasts a love of others, a sense of duty to them, a moral instinct, in short, which prompts us irresistibly to feel and to succor their distresses. . . ."[14]

The Americans were political revolutionaries but not *ethical* revolutionaries. Whatever their partial (and largely implicit) acceptance of the principle of ethical egoism, they remained explicitly within the standard European tradition, avowing their primary allegiance to a moral code stressing philanthropic service and social duty. Such was the American conflict: an impassioned politics presupposing one kind of ethics, within a cultural atmosphere professing the sublimity of an opposite kind of ethics.

The signs of the conflict and of the toll it was to exact from the distinctively American political approach were evident at the beginning. They were evident in Jefferson's proposal for free public education; in Paine's advocacy of a number of governmental welfare functions; in Franklin's view that an individual has no right to his "superfluous" property, which the public may dispose of as it chooses, "whenever the Welfare of the Publick shall demand such Disposition"; etc.[15]

The American Enlightenment, like the European, came to an abrupt end. "Its ideas were soon repudiated or corrupted," writes Herbert Schneider, "its plans for the future were buried, and there followed on its heels a thorough and passionate reaction against its ideals and assumptions."[16] It was a reaction prepared for by the Enlightenment itself, by its own philosophic deficiencies, by the seeds it had nourished and allowed to sprout—the seeds of an irrationalism it was not equipped to combat and an altruism it predominantly endorsed.

Philosophically, America was born a profound anomaly: a solid political structure erected on a tottering base.

The Founding Fathers did not know that the era in which they lived and fought and planned was on the threshold of yielding to its antipode. They did not know that they had snatched a country from the jaws of history at the last possible moment. They did not know that, even as they struggled to bring the new nation into existence, its philosophic gravediggers were already at work, cashing in on the period's contradictions: in the very decade in which the Founding Fathers were publishing their momentous documents, Kant was publishing *his*.

Symbolically, this is America's philosophical conflict, running through all the years of its subsequent history. The conflict is: the Declaration of Independence, with everything it presupposes, against the *Critique of Pure Reason*, with everything to which it leads.

6

Kant Versus America

The first form of the Kantian invasion was the movement that dominated the course of nineteenth-century American philosophy: German metaphysical idealism.

The impetus to this movement in America was the desire to save religion from the onslaughts of science and of the Enlightenment mind. Brushing aside the revolutionary era's approach to philosophy, generations of American intellectuals unearthed every old-fashioned form of its antithesis, including Platonism, Orientalism, and Puritan mysticism. But for their chief inspiration they turned to the latest trends, the ones coming out of Germany.

The first wave of this American Germanism, the *transcendentalism* of Ralph Waldo Emerson and his circle, represents an eclectic, "literary" version of German romanticism. After the Civil War, as this version waned, similar ideas moved into the colleges, assuming scholarly form; for decades, until the turn of the century, the greatest power in our philosophy departments was *Hegel*.

Throughout the century, the idealists converged on the same view of reality: reality as a supersensible, "organic" dimension, i.e., God, construed as a "universal mind," an "oversoul," an "Absolute Self," etc. Physical nature, being merely "appearance," is essentially unreal, these literati and professors taught the country—and so are individuals, who are not separate entities but merely fragments of a single cosmic consciousness.

To defend such claims, the transcendentalists invoked the standard romanticist method. They lavished praise on intuition, instinct, faith, feeling, the heart, mystic insight, etc., and heaped random abuse on the senses, the intellect, logic, consistency, science. Their later academic counterparts took a different tack. Like Hegel, they presented themselves as champions of rationality, while framing ponderous constructs aimed to undercut every essential element and premise of the Aristotelian concept of reason (such as the senses, science, the finite, and much more). In its own sedate fashion, it was more thorough an epistemological assault than anything that had emanated from the New England seers.

For the practical guidance of Americans, the idealists generally condemned any form of egoism and counseled love, Christian love as construed in Königsberg and Heidelberg. We must keep in sight always "the fundamental and everlasting difference between the Idea of Duty and the Idea of Interest," writes one leading transcendentalist; the "reward of moral approbation" belongs most of all to men "who have sacrificed themselves to a sense of duty." If a man gives total loyalty to an appropriate "social cause, which binds many into the unity of one service"—states Josiah Royce, the leading Hegelian of the period in America—he can thereby achieve "fulfillment of himself through self-surrender . . . through a willing abandonment of the seeking of his own delight."[1]

The collectivist tendency of transcendentalism was often hidden by an individualist veneer, which is, however, only a veneer. (For instance, Emerson's famous doctrine of "self-reliance" demands that a man rely not on his superficial self, but on his *real* self, the "universal mind." "All is of God. The individual is always mistaken"—this from Emerson, the alleged champion of individualism.) More philosophical than the transcendentalists, the Hegelians generally dispensed with any such veneer. Individualism, states Royce, is "the sin against the Holy Ghost." "We have been forced to abandon the notion of *exclusive* individuality," declares James Edwin Creighton (the first president of the American Philosophical Association), "and to recognize that individuals have reality and significance . . . just in so far as they embody and express the life and purpose of a larger social whole of which they are members."[2]

Some of the American Hegelians disseminated the principle of collectivism in broad philosophical terms, without reference to its political implications. Others counseled a modest shift in the direction of statism while affirming their allegiance to the American system. Others were not so reticent. One demands that the state control all property, explaining that true freedom "rests upon the choice of the state," and that individual liberty, so far from being true freedom, is actually "the most hopeless bondage." Another advocates "Civic Communism," stressing that "the Government is the very Self of man made real, made a true entity, which otherwise would be unreal, untrue, having no objective validity in the world." Another declares that the state has "original, absolute, unlimited, universal power over the individual subject, and over all associations of subjects. ...."[3]

During the nineteenth century it became a trend and then the rule for American students, especially in philosophy and theology, to spend a year or more in Germany absorbing the latest German culture. An army of American students absorbed it. They came home, and they repeated what they had learned. They repeated it throughout the country that had been founded on the ideals of an enlightened mind and man's inalienable rights.

While the collectivists were finding their chief inspiration in the trends of Germany, their establishment opponents—the defenders of the American system, capitalism—were looking for answers primarily to England. During the crucial, turning-point years between the Civil War and the end of the century, they were relying for philosophic support mainly on two movements: classical economics and evolutionary biology.

The most philosophical representative of the former is John Stuart Mill, widely quoted by American conservatives at the time (and since). A weary agnostic on most of the fundamental issues of philosophy, Mill bases his defense of capitalism on the ethics of *Utilitarianism*.

Utilitarianism is a union of hedonism and Christianity. The first teaches man to love pleasure; the second, to love his neighbor. The union consists in teaching man to love his neighbor's pleasure. To be exact, the Utilitarians teach that an action is moral if its result is to maximize pleasure among men in general. This theory holds that man's duty is to serve—according to a purely quantitative standard of value. He is to serve not the well-being of the nation or of the economic class, but "the greatest happiness of the greatest number," regardless of who comprise it in any given issue. As to one's *own* happiness, says Mill, the individual must be "disinterested" and "strictly impartial"; he must remember that he is only one unit out of the dozens, or millions, of men affected by his actions. "All honor to those who can abnegate for themselves the personal enjoyment of life," says Mill, "when by such renunciation they contribute worthily to increase the amount of happiness in the world. . . ."[4]

Capitalism, Mill acknowledges, is not based on any desire for abnegation or renunciation; it is based on the desire for selfish profit. Nevertheless, he says, the capitalist system ensures that, most of the time, the actual result of individual profit-seeking is the happiness of society as a whole. Hence the individual should be left free of government regulation. He should be left free not as an absolute (there are no absolutes, says Mill), but under the present circumstances—not on the ground of inalienable rights (there are no such rights, Mill holds), but of social utility.

Under capitalism, concluded one American economist of the period with evident moral relief, "the Lord maketh the selfishness of man to work for the material welfare of his kind." As one commentator observes, the essence of this argument is the claim that capitalism is justified by its ability to convert "man's baseness" to "noble ends." "Baseness" here means *egoism*; "nobility" means *altruism*. And the justification of individual freedom in terms of its contribution to the welfare of society means *collectivism*.[5]

Mill (along with Smith, Say, and the rest of the classical economists) was trying to defend an individualist system by accepting the fundamental moral ideas of its opponents. It did not take Mill long to grasp this contradiction in some terms and amend his political views accordingly. He ended his life as a self-proclaimed "qualified socialist."

Herbert Spencer, the thinker most admired by the conservatives of the Gilded Age, tried to defend capitalism by claiming with Kant that reality is unknowable, then by interpreting the "phenomenal" world according to the theory of evolution.

In Spencer's view, every aspect of nature (not just the origin of species) is governed by evolution; the lower forms of life thus become the metaphysical model, by reference to which human life is to be understood. The lower forms subsist by competing for a limited food supply available in nature; therefore, according to evolutionary theory, there is an inexorable "struggle for existence," in which the less adapted are doomed to perish. Ignoring the fact that man is a different kind of entity—that he survives by production and is able to create a constantly increasing amount of wealth—Spencer concludes that the "survival of the fittest" is the law of human life, also.

In time, Spencer holds, the process of evolutionary human breeding will weed out the weak, perfect the strong, and guarantee mankind's happiness; but this will happen only if men do not interfere, i.e., do not seek, by economic controls or welfare legislation or undue charity, to hamper the fit or nourish the unfit. Hence governments should adopt a policy of laissez-faire.

Spencer accepts the principle of individual rights, but it is not part of his own distinctive viewpoint. According to his theory, the freedom of the strong is justified not because man has rights, but because such freedom will ultimately advance the welfare of the species. To achieve the same end, the weak are to be allowed to perish. In both cases, the operative standard of value is not the life of the individual but, in Spencer's words, "the further evolution of Humanity," "the making of Man," the "life of the race."[6]

Spencer's defense of individualism, like Mill's, proceeds from the premise of collectivism, and from the moral code at its base.

Human nature, Spencer says, is now in a comparatively low moral state, but gradually it will be reshaped. In the course of eons of evolution, selfishness will atrophy. Eventually men will reach a level of altruism "such that ministration to others' happiness will become a daily need—a level such that the lower egoistic satisfactions will be continually subordinated. . . ." In this future Utopia, men will be eager to commit acts of self-sacrifice for their fellows; they will be so eager for self-immolation "that the competition of self-regarding impulses . . . will scarcely be felt."[7]

This is the kind of moral ideal handed on to his American followers by the leading nineteenth-century champion of the system based on the profit motive. The Americans listened. Moral conduct is "the disinterested service of the community," writes John Fiske, Spencer's leading philosophic disciple in the United States; immoral conduct is "the selfish preference of individual interests to those of the community";

the "all-important consideration" is "the well-being of the community, even when incompatible with that of the individual. . . ."8

William Graham Sumner, the best-known Social Darwinist in America, represents a different development of Spencer's ideas. Sumner respected the traditional individualist virtues and did not preach altruism. But being a sociologist, not a philosopher, he did not offer any philosophic defense of the way of life he admired and often unwittingly acted to undermine it. Thus he denied the concept of natural rights; proclaimed that laissez-faire is not "a rule of science," but a matter of mere expediency; and ended as a skeptic, holding that there are no objective moral standards, and that "an absolute philosophy of truth and right . . . is a delusion."9

The American defenders of capitalism had no answer to the ideas coming out of Germany, not in any branch of philosophy and especially not in the field of ethics. As a rule, they struggled not to resolve but to evade the moral issue confronting them. The economists were wont to say that man ("economic man") is selfish by nature, and that the capitalistic status quo is therefore unalterable, no matter what the moral dreams of visionaries; besides, they often added, the moral status of capitalism is not a proper concern for economists, to whom, they said, questions of good and evil are irrelevant. The followers of Spencer were even more ardently deterministic. Man, they believed, must accept his current low moral state, sit back for millennia, and await the millennium. In a remark to a contemporary, one American Spencerian eloquently expresses this conservative mentality: "You and I can do nothing at all [in regard to current social evils]. . . . We can only wait for evolution. Perhaps in four or five thousand years evolution may have carried men beyond this state of things. But we can do nothing."10

The defenders of capitalism spent their time broadcasting the vibrations of guilt and futility. Implicitly or explicitly, they were telling the country: human intelligence is impotent to control the course of society, men are helpless in the face of their own motivation, laissez-faire appeals to the evil in men, but men are stuck with it.

The United States had been founded by men who were convinced that man is *not* impotent. Once, that conviction, in conjunction with the Enlightenment code of values, had led

Americans to revolt against tyranny. Now, however, the conviction reversed its historic role: abandoned by the pro-capitalists, it was picked up by the burgeoning statist groups of the late nineteenth century. These groups became the wave of the American future. They had two invaluable assets on their side: they were applying to practical politics the fundamental ideas accepted for years by the country's leading intellectuals; and they encountered no *moral* opposition anywhere.

Some of the new statist groups invoked religion (e.g., the Protestant Social Gospelers). Others invoked a romanticist version of science (e.g., the Reform Darwinists). Some demanded bloodshed and socialism. Most urged peaceful "reform," i.e., a compromise between laissez-faire and socialism. But all drew their strength from the same credo. Man, they said, *is* the master of his social environment; he is capable of being good *now;* a system whose motive power is the antithesis of virtue can no longer be tolerated. As to the definition of "good," the reformists felt certain about it. "Sacrifice, not self-interest, is the life of the individual, of society, of the nation," says one. The "existing competitive system is thoroughly selfish . . . ," says another. Individualism "is the characteristic of simple barbarism," says a third—and laissez-faire must be replaced by "a new conception of the functions of government and consequent enlargement of its powers, and the sphere of its operations."[11]

Through most of the nineteenth century the original American system, although hampered and increasingly contradicted, continued to function, sustained by the remnants of the Enlightenment heritage still embedded in the American mind. It was the remnants of a philosophy that had never had a proper foundation or defense, and that had been further undermined by a century of philosophic assault. Such remnants could not hold out indefinitely.

Near the end of the century the heavy artillery of the statists was moved in. The bombardment against the Enlightenment *epistemology*, waged here earlier only by a relative handful of intellectuals, began on an unprecedented scale. The name of the new bombardment was *pragmatism*.

In Europe, pragmatism was merely one element of the post-Kantian trend; in America, it became the essential form of that trend, the one which more than any other swept the intellectuals and then the country. Among European thinkers, pragmatism remained a generalized tendency; in America, the tendency took specific shape, developing into a detailed, comprehensive philosophy. To listen to pragmatists in Washington is to hear only slogans which are a final result; to read William James and John Dewey is to discover the abstract theory which underlies such a result.

American pragmatism is a continuation of the central ideas of Kant and Hegel. It is *German metaphysical idealism* given an activist development.

Man cannot know facts that exist "antecedent" to the mind, say James and Dewey, but this is not a problem because it is not the function of the mind to know such facts. The mind, says Dewey, is *not* a "spectator." Knowledge—any kind of knowledge, whether in science or in ethics—is not "a disclosure of reality, of reality prior to and independent of knowing. . . ." "The business of thought," he says, "is not to conform to or reproduce the characters already possessed by objects. . . ."[12]

The business of thought, Kant had said, is to construct out of the data it receives a universe of its own making—the physical (phenomenal) world. The business of thought (the Absolute thought), Hegel had said, is to produce a universe out of itself, by its own operations. The essence of mind, both concluded, is not to be a perceiver of reality, but to be the *creator* of reality. This is the heart of German idealism, and this is the heart of the pragmatist metaphysics.

Men, the pragmatists allow, do receive some kind of data on which their thought operates. These data, however, which the pragmatists call "experience," do not represent a firm, "antecedent" reality to be identified by man, but an unformed material to be shaped, molded, *changed* by man. The function of thought is not to "spectate," but—to use Dewey's term—actively to "reconstruct" this material, i.e., to impose a specific character on it and thereby to bring a definite reality into existence.

The idealists, according to pragmatism, are mistaken: apart from thought, there *is* some sort of realm. But the non-idealists are mistaken, too: this realm is not something specific. Reality, the pragmatists state, is not "fixed and complete in itself"; it is not "ready-made"; in itself, it is "unfinished," "plastic," "malleable," "indeterminate."[13] In itself, reality is a spread of something—*without identity*; something—which is nothing in particular.

The spread is not infinitely malleable. Sometimes, the pragmatists observe, the data man receives prove intractable, and man fails in his attempted "reconstruction" of reality. Why this should be—how it is possible for nothing-in-particular to be recalcitrant—pragmatism does not say. (Any explanation would have to refer to the nature of "antecedent" reality, a concept which pragmatism rejects.) As to *when* success or failure in reshaping reality will occur, no one, according to pragmatism, can know it in advance. In each situation all one can do is try and see. Thought is "experimental," the pragmatists state, and the essence of the experiment is the attempt to discover whether in any particular case the malleable material will or will not yield to man's demands.

Kant and Hegel, each in his own way, had imposed certain limitations on the actions of the mind; they had held that, although mind is the creator of reality, the mind nevertheless has its own inner nature and fixed principles of functioning, which it has to obey. Pragmatism disagrees. Dispensing with all "rigidity," all principles, all necessary laws, whether of reality or of the mind, the pragmatists proclaim the final climax of the idealist view: human beings, they hold, are free to select their own thought patterns in accordance with their own unrestricted choice; they are free to "experiment" with any form of thought which they can imagine or concoct; and, therefore, they are free to attempt to create whatever reality they choose, no holds barred.

In selecting a pattern of thought, according to pragmatism, there is one guide for men to follow: the demands of *action*.

In the normal course of affairs, Dewey elaborates, men do not and need not think; they merely act—by habit, by routine, by unthinking impulse. But in certain situations the malleable material of reality suddenly asserts itself, and habit proves inadequate: men are unable to achieve their goals, their action is blocked by obstacles, and they begin to experience frustration, trouble, "dis-ease." This, according to pragmatism, is when men should resort to the "instrument" of thought. And the goal of the thought is not to learn facts or know reality, but to "reconstruct" the situation so as to escape the trouble, remove the obstacles, and resume the normal process of unimpeded (and unthinking) action.

Toward this end, the mind formulates an "idea"—which is, according to Dewey, simply a "plan to *act* in a certain way as the way to arrive at the clearing up of a specific situation." If the plan when acted on removes the frustration; if the re-shaping of reality suceeds; if, in Dewey's words, "existences, following upon the actions, rearrange or readjust themselves in the way the idea intends"—then the idea is true, pragmatically true; if not, then the idea is (pragmatically) false. The ruling epistemological standard, therefore, is consequences in action. "[An idea's] active, dynamic function is the all-important thing about it," writes Dewey, "and in the quality of activity induced by it lies all its truth and falsity."[14]

Since consequences in action determine truth (and since the success of man's "experiments" to reshape reality cannot be predicted), the truth of an idea, according to pragmatism, cannot be known in advance of action. The pragmatist does not expect to know, prior to taking an action, whether or not his "plan" will work. He accepts, in Dewey's words, "the fundamental idea that we know only after we have acted and in consequence of the outcome of action."[15]

Aristotle, and the Enlightenment shaped by his philosophy, had held that reality exists prior to and independent of human thought—and that human thought precedes human action. Man, Aristotle held, must first grasp the appropriate facts of reality; on this basis, he can then set the goals and course of his action. Pragmatism represents a total reversal of this progression. For the pragmatist, the order is: man acts; he invents forms of thought to satisfy the needs of his action; reality adapts itself accordingly (except when, inexplicably, it resists). First, action—second, thought—third, reality.

Given such a view, there is nothing (in thought or reality) to impose any fixed pattern on the course of human action. Men's actions, according to pragmatism, are subject to perpetual change in every respect, as and when men so decide—and, therefore, so is thought, so is truth, so is reality. Men not only make reality, this view holds; they make it and then, when the demands of their action change, they remake it according to a new pattern until, suddenly blocked and "dis-eased," they discard that pattern and "experiment" with a new model, and so on without end.

In the whirling Heraclitean flux which is the pragmatist's

universe, there are no absolutes. There are no facts, no fixed laws of logic, no certainty, no objectivity.

There are no facts, only provisional "hypotheses" which for the moment facilitate human action. There are no fixed laws of logic, only mutable "conventions," without any basis in reality. (Aristotle's logic, Dewey remarks, worked so well for earlier cultures that it is now overdue for a replacement.) There is no certainty—the very quest for it, says Dewey, is a fundamental aberration, a "perversion." There is no objectivity—the object is created by the thought and action of the subject. The only question for a pragmatist in this latter regard is: what version of subjectivism to adopt?

William James characteristically, although not consistently, adopts the personal version. Human actions and purposes, he holds, vary from individual to individual, and therefore so does truth. John Dewey, typifying the dominant wing of the movement, rejects this approach; his *social* subjectivism represents a more faithful adherence to the ideas of Hegel (whose disciple Dewey had been in the early years of his career). There is, according to Dewey, no such thing as an autonomous individual: a man's intelligence, he holds, is fundamentally conditioned by the collective thinking of other men; the mind is not a "private" phenomenon, it is a social phenomenon. In this view, the pragmatist "reconstructor" of reality is not the individual but society. Pragmatic truth, accordingly, is that which works for the group. Truth, like thought, is "public"; it is those hypotheses which facilitate the actions and purposes of the community at large.

In the field of ethics, too, James avows his subjectivism forthrightly. Value-judgments, he holds, can be based only on feeling—on arbitrary desire or demand, whatever its content. "Any desire," he writes in an early essay, "is imperative to the extent of its amount; it *makes* itself valid by the fact that it exists at all." Hence, "*the essence of good is simply to satisfy demand. The demand may be for anything under the sun.*"[16]

Not so, declares Dewey. Before men act on a desire, he says, they must first evaluate the means required to implement it and the consequences that will (probably) flow from acting on it. What standard is to guide this evaluation? There are no absolutes, answers Dewey; in each particular situation, men are to evaluate the desire at issue by reference to whatever values they do not choose to question at the time, although any one of these values may be questioned and discarded in the next situation. The test of a desire is its compatibility not with reality, but with the rest of men's desires of the moment. The operative standard, therefore, is feeling. In this way, despite his heated disclaimers, Dewey's ethical position reduces in the end to that of James. (Dewey regards his version of the pragmatist ethics as the method of being "intelligent," "scientific," and "objective" in regard to value-judgments.)

When pragmatists claim that action is the philosophic primary, the deeper meaning of their claim is: *feeling* is the primary, the metaphysical bulwark on which the pragmatist universe is built, the irreducible, all-controlling factor, which determines action, and thus thought, and thus reality. At the core of the pragmatist universe is emotion—raw, unreasoned, blind; or, in the traditional terminology, "will."

Pragmatism accepts fully the voluntarist irrationalism of the nineteenth-century romanticists. The typical romanticist, however, openly dismissed reason in favor of feelings. Pragmatism goes one step further: it urges the same dismissal and calls it a new view of reason.

By itself, as a distinctive theory, the pragmatist ethics is contentless. It urges men to pursue "practicality," but refrains from specifying any "rigid" set of values that could serve to define the concept. As a result, pragmatists—despite their repudiation of all systems of morality—are compelled, if they are to implement their ethical approach at all, to rely on value codes formulated by other, non-pragmatist moralists. As a rule the pragmatist appropriates these codes without acknowledging them; he accepts them by a process of osmosis, eclectically absorbing the cultural deposits left by the moral theories of his predecessors—and protesting all the while the futility of these theories.

The dominant, virtually the only, moral code advocated by modern intellectuals in Europe and in America is some variant of *altruism*. This, accordingly, is what most American pragmatists routinely preach. Typically, they do not crusade for it (there are no absolutes), or even adhere to it systematically (there is no system). They merely take it for granted as unquestionable whenever they feel like it—which, given their

Kantian-Hegelian schooling, is 90 percent (or more) of the time.

In politics, also, pragmatism presents itself as opposed to "rigidity," to "dogma," to "extremes" of any kind (whether capitalist or socialist); it avows that it is relativist, "moderate," "experimental." As in ethics, however, so here: the pragmatist is compelled to employ some kind of standard to evaluate the results of his social experiments, a standard which, given his own self-imposed default, he necessarily absorbs from other, non-pragmatist trend-setters. Dewey virtually admits as much when he declares that "the genuine work of the intellectual class at any period" is not to originate standards or ideals, but "to detect and make articulate the nascent movements of their time"[17]—which means: to take over and propagate whatever standards and ideals have already been launched by earlier intellectuals.

The "nascent movement" when Dewey wrote, the political principle imported from Germany and proliferating in all directions, was *collectivism*.

The Enlightenment, states Dewey, is wrong. The traditional liberals (these include Locke and the Founding Fathers) are wrong in their "rigid doctrine of natural rights inherent in individuals independent of social organization." They are wrong in holding that the individual possessed antecedent "liberties of thought and action . . . which it was the sole business of the state to safeguard." They are wrong in believing that an expanding government is "the great enemy of individual liberty. . . ." All these ideas, Dewey remarks, were "relevant" once, but they are not "immutable truths good at all times and places"; and today, he claims, these "negative" ideas are outdated. Today, we must abandon the Enlightenment's "peculiar idea of personal liberty": "atomistic individualism," laissez-faire capitalism, the concern with private profit and "pecuniary aims," the "regime of individual initiative and enterprise conducted for private gain"—all of it now must be discarded.[18]

Intelligence, says Dewey, is not "an individual possession," but "a social asset," which "is clothed with a function as public as is its origin. . . ." Hence, "property and reward" are not "intrinsically individual." Since the minds of scientists and industrialists are a collectively created social resource, so is the wealth these minds have made possible. What America needs now, Dewey concludes, is "organized action in behalf of the social interest," "organized planning" of the economy —in short, "some kind of socialism."[19]

He does not reject individualism, Dewey says, only the concepts of an independent individual and of individual rights. He calls his theory a "new individualism."

The process of spreading a philosophy by means of free discussion among thinking adults is long and complex. From Plato to the present, it has been the dream of social planners to circumvent this process and, instead, to inject a controversial ideology directly into the plastic, unformed minds of children—by means of seizing a country's educational system and turning it into a vehicle for indoctrination. In this way one may capture an entire generation without intellectual resistance, in a single *coup d'école*.

Rarely, if ever, has a free nation capitulated to this kind of demand as rapidly, as extensively, as abjectly, as America did. When the country surrendered its educational institutions—in countless forms, direct and indirect, public and private, from nursery school on up—to the legion of Progressive educators spawned by Dewey, it formally delivered its youth into the hands of the philosophy of pragmatism, to be "reconstructed" according to the pragmatist image of man. It was a development which, in a few decades, created a new intellectual establishment in America. It was the inauguration in the country of the Enlightenment of the formal reign of Kant and Hegel, not merely among a handful of intellectuals, but among the leaders of American life in every field.

The goal of the Progressive indoctrinators was not to impose a specific system of ideas on the student, but to destroy his capacity to hold *any* firm ideas, on any subject.

The theory of Progressive education begins with an attack on the traditional, reality-oriented, intellect-oriented approach to education. For the pragmatist, education is not a process in which knowledge of "antecedent" reality, already accumulated and logically organized by men, is transmitted to the minds of their young. The function of education, writes Dewey, is not to communicate "a ready-made universe of knowledge." A school is not primarily a place to learn "intellectual lessons." The "staple of the curriculum" is not to be academic subject matter, not "[f]acts, laws, information," not "various bodies of external fact labeled geography, arithmetic, grammar, etc."[20]

According to the Progressives, education is to be not subject-centered, but child-centered. ("We don't teach history, we teach Johnny.") Education is to be "relevant," relevant to the "real interests" of the child—above all, to his interest in self-expression. His self, in this context, is his "instincts" and his "spontaneous impulses." Their natural expression is action.

For pragmatism, the child (like the man he fathers) is not primarily a thinking being, but an acting being. He does not learn primarily by listening or by reading; he "learns by doing." Since he has not been taught "ready-made" knowledge, his classroom doings are to be "experimental." Like the adult pragmatist, he learns to resort to thought as a "practical instrument" to enable him to escape the obstacles of the moment, whenever these, inexplicably, occur—and then drops the instrument when things are "working" again, as determined by his feelings. Since action is inherently concrete, the child's doings are centered around disconnected projects, which cut across all the lines of traditional academic subjects, but dip briefly and randomly into whichever subjects the teacher (or the class) feels are relevant to the project of the moment.

Such bits of information as the child does manage to absorb by this method are not, the Progressives insist, to be presented or accepted as certainties. The teacher and the pupils must not be "authoritarian," but "tentative" and "flexible."

Except on one point. Since group demands, according to Dewey, have metaphysical primacy, the function of the school is not to develop a reality-spirit or an intellectual spirit, but a "social spirit." Since "mind cannot be regarded as an individual, monopolistic possession," the function of the school is to be a trust-buster: to recondition any aspiring "monopolist" of this kind (any intellectually independent student), by training him, in Dewey's words, "to share in the social consciousness," i.e., to submit his mind to the demands of the group. The fundamental goal of education, writes Dewey, "is the development of a spirit of social co-operation and community life. . . ." The goal is to foster the child's "social capacity"—by, among other things, "saturating him with the spirit of service. . . ."[21]

Despite their relativism, the Progressives do feature one absolute, one certainty, one iron thread on which the child's various doings and projects are strung: *society*, and the imperative of conforming to it. "Life-adjustment" for this movement means "community-adjustment." The school is to be centered on the child—and the child is to be centered on the collective. This is the "new individualism" translated into the field of education.

And this is still another reason why the child should not concentrate on facts and truths in his years at school. "The mere absorbing of facts and truths," writes Dewey, "is so exclusively individual an affair that it tends very naturally to pass into selfishness. There is no obvious social motive for the acquirement of mere learning, there is no clear social gain in success thereat."[22] In the Progressive school, the child learns something transcending facts, truths, and selfishness. The modern Johnny may not be able to read, or add, or spell, or think, but he does learn to serve, to serve others, to adapt to others, to obey their spokesmen. He does not absorb "a ready-made universe of knowledge." Instead, he absorbs a "ready-made," pragmatist contempt for knowledge (and for reason), combined with a "ready-made," "practical" philosophy: altruism, collectivism, statism.

For the most part, the American intellectuals who accepted the philosophy of pragmatism were under few illusions in regard to its meaning or consequences. They knew what they were doing. This was not true, however, of the general public, businessmen included. The American people were led to embrace the pragmatist philosophy not because of its actual, theoretical content (of which they were and remain largely ignorant), but because of the method by which that content was presented to them. *In its terminology and promises*, pragmatism is a philosophy calculated to appeal specifically to an American audience.

The method, perfected especially by the Deweyites, consists in describing the philosophy in reverse. The pragmatists adopt the traditional language of science and philosophy; they flaunt the long-established, value-laden words which name the ideas deeply admired by most Americans; and they do it while discarding and even *inverting* the meaning of such language. Thus they pose as champions of the very ideas which their own philosophy systematically attacks.

The American public, descendants of the era of Enlightenment, wanted a philosophy of this world; dismissing supernaturalism and religion, the Deweyites stress "nature"—and then construe the term as meaning a flux without identity, to be molded by the desires of the group. The Americans wanted a philosophy based on reason; the Deweyites stress "scientific method" and "intelligence"—then, in the name of these, propound a voluntarist irrationalism which denies the mind's capacity to grasp reality, principles, or fixed, causal laws. The Americans wanted a philosophy based on facts; the pragmatists stress "experience"—and deny that it yields information about facts. The Americans had little sympathy for self-indulgent wallowing in emotion; the Deweyites denounce "sentimentalism"—while raising feelings to a position of philosophic primacy. The Americans admired human self-confidence; the pragmatists stress man's "power"—not his power to know, but to create, reality.

The Americans wanted a morality relevant to life; so do they, say the pragmatists, as they disseminate a cynical amoralism. The Americans admired individualism; so do they, say the Deweyites, a "new" kind of individualism, which teaches social conformity as the fundamental imperative. The Americans, scornful of passive tradition-worship, were open to new ideas; in every branch of philosophy, the pragmatists stress "experiment," "novelty," "progress," then offer a rehash of traditional theories culminating in the oldest politics of all: statism. The Americans were unable to stomach the overt mysticism of the post-Kantian Germanic axis in philosophy; the pragmatists present themselves as the exponents of a distinctively "American" approach, which consists in enshrining the basic premises of such Germanism while rejecting every fundamental idea, from metaphysics to politics, on which this country was founded. Most important of all, the Americans wanted ideas to be good for something on earth, to have tangible, practical significance; and, insistently, the pragmatists stress "practicality," which, according to their teachings, consists in action divorced from thought and reality.

The pragmatists stress the "cash value" of ideas. But the Americans did not know the "cash value" of the pragmatist ideas they were buying. They did not know that pragmatism could not deliver on its promise of this-worldly success because, at root, it is a philosophy which does not believe in this, or any, world.

When the Americans flocked to pragmatism, they believed that they were joining a battle to advance *their* essential view of reality and of life. They did not know that they were being marched in the opposite direction, that the battle had been calculated for a diametrically opposite purpose, or that the enemy they were being pushed to destroy was: themselves.

Pragmatism is the only twentieth-century philosophy to gain broad, national acceptance in the United States. It is the last philosophic movement in our era to pretend to offer Americans practical guidance and an overall view of life. Its successors in our universities, for two generations now, have renounced even the pretense; they represent not a new kind of guidance or a new philosophy, but the collapse and disintegration of the field. The disintegration has taken two forms, both imported from Europe.

One, the analyst or British axis, rejects any commitment to any ideas, even of a skeptic or mystic kind. Philosophy, in this view, has no distinctive subject matter and no practical (or theoretical) purpose. It is not a study of facts or of values; it cannot describe the universe or define the good. It is a technical linguistic pastime based on arbitrary rules (and often replete with bristling, mathematical symbolism)—an academician's private preserve or game, detached from reality and irrelevant to life.

The other form of the disintegration, the nonanalyst or Continental axis, regards the analyst viewpoint as the unavoidable, sterile expression of *reason*. This axis holds that philosophy must deal with reality and with the crucial problems of human life, by rejecting reason.

The best-known version of this view, the Existentialism of the fifties and sixties, held that reality is absurd and that irrational passion is the only means of knowledge. In such a world, said Sartre, man is the controller of his destiny, except that he cannot control it because his mind is helpless; so freedom is a "curse," and man's fate is fear, trembling, nausea—from which there is "no exit," since thought is self-deception, system-building is self-deception, a rational ethics is self-deception. All one can do, therefore, is make a blind, activist commitment to some course, or join the Zen Buddhists in merging with a superior dimension, or praise Fidel Castro as the hero of the century, or do something else, anything else, whatever anyone chooses to feel. (This is what Existentialists described as "individualism.")

Today academic philosophy in America has disappeared. It has reached the dead end of the Kantian dichotomy of thought versus reality. With its practitioners divided between absurd word-chopping and wordy absurdity-worship, it has completed a full retreat: a retreat by one group from asking any significant questions, a retreat by the other from any means of answering them. The public, in consequence, has retreated from formal philosophy, which it now regards as an object of contempt.

Today Americans no longer seek philosophic guidance from philosophers, but from whoever fills the place philosophers have vacated: politicians, economists, psychologists, gurus, etc. Such men, however, do not originate philosophic ideas or change philosophic trends. They merely transmit the ideas they have been taught and push the trends ever closer to their final conclusion.

The men who still rule our era and our country are the men who *did* originate fundamental ideas, the men who created the current trends: the philosophers of the past centuries—particularly, Kant and Hegel. The evidence of their continuing power is the dead ideas alive in America today, the ideas alive and dominant by default, not because there are crusading philosophers any longer, but because there *aren't.*

In the battle between the *Critique* and the Declaration, the *Critique,* so far, is winning hands down.

PART TWO

PRACTICE

7

United They Fell

Because philosophy deals with broad abstractions, most people regard the subject as detached from life. They regard philosophy as they would a political-party platform—as a set of floating generalities unrelated to action, generalities which are part ritualistic piety, part rationalization or cover-up, and part rhetorical hot air.

What, people ask, do these generalities have to do with the real issues of life, the issues which are immediate, topical, practical: the fierce debate in the Senate between the liberals and the conservatives, or the crisis of the economy, or the failure of the schools, or the mood of the new generation on the campuses, or the bitter controversy over the latest, shocking movie, play, painting, novel, or psychotherapeutic method.

People cannot explain the developments in the fields that do interest them because they do not know the source of those developments. In every field, the source is the choices men make, which rest ultimately on their *basic* choices. Knowingly or not, those choices flow from men's basic ideas and values. The science of basic ideas is philosophy.

If a man is skeptical about the role of philosophy in life, let him put aside philosophy books. Let him leave the cloistered ivory tower of theory and plunge into the sprawling realms of practice. Let him observe the concretes of his society's *cultural life*—its politics, its economics, its education, its youth movements, its art and religion and science. In every area, let him discover the main developments and then ask: why?

In every area, the actors themselves will provide the answer. They seldom provide it in the form of philosophical speeches. Frequently they offer moral declarations. Predominantly, however, they offer passing references, vague implications, and casual asides—which seem casual, except that the actors cannot avoid making them and counting on them. The references are the tip of the iceberg: they reveal the basic premises motivating a given development.

When a man discovers that those references, in every area, reveal the same fundamentals at work, when he sees the same broad abstractions setting the terms for every action, issue, alternative, and turning point, then he will know the power that integrates the concretes of human life and moves human history.

To understand the state of a society, one must discover the extent to which a given philosophy penetrates its spirit and institutions. On this basis, one can then explain a society's collapse—or, if it still has a chance, forecast its future.

This is what can make intelligible the fact of Hitler's rise, and the possibility of America's fall.

* * *

At 3:15 P.M. on February 6, 1919, an historic National Assembly, comprised of 423 freely elected delegates, was formally convoked in the city of Weimar, Germany. Its purpose was to replace the imperial regime of the Hohenzollerns, which had collapsed after the country's defeat in the war, with a new German government, operating in accordance with a new, republican constitution to be written by the delegates.

The delegates appreciated the significance of their meetings. The product of their debates, they knew, was to be not a paper formality, but the document that would determine the political system and thus the future of the country.

The leaders of the interim government (who were Social Democrats) had decided not to hold the assembly in Berlin, because the risk of violence was too great: Germany's Communists, refusing to participate in any parliamentary process, had taken to the streets, crying "All power to the Soviets." Besides, the leaders wished to emphasize the postwar desire to be "free from Berlin," i.e., from rule by Prussia.

Prussia, the largest and most powerful German state—a semifeudal, militarist verboten-ridden tyranny—had dominated the nation's affairs since the first united Germany was formed in 1871. The new Germany, its leaders vowed, would be made in the image not of Potsdam but of Weimar. Weimar was the longtime home and symbol of Germany's non-Prussian tradition: the tradition of Goethe and Schiller, of classical humanism, of political liberalism. It was, in effect, the symbol of the German Enlightenment.

The German Enlightenment was essentially different from its counterparts in England, France, or America. The difference may be condensed into a single fact: whatever the greatness of its artistic representatives or (as in the case of Schiller) their love of liberty, the top *philosopher* of the German Enlightenment, the figure universally taken as the country's leading champion of man, reason, and freedom, the most influential thinker of "the Weimar tradition," is Immanuel Kant.

In the meetings of the Weimar Assembly, however, during the fateful spring of 1919, the contending parties had little time to be concerned with philosophy or with Kant. They were concerned with politics and with Marx. The major contenders were the Social Democrats—an officially Marxist group carried over from the imperial period, who had emerged from the postwar elections as the nation's largest party—and various groups of conservative nationalists, who opposed the creation of a republic.

The Social Democrats continued all the longtime traditions of their party and sought support in essence from only one segment of the electorate: the "proletariat," i.e., the urban workers. The party's goal, in the words of one resolution, was "to unite the entire strength of the proletariat in the struggle against the common enemy, capitalism and reaction."[1]

The purpose of the struggle, Social Democratic leaders told the workers, is to achieve a single ideal: socialism. Socialism, they said, means public ownership of property; it means an end to rule by bourgeois greed; it means a selfless, egalitarian, classless society, in which all men live to serve the common good. Until the withering away of the state, the leaders added, socialism also means a powerful government. We must fight against the "night watchman" view of government, in order "to protect the age-old vestal fires of all civilization, the state, against the [liberal] barbarians," said Ferdinand Lassalle, the most influential source of German Social Democracy in the nineteenth century and "the greatest single figure in the [party's] history." "The state is this unity of individuals in one moral whole . . . ," said Lassalle. "The purpose of the state is, therefore, not that of protecting the personal freedom and property of the individual which, according to the bourgeoisie, the individual brings with him into the state."[2]

The single most eloquent presentation of the Social Democrats' view of life is *The Weavers*, a play by the famous late-nineteenth-century dramatist Gerhart Hauptmann. *The Weavers*, which helped to make Hauptmann "the idol of the Socialist masses," deals with the German weaving industry in the 1840's. The play depicts a mass of oppressed toilers, "flat-chested, coughing creatures with ashen gray faces . . . broken, harried, worn out," creatures bowed by servility and tortured by constant hunger (one old man must eat his pet dog in order to stay alive). The cause of all the misery, says the play, is the forces of the establishment—above all, the fat, rapacious "devils of manufacturers," who live in palaces, gorge on pastries, and bathe their babies in wine and milk. Such men, the weavers cry, are "hangmen all . . . demons from the pit of hell. . . . Your goal is known to everyone, To bleed us poor men dry." In the end the weavers, pushed too far, rise up in the name of social justice, sack the homes of the capitalists, wreck all their possessions, and then march off to smash once and for all the workers' chief enemy: "From here we'll go over to . . . the steam power looms. . . . All the trouble comes from those factories."[8]

The Weavers conveys perfectly the basic emotion, and emotionalism, which animated Germany's Marxists of both kinds, Social Democrat and Communist. In their bitter, sweeping denunciations of the "class enemy" and in their fiery predictions of its "revolutionary" overthrow, the two groups, whatever their differences in regard to tactics, were at one.

In practice, however, the Social Democrats did not approve of sacking homes or smashing up power-looms—and their struggle was not so much against class enemies as against Communist guns. The Social Democrats opposed violence, a proletarian putsch, and Bolshevist Russia—not its ends, which they regarded as noble, but its methods, which they regarded as uncivilized and brutal. Socialism, they said, must come to Germany lawfully, by parliamentary decision; which, they said, meant a slow, evolutionary process, inasmuch as a majority of the German people was anti-Marxist and would have to be reeducated.

In the interim, party leaders decided, they would continue to preach Marxist ideas with all the party's traditional zeal, but would confine themselves in practice to pursuing a limited, "Reformist" program in the Reichstag. "Reformism" in this context means a form of welfare statism. It means the policy of working within the framework of a semisocialist, semicapitalist "mixed" system, in order to secure the passage or strengthening of piecemeal pro-labor programs, including such items as the extension of union power, the eight-hour day, minimum wages, unemployment insurance, government housing, socialized medicine, government controls over industry, and higher, graduated taxes on upper-income individuals and on business profits.

The party, said its Marxist oratory, rejects the kind of temporizing, social-welfare measures introduced in the imperial era by Bismarck—measures which merely delay and subvert the coming revolution. Such measures, said the party's Reformist practice, are precisely what the party is fighting for.

We stand solidly, said the Democratic face of Social Democracy, with the moderate bourgeois parties in defense of the republican system, which protects the civil rights and liberties of all men. This "capitalistic" republic, said the Social face of Social Democracy, is merely a transitional stage, a necessary evil, on the road to a truly moral society, in which men will enjoy something greater than liberty: economic equality. "The worker," said August Bebel (a revered prewar party leader), "has little interest in a state in which political liberty is merely the goal. . . . What good is mere political liberty to him if he is hungry?"[4]

Down with the sham liberty of capitalism, shouted impassioned speakers at party rallies. Not now, pleaded the same men the next morning; first we must give the capitalists a chance to rebuild the country after the war: "[I]t seems impossible for us to transfer industry into the possession of the community at a time when the productive forces of the country are almost exhausted. It is impossible to socialize when there is hardly anything to socialize."[5]

"Give me chastity and continence, but not yet," said Augustine in a famous prayer, expressing the torture of a profound inner conflict. Transposed to the political arena, this in essence was the conflict and the torture of postwar Germany's leading party.

The Social Democrats have been condemned as ineffectual by virtually all commentators on the Weimar Republic. The standard explanation is that the party leaders' moral character or experience or strategy was inadequate. In fact, the root of the party's deficiency was not personal or tactical; it was ideological. In their Marxist ideals, the Social Democrats were heirs to Germany's central, collectivist tradition. In their republican methods, they were clinging to remnants of an opposite (and in Germany weak and peripheral) tradition: the Enlightenment world view. The result was a party incapable by its nature of providing a nation with decisive leadership, a party impaled from the outset on a fundamental contradiction.

It did not take long for the political jokes to begin. Their butt was revolutionists who wanted peace and quiet; proletarian militants who made collaboration with the bourgeoisie an essential policy; socialists who refused to socialize.

Such were the men whom the German conservatives at the time took to be the champions of a scientific approach to life.

The conservatives, whose main political outlet was the Nationalist party, were the groups that sought a restoration of the monarchy (or, failing this, rule by a military junta). These groups included most of the leaders of the imperial establishment, such as the wealthy Junker landlords, the powerful Officer Corps, and many prominent German judges, bureaucrats, industrialists. Two groups in particular were the most influential in proselytizing for the conservative viewpoint. One was the country's largest religious denomination, the Lutheran Church, which, faithful to the ideas of its founder, had long been a bulwark of Prussianism. The other was the profession trained to teach young minds, the educational-professorial establishment, which, transferred intact from the empire to the Republic, remained to the end a loyal product of the Kaisers.

What socialism was to the leftists, nationalism was to the conservatives: it was their ideology, their political ideal, their common bond. "Nationalism" in this context means the belief in the superiority of the "German soul" over "Western decadence," and, as corollary, the belief in the historic mission of the Fatherland, its mission to guide (or rule) the world's lesser peoples.

The conservatives did not attempt to prove the inherent superiority of all things German. They felt it, and that was enough for them. The German soul, they often said, rejects intellectual analysis; it functions decisively, by instinct. It rejects the plodding debates of "isolated" individuals, which characterize parliamentary government; instead, it demands "organic unity" and a state embodying "the principle of authority." It rejects all talk about man's rights as mere "Western selfishness." What it cherishes is duty, and self-sacrifice for the Fatherland.

Most of the conservatives were religious men, who regarded their basic ideas as inherent in a Christian approach to life. Typically, the public statements of these men dwelt on such themes as the value of faith, the evil of atheism, the importance of church and family, and the need of religious schools to guide the young and immunize them against radicalism. Whether they invoked religion or not, however, the conservatives characteristically reviled "the rational Republic." This was not meant as sarcasm; in their opinion the Republic *was* rational. On this subject, all were prepared to agree with Luther. "There is on earth among all dangers no more dangerous thing than a richly endowed and adroit reason," Luther had said. "Reason must be deluded, blinded, and destroyed."[6]

In economics, as in philosophy and politics, the conservatives stood for tradition, German tradition.

Faithful to its dominant nineteenth-century ideas, Germany, alone among the major Western nations, had never entered the era of classic liberalism; in varying forms and degrees the German states had characteristically been regulated economies. Then, in the Prussian-dominated empire, Bismarck and his successors had entrenched many new controls, including the policy of awarding special favors from the Reich government—subsidies, protective tariffs, and the like—to the country's big landowners and industrialists. In addition, to placate the rising labor movement, Bismarck in the 1880's had created in Germany the world's first welfare state, complete with programs for compulsory health insurance, workmen's compensation, and old-age and disability insurance.

Bismarck's conservative supporters at the time, including the professorate and the Lutheran Church, had accepted such programs enthusiastically, as a natural expression of Prussian paternalism, social-mindedness, and sense of duty. The base of Bismarck's approach was established by the so-called "socialists of the chair," a group of highly influential social-science professors at the German universities. The ideas of these men, notes von Mises, "were almost identical with those later held by the British Fabians and the American Institutionalists. . . ." As to the Lutherans, most had followed the lead of such figures as Pastor Adolf Stoecker; they had rejected capitalism as an evil, Jewish idea, incompatible with the spirit of Christianity. "[I]n no other country had the idea of social reform taken hold of people's minds as thoroughly as in Germany . . . ," summarizes one historian (who makes no attempt to explain the fact).[7]

The Weimar conservatives followed their Bismarckian mentors. They advocated all the imperial types of controls, programs, taxes, and rejected two policies. One was unhampered Western capitalism (which they often described as plutocracy, pacifism, or "Jewish greed"); the other was "radical experiments," i.e., any *new* government programs designed to tip the balance of power in favor of labor. In place of both policies, the conservatives demanded private property "in the German sense." The German sense, they said, means a recognition of private ownership (in some areas), combined with the principle that property must be used to serve the welfare of the nation, as determined by the authorities of the state.

The deadliest enemy of the country, the conservatives declared, is socialism. Their working definition of socialism was: state control of the economy for the sake of benefiting the lower classes. They fumed against it, demanding state control of the economy for the sake of benefiting the upper classes.

The Nationalist party (and a somewhat similar group, the People's party) was regarded in Germany as the political right. The term "right," in Germany, had nothing to do with and did not mean classic liberalism, individual rights, a market economy, or capitalism. It stood for the opposite of all these ideas. It stood, in economics as in politics, for an explicit version of *statism*.

In 1919 the conservatives knew that it was still too soon

for them to achieve their social goals. They knew that they had to give the new government a chance. They resolved to bide their time and see what the defenders of the "rational Republic" would do.

The defenders did not consist only of Marxists. The Social Democrats had two indispensable "bourgeois" allies, without whom neither the new Constitution nor the Republic to which it gave birth would have been possible. These two allies were the Center party and the Democratic party.

The Center party (which regularly drew nearly 20 percent of the vote in the Weimar years) had been organized in 1870 to serve as the political arm of the Catholic Church in Germany.[8]

Whatever their disagreements on other issues, the Centrists prided themselves on being united as a *moral* force able to combat the spread of decadence in postwar Germany. The moral values which party leaders upheld included faith in God, a return to the commandments of traditional Christianity, and obedience to authority, not only religious but also political (since, according to Catholic teaching, political power derives from God). The chief cause of the country's spiritual decay, the leaders said, was the modern trend to secularism and freethinking. Freethinking, to these men, did not mean merely atheism; it meant independent thought on any philosophical question. A member of the Reichstag once declared: "It is impossible for me to recognize the moral basis of any action if I do not understand it." The Centrists present responded by calling out: "Materialism! Materialism!"[9]

Like their counterparts in other lands, the Centrists did not rely only on the methods of persuasion to spread their ideas. They sought to impose their moral code on the rest of the country by force of law, urging measures such as the prohibition of abortion, restrictions on sexual practices condemned by the Church, the censorship of pornography, and a statute to protect German youth from "worthless and obscene literature."[10] The party also demanded state financing of Catholic public schools.

On matters not decreed by their religion the Centrists often differed with one another. Some were political conservatives, who did not approve of the new German system; others were liberals, who did. ("[E]very government enjoys God's blessing, whether it be monarchic or republican," a party spokesman told the Weimar Assembly.)[11] On one basic question of politics, however, all factions were in agreement: the party rejected both capitalism and socialism.

Capitalism, the Catholics held, is a godless system. Capitalism, they said, represents an inherently secular approach to life, one which counts on man's unaided intellect and rewards his striving for material success. It also represents an amoral approach: it claims a man's right to act on his own judgment, which implies a "sinful permissiveness" on sexual and political questions. Above all, in historian Koppel Pinson's words, "the motive of self-interest and the incentive of competition ran counter to Catholic religious belief, which espoused a social rather than an individual ethic. Society was a *corpus christi mysticum* [mystical body of Christ], and the individual was not to be considered an isolated phenomenon."[12]

As to socialism, the Centrists rejected it for one fundamental reason. Socialism, the party argued, is impractical idealism; Marx's vision of a perfect, egalitarian society on earth is noble, but impossible. It is impossible because of Original Sin, which, no matter what man's aspirations, dooms him to greed and failure. "To suffer and to endure . . . is the lot of humanity," Pope Leo XIII had said; "let men strive as they may, no strength and no artifice will ever succeed in banishing from human life the ills and troubles which beset it."[13]

Since capitalism is evil and socialism is too good for man, the party held, a compromise is necessary. "On the one hand," said a prominent German Catholic leader in 1848, "we see a rigid clinging to the right of property and on the other hand an equally determined denial of all property rights and we desperately seek some mediation between these two extremes."[14] The "mediation" he (and the Center party) reached was the idea that man does have a right to property, but that this right is not unlimited: it is conditioned by man's overriding moral obligation to use his property in such a way as to serve the general welfare.

Since every German group repudiated individualism, "centrism" in the Weimar Republic meant a middle ground, not between socialism and capitalism, but between statism of the Marxist variety (to benefit the lower classes) and statism of the conservative variety (to benefit the upper classes).

In the early postwar years the conservative Centrists, like monarchists throughout the nation, were relatively subdued, and the party's left wing was in the ascendancy. It was a wing eager to form a working coalition with the Social Democratic Reformists.

The final member of the "Weimar coalition" was the Democratic party, a middle-class liberal group organized in 1918, which included among its supporters a roster of famous names from the academic and business worlds unmatched by any of the other groups. This party, in Pinson's words, was the one "most committed to the ideals of a democratic republic, and it made its appeal largely to those in Germany who were truly democratic and socially minded but who rejected all notions of a class [or religious] party. . . ."[15] In the January 1919 elections, there was an impressive show of support for such an approach (over five million votes, about 19 percent of the total).

At the Weimar Convention, Friedrich Naumann, the party's first elected leader, stated the Democratic viewpoint in politics. The new Republic, he told the delegates, should represent a "sort of compromise peace between capitalism and socialism."[16] Such a compromise, the Democrats said, means the acceptance of individual rights—and of a powerful state, one strong enough to ensure that citizens exercise their rights in the service of the community. It means the sanctity of private property, and the socialization of monopolies. It means the rejection of egalitarianism, and a large-scale redistribution of income to benefit the poor.

In the mid-twenties, one of the party's election posters eloquently depicted its animating viewpoint. The poster, which would have been suitable for all the republican groups, featured a beefy Olympic runner symbolizing determination, along with a banner reading: "NOTHING WILL SWAY US FROM THE MIDDLE ROAD."

On the whole, the Democrats did not feel the need to defend their politics by reference to any abstract theory, such as dialectic materialism or the dogmas of faith. If, as has often been said, the essence of modern liberalism is "social conscience unencumbered by ideology," then the Democratic party was the purest representative of liberalism in Weimar Germany.

Even this approach, however, rests on an *implied* philosophic base, which was voiced occasionally by certain party members. Thanks to these men, Germany's "secular, bourgeois liberals" *can* be said to have stood for something intellectually distinctive. What they stood for was eloquently expressed a year before his death by the sociologist Max Weber, a major influence on the social sciences in Germany and one of the Democratic party's most illustrious founders.

In 1919, a group of students at the University of Munich, agitated by the Weimar Assembly debates and shaken by the violence in the country, invited Weber to address them. The students wanted guidance; they wanted this famous scholar-scientist to tell them what political system to endorse, how to judge values, what role science plays in the quest for truth. "Weber knew what was on their minds," writes Frederic Lilge. "He also knew that a distrust of rational thought was already abroad, a feeling which at any time might assume alarming proportions. . . . He therefore decided to impress upon his young audience from the outset the need for sanity and soberness of mind. . . ."[17]

They must not, Weber told the students, be taken in by religious dogmatists, or by irrationalist charlatans, left or right, who pretend to offer solutions to the world's problems. The fact is, he explained, there are no solutions. Certainty is unattainable by man, knowledge is provisional, values are relative, scholars are merely specialists doing technical jobs detached from life, science has nothing to say about morality or politics—and (in Lilge's synopsis)

> [it] was therefore an error on the part of students to demand from their academic teachers positive moral guidance and decisions, such as would be involved in answering the question as to what is the meaning of life. To attempt such an answer would transcend not only their work as scientists; it would also be a violation of the liberalism which Weber did his best to defend.

Liberalism, according to Weber, means an end to illusions, including the "illusion" of human progress—along with an attitude of endurance, "endurance [in Lilge's words] to bear the destruction of all absolutes, with no sentimental turning back or rash embrace of new faiths, only the strength to hold out in the radical though bleak veracity of a cleansed mind." As to selecting the proper course of action, Weber told the gathering, each individual has to decide the ideals that are right "for him." Since only questions of means, not of ends, fall within the province of science, he said, ends must be chosen subjectively, by reference to feelings.[18]

The liberals of Weber's kind, equating absolutism with fanaticism, believed that the precondition of freedom is skepticism. To restrain mob violence and induce respect for reason, they believed, one should tell the mob that reason is helpless and that man must act on feeling. To slow the march of the all-powerful state, they believed, it was proper to endorse it in principle, so long as one added that Germans should not act on principle, i.e., go to extremes. To discredit the totalitarians, to silence the noisy cry that *they* had the answer to Germany's crisis—these men believed—one should tell a desperate country, in weary, muted tones, that sane men have no idea what to do and never will.

This was the contest in the Weimar Assembly: the romanticist-nationalist groups (along with a transitional party of Independent Socialists, who sought a proletarian dictatorship) against the groups widely identified as the exponents of *reason*. These exponents were a coalition of halfhearted Marxists, dogmatic Catholics, and quaking skeptics.

The debate on the Constitution began on February 24, 1919. The final draft was approved by a vote of 262 to 75 on July 31 and took effect as the country's fundamental law on August 14. The conservative parties (and the Independent Socialists) voted against the draft on the grounds that it offered the country too much freedom. The members of the Weimar coalition voted yes unanimously. They recognized in the document not a partisan viewpoint, but the common base on which Germany's republicans were prepared to stand in their battle to win the allegiance of the country.

The Weimar Constitution is not a traditional Western charter of liberty. It is a distinctively twentieth-century document.

Article 7 alone, for instance, confers on the Federal government unlimited power to legislate on twenty subjects, including: "The press . . . Public health . . . Labour laws . . . Expropriation . . . banking and exchanges . . . Traffic in foodstuffs and articles of general consumption or satisfying daily wants . . . Industry and mining . . . Insurance . . . Railways . . . Theatres and cinemas." In subsequent articles, the state is assigned further powers. Some of these are: the power to lay down "general principles" concerning "The rights and duties of religious bodies . . . Public education, including the universities . . . housing and the distribution of the population . . ."; the power to preserve "the purity and health and the social furtherance of the family . . ."; and the task of supervising "the whole of the educational system."[19]

Having established its basic approach to government, the Constitution, striking a more traditional note, goes on to guarantee the protection of man's "fundamental rights." It promises to protect the freedoms of expression, association, movement, emigration, the ownership of property, the inviolability of a man's home, and several other rights. In every essential case, however, the document makes its priorities clear: it reserves to the government unlimited power, at its discretion, to attach conditions to the exercise of these rights. The promise of freedom of movement, for instance, concludes with the words: "Restrictions can be imposed by federal law only." The promise of the secrecy of correspondence concludes: "Exceptions may be admitted by federal law only." There is to be "no censorship"—except in the case of movies or "for the purpose of combating base and pornographic publications. . . ." The education of their children is "the natural right of the parents"—but "the state has to watch over their activities in this direction." "Personal freedom is inviolable," sums up Article 114, which continues directly: "No restraint or deprivation of personal liberty by the public power is admissible, unless authorised by law."[20]

The most famous statement of this kind is Article 48, which was invoked by the German government in 1930 to justify the establishment of a Presidential dictatorship. "If public order and security are seriously disturbed or endangered. . . ," the article says, without further definition, the President "may take all necessary steps . . . he may suspend for the time being, either wholly or in part, the fundamental rights" recognized elsewhere.[21]

The Founding Fathers of the United States accepted the concept of *inalienable* rights. The public power, they said in essence, shall make no law abridging the freedom of the individual. The Founding Fathers of the Weimar Republic rejected this approach as rigid and antisocial. The public power, their document says, shall make no law abridging the freedom of the individual—except when it judges this to be in the public interest.

As a rule, the German moderates held, *political* freedom works to benefit the public and therefore it should not often be abridged. Besides, they felt, such freedom pertains primarily to man's inner life or spiritual concerns, which can safely be left to the decisions of the individual.

Neither of these points, they held, applies in any comparable degree to *economic* freedom. A businessman, they said, works for his own welfare, not the public's. Besides, he is up to his neck in "materialistic concerns." This, the more religious republicans felt, is a realm that involves the lowest side of man, which must be firmly controlled by the authorities. This, the skeptics felt, is a realm vital to human survival, in which there can be no excuse—not even skepticism—for government inaction. This, the Marxists said, is the realm which counts in history and, therefore, which belongs to the people.

In the Weimar Assembly debates, the delegates never considered the possibility of extending freedom to the realm of production and trade. The moderates demanded that the government give up (much of) the Kaiser's control over the minds of the citizens; but they took it for granted that the government must never relinquish its grip over the citizens' productive actions.

Imperial Germany had not been a purely statist economy, but a mixture of controls and an element of economic liberty, with the emphasis on the controls. The Social Democrats in 1919 wanted just such a compromise as a transition measure. The liberals in the various groups wanted it as an end in itself. The conservatives wanted it in the name of tradition. Whatever their differences, the moderate consensus was: We do not want socialism (at least not now); we do not want capitalism (ever); we want a *mixed economy*. They got it, along with everything to which it leads.

The essence of Weimar economics is stated in Article 151 of the Constitution. "The organisation of economic life," it says,

> must accord with the principles of justice and aim at securing for all conditions of existence worthy of human beings. Within these limits the individual is to be secured the enjoyment of economic freedom.
>
> Legal compulsion is admissible only as far as neces-

sary for the realisation of threatened rights or to serve overriding claims of the common weal.[22]

"Property is guaranteed," says Article 153, but "Property entails responsibilities. It should be put to such uses as to promote at the same time the common good." Property, therefore, may be expropriated "in the public interest." For the same reason, "the distribution and the use of land are under state supervision. . . ." In addition, the government may "convert into social property such private economic undertakings as are suitable for socialisation," or it may demand the merger of such undertakings "in the interests of collectivism."

The Weimar Constitution concludes by mandating the programs of the welfare state, and by promising that the government will take special steps to protect the interests of "the independent middle class" and of "the labouring classes everywhere."[23]

The German Republic has been called "the freest republic in history." It is often described as an experiment in freedom which tragically failed. If so, it was a special kind of experiment, one that proved to be a pacesetter for the rest of the world.

The German Republic was an experiment in political freedom combined with economic authoritarianism and defended by reference to the ethics of altruism.

The country's republicans did not wish to choose between freedom and altruism. They thought that they could have both. "Every German," says Article 163, "is under a moral obligation, without prejudice to his personal liberty, to exercise his mental and physical powers in such a way as the welfare of the community requires."[24] In fact, however, it is either-or, and the moderates did have to choose; and they wrote their priorities all over their founding document.

The transition from document to reality did not take long.

* * *

While the contest between socialists and nationalists was taking place in the form of solemn debates at Weimar, a different version of the same contest was taking place in the streets of Berlin, Munich, and other German cities. In this arena, the contending forces were the *Communists* and the *Free Corps.*

During the war, a faction of young Marxists had broken away from the Social Democrats, denouncing the party's pro-war policy as a betrayal of the class struggle. These youths soon formed themselves into the Spartacus League (named after the rebellious Roman slave), then, after the war, reorganized the group as the Communist party of Germany. The party's support came from two sources: a militant minority of workers, and an influential elite of middle-class intellectuals centered in Berlin.

In contrast to the Social Democrats, whom they despised as "social Fascists," the Communists experienced no ideological conflicts; they were not tempted to dilute their fundamental approach by mixing into it remnants of an opposite viewpoint. They did not vacillate over the issue of individual rights; they dismissed the concept as a rationalization designed to justify "bourgeois privilege." They did not try simultaneously to uphold liberty and economic equality; they rejected the idea of liberty. Until we reach the classless society, they held, there can be no such thing as a society without rulers; until the state withers away, the absolute state is an absolute—and now it is the turn of the workers. The workers, they said, echoing the words of Lassalle, will offer the nation a "social dictatorship, in contrast to the egotism of the bourgeois society."[25]

Unlike their former colleagues among the Social Democrats, the Communists were not willing to postpone the socialist revolution; they were impatient to have their ideal *now*. It is pointless, said party leaders, to spend time trying to persuade or educate the "class enemy"; since men's thought is a mere by-product of economic factors, they claimed, and since proletarian logic is beyond the grasp of the bourgeoisie, enemy ideas cannot be dealt with by argument or discussion; they can be answered effectively only by the forcible overthrow of the existing social system. For the same reason, the leaders said, the party refuses, even as a transition measure, to participate in any parliamentary form of government. The alleged political equality of men under such a government, declared Rosa Luxemburg, the top Spartacist theoretician, "is nothing but lies and falsehoods so long as the economic power of capital still exists." "[T]he idea that you can introduce socialism without class struggle and by parliamentary majority decisions is a ludicrous petty-bourgeois illusion."

"Socialism," said Rosa Luxemburg, "does not mean getting together in a parliament and deciding on laws. For us socialism means the smashing of the ruling classes with all the brutality that the proletariat is able to develop in its struggle."[26]

The Russian Bolshevists, who were turning Moscow at the time into the world center of Marxist ideology, were eager to support those who shared their viewpoint. They supplied their German counterparts unstintingly with every necessity, including trained organizers, strategic guidance, literature, funds, and weapons.

The German Communists' first demand after the war was "All power to the Soviets," i.e., not to a representative national assembly, but to the (unelected) councils of workers and soldiers that had sprung up across Germany in the wake of the Kaiser's collapse. The radicals

> come in from the street [said one Social Democrat at the time] and hold placards under our noses saying: All Power to the Workers' and Soldiers' Councils! At the same time, however, they let you understand: If you do not do what we want, we will kick you out. . . . They can only represent a force as long as they are in possession of the majority of machine guns.[27]

In December 1918, a general congress of such councils convened in Berlin. By a large majority, the delegates backed the movement for a parliamentary republic and rejected the idea of a workers' dictatorship. The will of "the people," it seemed, was unmistakable. The Spartacists, however, had grasped the lesson of Hegel and were undeterred: they understood that the people does not know what it wills.

For six months, through the summer of 1919, the Communists proceeded to act as the people's vanguard: the party staged a nationwide campaign of violence designed to precipitate a civil war and overthrow the Republic. These months were filled with Communist-instigated riots, insurrections, putsches, marches on Berlin, seizures of buildings, angry mass strikes, and bloody street fighting—all of it adding up to an orgy of anarchy and murder. The chaos in the country may be glimpsed from the fact that Bavaria in April 1919 had three competing governments: an elected one, which was ousted by a "Soviet Republic" announced by a group of left-wing (but non-Communist) intellectuals, which was challenged by another "Soviet Republic" led by the Communists.

The Social Democrats leading the national government abhorred the eruptions of violence. They did not cease to preach the revolutionary exhortations of Marxism, which were their stock in trade. But at the same time they urged their followers, who numbered in the millions, to take up arms against the Communists. "Do you want the German Socialist Republic? . . . Then help us create a people's force for the government that will be able to protect its dignity, its freedom of decision and its activity against assaults and putsches. . . . A government . . . that cannot assert itself has also no right to existence."[28]

The government's plea evoked no response from the workers. The party faithful were not Communists, but they took the slogans of the Social Democrats seriously. They *did* want socialism, and they heard the Communists demanding it, too. However much the workers may have disliked the radicals' violence, they could not bring themselves actively to resist it; they were reluctant to fight against men who were—according to all the speeches of their own leaders—fellow proletarians, fellow comrades, fellow idealists. (The workers *were* capable of decisive action against an enemy identified as rightist: a year later a nationalist putsch in Berlin was defeated by a massive general strike.)

The Social Democratic leadership itself showed signs of a similar ambivalence. The party that was working to put down the Spartacist rebels was even capable on occasion of cooperating with the rebels' disruptive tactics. In March 1919, for instance, the Communists called for a general strike in Berlin, flaunting such slogans as "Down with the National Assembly!" and "The revolution can only advance over the graves of the Majority Social Democrats." The Social Democrats in Berlin first opposed the strike call, then abruptly decided to join the strike committees themselves (and finally, alarmed by the threat to life, resigned from them). The moderates joined in, despite the Spartacist call for their slaughter, largely because of what has been called "the rivalry of radicalism." The other left-wing groups had to try to surpass the Spartacists in revolutionary zeal. Such groups had to justify their existence; they had to show their followers and themselves that they, too, could be counted on for moral fervor and political action—as defined by the basic philosophy which all these groups shared.[29]

Qua republicans, the Social Democrats did not want the Communists to win. Qua Marxists, the Social Democrats did not want the Communists to lose. The result was a party that could do little during a momentous national crisis except appease, vacillate, temporize, and hope that someone else would act.

The Social Democrats found someone else. In a fateful step, the party leadership turned to the one German group able and eager to put down the Communists: the remnants of the Kaiser's army and of the old Officer Corps—and asked them to save the country. These men were open enemies of the Republic, but they preferred it to a communist state for tactical reasons. A republic, they felt, would buy them time, until conditions favored the establishment of a truly "German" system of government.

In this manner, by the default and decision of the moderate left, the initiative in Germany and the basic responsibility for its future passed to the country's nationalist forces—specifically, to the troops known at the time as the *Free Corps*.

The Free Corps were bands of armed adventurers—primarily, bitter young soldiers returned from the front—who, unable or unwilling to find employment, roamed the country and acted according to their feelings; in many cases they were led by former junior army officers. Although mostly of middle-class origins, these soldiers hated the same basic enemy as the Communists: the bourgeois mentality and way of life (some even called themselves "Bolshevists of the Right"). In place of the money-grubbing bourgeois system, they said, Germany needs "idealism," passion for the Fatherland, a Führer, and, most important of all, action. They were seldom more specific. "We could not," one of them said, "answer the question that so often echoed from the other side of the gorge [i.e., from the middle-class establishment], 'What do you really want?' "

> We could not answer because we did not understand the question, and they could never have understood the answer. . . . Over on the other side they wanted property and permanence . . . and we wanted no system, no order, no platitudes and no programs. We acted according

to no plan, toward no established goal. Indeed, we did not act at all, something acted in us. . . . "What do you believe in?" you ask. Nothing besides action.[80]

When asked by an old monarchist what was the sense of their actions, one of them answered: "There is sense only in danger. Marching into uncertainty is sense enough for us, because it answers the demands of our blood."

Their blood led these fighters—who defiantly called themselves "freebooters," "outlaws," "nihilists"—to loot and to smash. They fought the "red terror" of the Spartacists by unleashing a "white terror" of their own. They fought the Reich's attempt to disband their units (in 1920), by marching on the capital in an abortive attempt to overthrow the government (the Kapp Putsch). In the name of "German honor," they pronounced secret death sentences in vigilante courts, then carried out the sentences in wave after wave of political assassinations. What the Free Corps stood for, summarized one enthusiastic member, was "robbery and plundering, arson and murder—a mixture of every passion and demoniacal fury."[81]

The Free Corps did not consist only of soldiers. "Next to the war veterans," writes one scholar, "students formed the largest group in the Free Corps. For the most part, they were young idealists" who despised "peace and money-grabbing." "Next to the racist officers," said the leader of Hitler's Storm Troopers, Ernst Röhm, recalling his Free Corps days, "it was primarily the aggressiveness and loyalty of the students that strengthened us."[82]

Such were the men who, in a series of brutal armed confrontations (brutal on both sides), decisively crushed the Spartacist threat—thereby gaining, at the expense of the hand-wringing moderates, the prestige of national heroes. From this time on, the Communists were forced, despite their ideology, to try to gain power by electoral means. "The German nation," observes Ludwig von Mises, "obtained parliamentary government as a gift from the hands of deadly foes of freedom, who waited for an opportunity to take back their present."[83]

Ideologically, the clash between Communists and Free Corps was a clash between champions of the all-powerful state and seekers after an all-powerful leader; between activists eager for an unselfish (socialist) Germany and activists eager for an "idealistic" (non-capitalist) Fatherland; between brute force justified by economic determinism or "dialectic logic" and brute force justified by "the demands of the blood."

The clash was only a variant of the basic alternative that was being offered to the nation in the meetings of the Weimar Assembly.

Wherever the German turned—to the left, to the right, to the center; to the decorous voices in parliament or to the gutters running with blood—he heard the same *fundamental* ideas. They were the same in politics, the same in ethics, the same in epistemology.

This is how philosophy shapes the destiny of nations. If there is no dissent in regard to basic principles among a country's leading philosophic minds, theirs are the principles that come in time to govern every social and political group in the land. Owing to other factors, the groups may proliferate and may contend fiercely over variants, applications, strategy; but they do not contend over essentials. In such a case, the country is offered an abundance of choices—among equivalents competing to push it to the same final outcome.

It is common for observers to criticize the "disunity" of Weimar Germany, which, it is said, prevented the anti-Nazi groups from dealing effectively with the threat posed by Hitler. In fact, the Germans were united, and this precisely was their curse: their *kind* of unity, their unity on all the things that count in history, i.e., on all the *ideas*.

The effect of this unity was a world convulsion. The cause, however, like a silent tremor, had been hard to notice.

It was only some deadly marks on paper made one hundred and fifty years earlier by a purposeful figure at a solitary desk in the peaceful little town of Königsberg.

8

The Emotionalist Republic

Just as Germany's political movements, despite their clashes on the surface, were united in essence by one viewpoint, so were the nation's cultural movements. They were united on the kinds of issues that alone could give rise to the country's monolithic politics. One fundamental principle was everywhere in the ascendancy—among artists and educators, radicals and traditionalists, young and old alike.

For a country ruled by such a principle, several names are possible.

The "rational Republic" is not one of them.

* * *

More than any other form of human expression, art is the barometer that lays bare a period's view of reality, of life, of man. A work of art reflects its creator's fundamental ideas and value-judgments, held consciously or subconsciously. Since most artists are not independent theoreticians, but absorb their basic ideas from the prevailing consensus (or some faction within it), their work becomes a microcosm embodying and helping to spread further the kinds of beliefs advocated by that consensus.

The leading art school of Weimar Germany, especially in the Republic's earlier, formative years, was *Expressionism*, the product of a middle-class youth movement that had been growing since the turn of the century. According to admirers and enemies alike, this school, which reached its greatest influence after the war, was the perfect cultural embodiment of the new, anti-Kaiser spirit.

What Expressionism expressed was an open break with the intellect, with material reality, and with the entire spectrum

161

of "middle-class" values, from emphasis on work and personal success, to industrial civilization, money, business, to sexual standards, to law and order.

> The profound recoil against the mechanization of life, the wholesale attack on bourgeois morals, the emphasis on nudity and sexual license, the affinity for anarchist tactics, the search for exotic states of mind and exotic forms of dress, the yearning for pastoral freedom, communal living and generational solidarity, above all, perhaps, the cult of the irrational . . . [wrote *The New York Times'* art critic in 1969]—all of these features of the revolt we are now witnessing were crucial to the Expressionist program.[1]

Some of the Expressionist rebels were apolitical, some were moderate socialists, some flirted with the Nazis. Most, however, were drawn by their viewpoint to a different group. They were either members of the Communist party or, more commonly, its freewheeling sympathizers and fellow travelers.

The essence of the new approach to art was on stage nightly in Weimar Germany: the Expressionists took the theater over completely, making it their leading, most controversial, and most highly publicized showcase.

The themes featured in the new plays included the stifling "prison" of bourgeois life; the threat of the machine age to religion or the soul; the anguished cry of the heart before the abyss of nothingness; the frustration and agonizing loneliness of modern man; his need for love; his disgust with "the system" and with the older generation. A favorite motif in these works was the praise of patricide, i.e., of the new youth's passion to kill his father.

These themes were offered to the public not in the form of coherent statements, but as occasional flecks of meaning surfacing in a torrent of inarticulate rage. Art, the playwrights explained, must be an agent of cultural revolution. It must be designed to shock the bourgeoisie out of their wits and their "self-satisfied complacency." It must reject the old-fashioned "lie" of beauty in order to tell the truth about man: the truth that he is a huddle of impotence caught in an apocalyptic universe, doomed to a nightmare existence of horror, torment, defeat. Above all, the new authors said, a play must not make concessions to the nineteenth century: it must be willing to dispense with "intellectualism," to "experiment" with the nonobjective, to flaunt the nonintelligible.

Rejecting the concept of plot, leading playwrights such as Georg Kaiser offered the theatergoer collages of random episodes and moods, devoid of progression, structure, even adequate lighting—and pocked with deliberate absurdities. (For example, in Kaiser's most famous play, *From Morn to Midnight*, first produced in 1916, a man's refusal to eat his pork chops causes his mother to fall dead; a man, meeting a woman with a wooden leg, proceeds to water it with champagne; etc.) Rejecting characterization, the Expressionists presented nameless figures—e.g., "Cashier," "Lady," "Stout Gentleman"—figures without individuating traits or intelligible motives, but exuding an unmistakable aura: strident hysteria, alienated bitterness, frenzied disorientation. Rejecting "beautiful phrases" and contemptuous of clarity, the Expressionists specialized in plays filled with mad dialogue, raving confessions, disjointed screaming at the audience, and delirious word salads, such as: "Space is loneliness. Loneliness is space. Coldness is sunshine. Sunshine is coldness. Fever heat burns you. Fever heat freezes you. Fields are deserted. Ice overgrows them. Who can escape? Where is the door?" These new modes of theatrical speech were hailed as the "liberation" of language, its liberation from the shackles of grammar, syntax, and logic.[2]

The Expressionist plays were offered as a cry from one heart to another, bypassing any intermediary, such as the brain. They were offered as an expression of pure feeling—a kind of feeling reveling in its own willful subjectivity, pulsing with the terror of its own helplessness, chuckling at the consternation of the audience, and begging for the moral ideal, conceived as mystic union with God or Community or Humanity. It was a prayer to the ineffable—and a thumbing of one's nose at the "philistine" elders.

To feel is human; to extol feeling above reason is philosophy, a special kind of philosophy, the kind that the Germans had been taught for over a century.

The conservatives in Germany hated the new theater and its counterparts in the rest of the arts and every other social symptom which, in their view, was a product of the postwar culture, such as pornography, prostitution, public nudity, rising juvenile delinquency, blatantly flaunted homosexuality. They cursed all of it as "cultural Bolshevism." This is a loose term signifying antipathy to any innovation, of whatever nature; or antipathy to the pro-Communist politics of the avant-garde; or, more often, antipathy to what an enraged segment of the population sensed about the new manifestations: that they were a monstrous aberration overrunning the country, something decadent, wanton, anarchist, degenerate.

This aberration, said the conservative intellectuals, is the price Germany is paying for rejecting the tradition of Prussia, Luther, and the German heart, in favor of freedom, secularism, and the Western intellect. The modern corruptions, they said, are the product of *reason.*

Reason, they said, is precisely what man cannot live by. Life, explained Oswald Spengler, the world-famous nationalist historian, "has no system, no program, no reason. . . ." It cannot be analyzed or "dissected" according to intellectual principles. "[T]he profound order in which it realizes itself can only be grasped by intuitive insight and feeling. . . ."[3]

The political left demanded the new in art, the youth-oriented, the radical. The rightists, by contrast, revered tradition and flocked to the artistic heroes of an earlier era. One of their top favorites in this regard, which indicates the nature of their "intuition and feeling," was Richard Wagner.

Wagner intoxicated the nationalists by re-creating the world of ancient Teutonic mythology—in Shirer's evocative description, "an irrational, heroic, mystic world, beset by treachery, overwhelmed by violence, drowned in blood, and culminating in the *Götterdämmerung,* the twilight of the gods, as Valhalla, set on fire by Wotan after all his vicissitudes, goes up in flames in an orgy of self-willed annihilation. . . ." Here was a vision of life congenial to the deepest feelings of the German chauvinists. They knew what alternative they would accept to the wanton decadence of "cultural Bolshevism." It was the wanton barbarism of the savage Nibelungs.[4]

Wagner presented his vision of life in appropriate musical terms. Through his unprecedented use of chromaticism and dissonance he became the major transition figure leading from traditional harmony to modern atonality. Thus the prophet of Wotan became the hero not only of Goebbels and Hitler, but also of Arnold Schoenberg.

The Weimar conservatives admired certain contemporary artists, too—for instance, the highly influential poet-seer Stefan George. Idol of the rightist literati and center of a prolific circle, George, who was given to holding "seances" in darkened salons, sought to unite in his work such values as Spartan aristocracy, German community, Catholic communion, and the "nobility" of force.

What the youth of Germany learned from George may be gleaned from one of his disciples, the influential psychologist (and graphologist) Ludwig Klages. The intellect, according to Klages, is a "hostile power, asphyxiating the originally intuitive and prophetic mind of primeval man and culture." The proper course for psychology, therefore, "is to turn away from rationalist and causal procedures to the primeval level," which is to be grasped by "divination."[5]

Between 1929 and 1932, Klages published his three-volume masterwork, *The Intellect as Adversary of the Soul*. The title is an eloquent statement of the cultural credo of the German conservatives—and of their mortal enemies.

The "change from the realistic to the non-objective plane" is a change "from the logical to the illogical," wrote the modernist painter Wassily Kandinsky, a disciple of Madame Blavatsky and a leading teacher at the Bauhaus, the center and bastion of Weimar Germany's left-wing avant-garde. "In this world," said Paul Klee, another leading Expressionist painter and Bauhaus teacher, "I am altogether incomprehensible."[6]

The task of the visual arts, according to the Expressionists, is not to depict physical objects, but an "invisible reality," consisting of emotions or the supernatural or the ineffable. Some artists implemented this viewpoint by means of a streaky, smeary style that featured flat, blurred (but still recognizable) objects, incoherent spatial relationships, and a deliberately primitive technique. Typically, these paintings presented distorted human figures dwarfed by ominous, swirling backgrounds, figures with faceless heads or agonized, unseeing eyes or vicious, piglike snouts.

The more "liberated" artists, following the lead of men such as Kandinsky and Klee, dispensed with the depiction of physical objects of any sort in the name of fidelity to a world of non-objects, which the artist purported to render by means of shapeless "abstract" blobs, or arbitrary juxtapositions of lines and circles, or collages made of paper, cardboard, wood, and tram tickets.

The counterpart of this approach in music was the composers who followed the lead of Arnold Schoenberg, the man who pioneered the assault on the concept of tonality. The musical Expressionists dispensed with the establishment of a key, with modulation, with harmony, with melody. Instead, their "atonal" compositions offered the listener an unintegratable series of agitated, dissonant sounds featuring apocalyptic pounding, muffled dribbles, and hysterical bleating-wailing. The new music, said Schoenberg, "treats dissonances like consonances" and thus represents the "emancipation of the dissonance"—in other words, Noise Lib. It is not beautiful, said its admirers at the time, but it is profound. It is profound because it is ugly, because the public hates it, and because it is unintelligible. "I cannot be understood," wrote Schoenberg in a 1924 letter, "and I content myself with respect."[7]

For the educated German in the twenties there was no escape. Everywhere, he encountered offshoots of the Expressionist view of life or kindred developments reflecting the same spirit. When he reached for the newspapers, he was struck by the horror cartoons of George Grosz, which depicted prostitutes, mutilated veterans, porcine industrialists, in an attempt, as Grosz put it, "to convince this world that it is ugly, ill, and hypocrit[ical]."[8] When the German went to view the new buildings, he saw—offered as the alternative to arbitrary, Classicist ornamentation—the International Style, i.e., flat-topped, deliberately barren structures devoid of ornament. When he went to the movies, he could hardly avoid the wave of horror films spawned by *The Cabinet of Dr. Caligari*. When he took a quiet moment to read the new poetry, he was assaulted by images of dirt, madness, rats, stinking suns, rotting corpses, or by page after page of neologisms.

If he did try to escape all of it, if, seeking some vision of man other than horror-freak or Teutonic brute, he fled to the more civilized among the conservative writers, he was offered the kind of human projection they specialized in. They specialized in the presentation of religious mystics, men oblivious to this world and in quest of God.

Sometimes the heroes of the conservative writers were mystics in quest not of God, but of "nature." If the German did not care to read the so-called "asphalt (city-oriented) literature" of the modern writers, reeking as it did of Joyce, genitals, and socialism, his alternative was to turn to the romanticists' "literature of the soil," which brushed aside as contemptible distractions all human achievements, including machinery, wealth, cities, and extolled instead the simple, mindless life of the village peasant.

Although the German left had growing doubts about the process of industrialization, most Marxists in the twenties were still defenders of technology. On this point the conservatives were ahead of their time. Germany's Old Right beat America's New Left by fifty years: it took the soil seriously. The Industrial Revolution and all its products, said some of the loudest right-wing voices, is a secular, soulless, capitalistic (and essentially American) evil, an evil to be swept away and replaced by a return to nature, in the form of unmechanized rural subsistence.

Life without technology, its advocates admitted, might not advance human comfort, ease, or enjoyment. But happiness, these brooding nature-apostles felt, is not man's destiny. By its very essence, they said, life is war, suffering, death—in Spengler's words, "death of the individual, death of a nation, death of a culture."[9]

Both sides in Germany's cultural battle elevated feeling above reason. And both sides experienced the same basic *kind* of feeling. The left called it alienation or the angst of nothingness. The right called it götterdämmerung or the philosophy of Schopenhauer. The common denominator is the conviction of doom.

It is an understandable conviction on both sides. Man without his mind *is* doomed.

The same epistemological cause leads ultimately to the same social effect. The left culturati called their political ideal "socialism." The right culturati called theirs "Prussianism." But, as Spengler pointed out in an influential work entitled *Prussianism and Socialism*, there is no essential difference between these two concepts. Under both approaches, he noted, "Power belongs to the whole. The individual serves it. The whole is sovereign. . . . Everyone is given his place. There are commands and obedience." The first conscious socialist, Spengler concluded, was not Marx, but Friedrich Wilhelm I.[10]

Like their elders of both types and for the same kind of reason, the youth in Germany were eager to serve "the whole." This was particularly true of the country's organized youth groups, most of which, thanks to the chauvinism of the German schoolteachers, were avidly nationalist. (Prior to World War I the German youth movement was called the Wandervogel; in the Weimar years its counterpart was referred to as the Bünde.)

The youth, taught by their bourgeois teachers to despise the bourgeoisie, proceeded on cue to stage a rebellion. As early as the 1890s, children ranging in age from eleven or twelve through the twenties began to declare their rejection of their parents, their commitment to "German" values, and their need of fundamental social change. The young rebels represented a kind of elite: for the most part they were urban high-school students—Protestant, middle-class, well-educated.

Widely regarded as gentle, if peculiar, idealists, the German schoolboys acted out literally the ideas they had learned. Whenever they could, they escaped from the "cold," "mechanistic" cities they had been taught to hate, in order to become addicts of restless "rambling"—roaming the countryside in groups, hiking, camping, singing German folk songs, visiting venerable ruins, etc. In one observer's words, the Wandervogel were "long-haired, untidy bacchants . . . strumming on their guitars their collective revolt against bourgeois respectability."[11]

The same ideas which led to the rise of Expressionist art in Germany and of medieval Wotan-worship led also to the rise of a whole army of hippies, half a century before Haight-Ashbury.

Like their elders, the German ramblers dismissed "the whore of the Enlightenment," which is what many of them called the faculty of reason. Like their elders, they sought instead to experience a certain kind of feeling ("warm," "vital," "spontaneous"), the kind of feeling, they said, which could be found in primitive societies or in primitive nature or in the Orient—if one gave up one's individuality and merged oneself into an appropriate, "organic" youth group. Such merger, the youngsters added, requires a leader, a man whom the group members accept, respect, and obey. As a rule the leaders selected were three to six years older than the membership—old enough to be authoritative figures, but young enough to remain part of a crusade directed against adults.

The movement's description of this policy was "youth led by youth."

On the whole, Germany's youth movement was socialist but antipolitical. Committed to freewheeling "German instinct," eager to escape the restrictions of ideology, the members were not much interested in the theory or practice of socialism; typically, they flaunted their disdain for political parties and programs. "Our lack of purpose," they often said, "is our strength."

The youth groups did seek action, but in the words of one observer it was action of a special kind: "action without any conscious purpose, without any goal whatsoever. . . . '[I]t would be hard to find a "purer" type of irrational social action in any society.' This 'goalless' activity, motivated more by feeling than by thought, was encouraged by the leaders."[12]

The "youth led by youth" were being led in fact by the adults. The group leaders were merely following the national trend. They were doing to their unformed charges what the country's erudite professors were doing every day to their graduate students—and what the new playwrights were doing every night to their audiences.

The Weimar left was disturbed by the country's youth groups, and especially by the politics of these antipolitical ramblers. When Walther Rathenau, for instance, was murdered by Free Corps assassins in 1922, the graves of the assassins, who committed suicide, were strewn with flowers and were for years regarded as a shrine, which was regularly visited by reverent youngsters.

The Social Democrats and their allies knew that they had somehow to produce a different kind of German youth. Since the school and university system remained in the hands of the nationalist professorate, there was not much that the socialists could do in the way of educational reform, but they did make some attempts, enough to indicate *their* ideas on the subject.

What the socialists did, primarily, was to try to spread Progressive education.

The German Progressives purported to foster gentleness and tolerance in the schools as against the harshness of Prussian discipline. Like the nonobjective artists, they spoke of novelty and experiment as against tradition; of free self-development as against what they called the stifling dogmas of the nineteenth century; of peaceful, humanitarian values as against the bloodthirsty nationalism of the regular schools.

The Progressives' method of achieving these goals was to declare that education is not to be subject-centered but child-centered; that the child learns not by thinking, but by feeling and doing; that the schools must get away from "the one-sidedness of a barren intellectual culture"; and that what counts is not the student's mind or "the logical development of a school subject," but "the whole child," especially his heart (or "soul"). "The highest thing is not learning and not subject matter, but the human soul!" said the prominent educator Alfred Lichtwark, who founded the radical Lichtwark-schule in Hamburg.[13]

The same words could as easily have been spoken by Spengler, or by the Nazi educator Hans Schemm, or by the faculty of the Bauhaus.

While the rightist schools, using the methods of Prussia, were pounding into their students the virtue of unrestrained "instinct," the Progressives were trying to stem the tide by teaching *their* charges the virtue of unrestrained "spontaneity." The Progressives, however, did not pound; their method was to eliminate restrictions, i.e., all educational standards and requirements. In many schools, according to two admiring American observers in 1929, "[t]ime schedules were torn down. . . . Prescribed curricula vanished. . . . Subject lines were blotted out. . . . Children were allowed to choose their own teachers, direct their own work or study and control their own behavior."

"The immediate result," these observers write, "was chaos. Not in every school, for there were many which made a more gradual extension of liberties, but in several of those which regarded anarchy as the first step toward freedom there was an era of 'wildness.' " The new schools, however, placed a certain limitation on the wildness.

> Yet to-day the individual is not overemphasized. He is not set apart from his connections with the group as if he were an entity, but he is generally looked upon as one whose development and interests are closely bound up with those of society. Room for individual variation is allowed, but the good of the group is to set the limits of personal freedom.[14]

In the most famous Progressive institution of the Weimar era, the Karl Marx elementary school in Berlin, the group (the child's peers) became the arbiter not only of freedom, but also of morality and truth. Objective standards of performance were dropped. "The judgment of the group is the standard by which the work and conduct of the individual is measured." As to any nonconformists in attendance, they soon discovered how much "peaceful tolerance" they could expect from their classmates. In the Karl Marx school, notes E.A. Mowrer, "anything but radical socialism among the pupils was for several years punished by the other pupils with violence and boycott."[15]

The socialists' plan for undercutting the educational establishment was to replace one set of Hegelian disciples by another: to fight brutal, mind-deadening authoritarianism à la Bismarck by means of gentle, mind-deadening subjectivism à la Dewey; to fight elitist romanticism by means of "democratic" anti-intellectualism; to eradicate passionate collectivism (of a nationalist variety) by instilling in the children passionate collectivism (of a socialist variety).

While the children of the bourgeois establishment, trained to be obedient, were taking to the countryside as whim-ridden ramblers, the children of the Progressive institutions, encouraged to be "free" and "wild," were learning to be socially adaptable, i.e., obedient. Regardless of their teachers' intentions, both groups were being prepared. They were being prepared interchangeably for the illogic of Kandinsky, the "liberation" of Schoenberg, and the orders of Hitler. As it happened, the wildness of the children proved to be merely a phase; the obedience lasted.

During the twenties, Germany's youngsters (both rightist and leftist) were in the vanguard of the growing rebellion against the Weimar Republic. The youngsters were rebelling against the establishment in the name of every fundamental idea which they had been taught by every influential spokesman of that establishment. Their parents and teachers, reluctant at first to go along, sought to preach the standard slogans of German ideology, while permitting some remnants of the Enlightenment spirit to be smuggled into the country's life and institutions. The children rejected the attempt as hypocrisy. They insisted that the adults practice the slogans fully.

In 1890, the signs of what was to come in Germany from

the undiluted reign of German philosophy were just beginning to be perceptible. By the 1920s, on both sides of the cultural-political divide, the signs had become blatant.

Such was the nature of the zeitgeist during Germany's first era of comparative freedom after generations of autocracy.

In any culture, however, there can be exceptions to the dominant trend. The comparative freedom of Weimar Germany gave rise to a flowering of authentic talent which, despite everything else, still gives the period a retrospective glow of light and life. There was an abundance of great names and achievements in the physical sciences and the performing arts. There were Berlin's celebrated cafes and nightlife—in part, decadent; in part, imaginative and colorful. There were the fading, often magnificent, remnants of an earlier, stylized view of art and of man—e.g., the film direction of Fritz Lang and Jo May, and the operettas of Franz Lehar and Emmerich Kalman.

Elements such as these were the products of a brilliant, foredoomed minority. They were the products of men with no intellectual base in the culture and no long-range hope; men who represented the Western past, not the German future, because they had no weapons with which to counter the dominant trend, the irrationalism that called itself Prussia or "progress."

The European avant-garde did not always cling to the term "progress." Some groups, such as the Dadaists of France and Germany, were more explicit.

Their purpose, the Dadaists said in 1916, is to cultivate the senseless by unleashing on the public every imaginable version of the unintelligible, the contradictory, the absurd. "Dadaism," said its advocates, "is against everything, even Dada." It is against every form of civilization and every form of art. "Art," they said "is shit"—a dictum faithfully implemented by pictures of the Mona Lisa wearing a mustache, or by collages pieced together from the leavings in somebody's gutter, or by exhibits such as Max Ernst's in Germany in 1920. One entered the exhibit through a public urinal, in order to contemplate, among other items, a block of wood with a notice asking visitors to chop at it, an aquarium containing sundry objects immersed in a blood-colored fluid, and a young girl in a communion dress loudly reciting obscene poetry.[16]

Dadaism is a consistent extreme of the cultural trend of

the period. It is the voice of unreason in art gleefully taking on the forms of madness. This is the movement which a prominent American philosopher, some years ago, hailed as "one of the *valid* eruptions of the irrational in this century,"[17] and which the German avant-garde at the time praised as daring, witty, and anti-middle class.

If art is the barometer of a society, then madness in the realm of art portends certain existential consequences. In the end, the equivalents of such madness, stemming from the same fundamental cause, will permeate and take over every social field.

In Weimar Germany, in the *economic* sphere, the wait was mercilessly brief. In 1923 one such development transfixed the nation.

* * *

The culture of Weimar Germany advocated irrational emotion. The economy demanded it. It provided conditions which allowed men no other mode of functioning.

The Republic was a mixed economy, the kind established by Bismarck and mandated by the nation's new constitution. There was an element of economic liberty, and there were growing government controls—direct or indirect; federal, state, or municipal—over every aspect of the country's productive life. The controls covered business, labor, banking, utilities, agriculture, housing, and much more. As a rule each new set of controls conferred benefits on some German group(s), at a cost. The cost was incurred by other groups, whose forced sacrifice paid for the benefits. The victims responded predictably.

Confronted with increasing British exactions one hundred and fifty years earlier, the American colonists did not decide to beef up their lobby in the English court; they heralded the rights of man and decided to throw off the yoke. There were no such ideas in Weimar Germany. The Germans did not question the code of sacrifice or the principle of statism. *These* ideas, they had been taught by every side and sect within their culture, specify how man ought to live and the only way man *can* live. They define the moral and the practical.

The Germans, therefore, practiced them. In order not to be eaten alive by the next round of legislation, virtually every-

one joined or identified himself with a group (since an isolated individual had no chance against large, vocal blocs).
And every group knew only one policy: to demand new
economic benefits from the government and/or new legislative sanctions against the other groups.

The hostile forces included big business versus small
business, importers versus domestic producers, employers' associations versus labor unions, blue-collar workers versus
white-collar, the employed versus the unemployed, industrialists versus Junkers, Junkers versus peasants, farmers versus
city dwellers, creditors versus debtors, the lower classes versus
the middle, the lower middle versus the upper middle, the
middle versus the upper. The plea which all these groups
addressed to the Reichstag was a cacophony of contradictions, such as: higher tariffs/freer trade; more subsidies to
business/less government intervention; tight money/easy credit; longer hours/shorter; higher prices/lower; bigger profits/
smaller; more competition/less; more public works/fewer;
more public ownership/no more; higher wages/give us jobs;
more social benefits/stop the inflation; what about us?/cut
the taxes.

The authors of the Weimar Constitution had believed that
a controlled economy in the hands of a democratic government would foster peaceful cooperation among men, as
against the "ruthless competition" and "war of all against all"
which they held to be inherent in a free market. What the
mixed economy produced instead was a ruthless competition
among groups, a *collectivist* "war of all against all."

It was not his own selfish advantage that he sought—said
the laborer, the businessman, the farmer, as he fought to impose legal restrictions or hardships on the others—but the
welfare of his group: the livelihood of the workers, the
progress of industry, the preservation of agriculture. His
group, he said, was deserving, because of the services it had
rendered to an overriding entity: the nation as a whole. The
Germans were marching into the future under the same banner while vying for its possession. The banner was inscribed:
sacrifice for the Volk—or for the Fatherland, or for the public interest, or for the common weal.

The political parties, which had formally mandated this
kind of approach in 1919, survived by cashing in on it. They

handed out economic favors to their constituencies in exchange for votes at the next election.

Neither the warring groups nor the parties which courted them had any means to know *what* favors to insist on, when, or at whose expense, or when to yield to the demands of their antagonists, who also had to survive. By the nature of the system there was no principle to follow: no one could devise a rational way to divide a nation into mutually devouring segments, or an equitable way to conduct the devouring. Every group, therefore, swung at random from the role of beneficiary to that of victim and back again, according to the passions, the tears, the fears, the alliances, the front-page propaganda, the back-room deals, and the expediency of the moment.

Life, Spengler said, has "no system, no program, no reason." It is not necessarily true of life as such. It *was* true of life in Germany's mixed economy.

That kind of life has consequences. In 1923 the Germans discovered one of them.

Since 1914, Germany's governments had needed vast sums of money—far more than the nation's leadership dared try to raise by taxation—for two reasons: in part, to pay for the state's growing socioeconomic programs; in part, to pay for war or war-related expenditures. (In the Weimar years, this last included but was not restricted to the payment of reparations.) To deal with its financial needs, the imperial cabinet at the onset of the war had inaugurated certain novel monetary and fiscal policies. The same policies were continued after the war by the republicans.

Both regimes amassed huge deficits. They sought to finance them, in essence, by means of borrowing and, ultimately, by reliance on the printing press.

Imperial and republican ministers alike refused to consider the possibility of reducing their outlays. The government's programs, they said repeatedly, cannot be significantly curtailed; the programs are necessary to save the poor or help the workers or protect industry or glorify the Fatherland; they are mandated by Christian compassion, or a progressive conscience, or German tradition, or love of country.

The ministers felt that their ends were noble, they felt that the pursuit of these ends was essential to their own political survival, and they felt that no other considerations had to be considered. Ultimate ends, they had long been taught, are matters to be decided not by reason or logic, but by instinct and feeling.

And as to means, they had been taught, there are no absolutes. The imperial leadership, more old-fashioned in this regard, had doubts about the ability of a government to spend with impunity what it did not have; these men expected to balance the books someday by winning the war. The republicans did not have even this chimerical hope. Many of them, in fact, had no desire to see the books balanced. They believed that a permanent policy of deficit financing and monetary expansion would work to their own advantage. Like the modern artists and educators, they, too, were eager to "experiment with the nonobjective"—in this case, by flooding the country with fiat currency unbacked by any objective value or tangible commodity.

In July 1914, the German mark had been trading at 4.2 to the dollar. In July 1920, the rate was 39.5 to the dollar. In July 1922, the rate was 493.2 to the dollar.

Despite such figures, the moderates running the Weimar government did not question their ends or means. They did not seem to be concerned about the results of their policies, or about cause and effect. They did not cease their orgy of spending. They merely created money faster and faster. By 1923, "150 printing firms had 2,000 presses running day and night to print the Reichsbank notes."[18]

If the politicians were ignoring causality and defying reality on a giant scale, evidently they expected to get away with it. Causality and reality—Germany's teacher had assured his compatriots—are only subjective human ideas or "categories." Reality, added one of his disciples (a fashionable Expressionist) disdainfully at the time, is merely a capitalistic concept.[19]

Kant to the contrary notwithstanding, however, reality in 1923 remained real. The German mark continued to fall—hour by hour, across the course of a single day.

> By the middle of 1923 [writes one commentator], the whole of Germany had become delirious. Whoever had a job got paid every day, usually at noon, and then ran to the nearest store, with a sack full of banknotes, to buy anything he could get, at any price. In their frenzy,

people paid millions and even billions of marks for cuckoo clocks, shoes that didn't fit, anything that could be traded for something else.[20]

In November 1923, Germany's Great Inflation reached its climax. The mark sank to its final level: 4,200,000,000,000 to the dollar. Everyone counting on monetary assets or fixed incomes—on savings, insurance, bonds, mortgages, pensions, and the like—was wiped out. "The intellectual and productive middle class, which was traditionally the backbone of the country," said one German leader at the time (Gustav Stresemann of the People's party), "has been paid for the utter sacrifice of itself to the state during the war by being deprived of all its property and by being proletarianized."[21]

The Germans could hardly believe that it was happening. Many seemed to become disoriented or even unhinged, and never fully believed in sanity again.

> All values were changed, and . . . Berlin was transformed into the Babylon of the world [said Stefan Zweig, a Weimar writer]. . . . Even the Rome of Suetonius had never known such orgies as the pervert balls of Berlin. . . . In the collapse of all values a kind of madness gained hold particularly in the bourgeois circles which until then had been unshakeable in their probity.

"Barbarism prevailed," said the painter George Grosz. "The streets became dangerous. . . . We kept ducking in and out of doorways because restless people, unable to remain in their houses, would go up on the rooftops and shoot indiscriminately at anything they saw."[22]

The German intellectuals had no cause any longer to curse "the whore of the Enlightenment." Its last vestiges were gone. The ideal they had sought instead—the passage, in Kandinsky's words, "from the logical to the illogical"—was all around them. Now they could meditate on *Dadaism in economics,* along with its corollary: a rain of bullets.

The Great Inflation was not the product merely of a practical miscalculation. Its fundamental cause did not lie in the realm of finance, but of philosophy—especially, epistemology. In essence, the inflation was an expression in the economic sphere of the basic spirit of Weimar German culture. There is a limit to how long a nation's thinkers can extol the contradictory, the irrational, the defiantly absurd; one day, in every field, they achieve it.

In November 1923, the German government was finally forced to act. It introduced a new currency, the Rentenmark, which was redeemable in dollars, and refrained thereafter from papering the country with it.

This kind of response, however, though economically appropriate, was too little and too late. The basic cause of the disaster, untouched, continued to act. And the signs for the nation's political future were already growing ominous.

One sign came from the nation's moderates. On October 13, 1923, by a vote of 316 to 24, the members of the Reichstag passed a bill designed to deal with the inflationary crisis. The bill did not strip the government of the power to engage in deficit financing or currency debasement. Instead, the new law "authorized the government to take any and all measures it deemed necessary in the financial, economic and social sphere. It might even, if it saw fit, disregard the fundamental rights of citizens laid down in the Weimar constitution." The bill did, however, prohibit the cabinet from tampering with certain items, including the eight-hour day and the welfare-state programs.[23]

Freedom, the German democrats were announcing to the country, is dispensable, but "social legislation" is an absolute.

Several weeks later, at the height of the inflation, another group of Germans was heard from. They, too, believed in the supremacy of "society," though not of a republican form of government: "[This is a] robbers' state! . . . [W]e will no longer submit to a State which is built on the swindling idea of the majority. We want a dictatorship. . . ."[24]

On the morning of November 9, 1923, in the city of Munich, the leader of this group decided to act. Adolf Hitler staged the Beer Hall Putsch.

It was too little and too soon.

9

The Nazi Synthesis

The German right characteristically denounced socialism, while supporting the welfare state, demanding government supervision of the economy, and preaching the duty of property-owners to serve their country. The German left characteristically denounced nationalism, while extolling the feats of imperial Germany, cursing the Allied victors of the war, and urging the rebirth of a powerful Fatherland. (Even the Communists soon began to substitute "nation" for "proletariat" in their manifestos.)

The nationalists, at heart, were socialists. The socialists, at heart, were nationalists.

The Nazis took over the essence of each side in the German debate and proudly offered the synthesis as one unified viewpoint. The synthesis is: national socialism.

Nationalism, said Hitler—echoing German thinkers from Fichte through Spengler—means the power of the nation over the individual in every realm, including economics; i.e., it means socialism. Socialism, he said, means rule by the whole, by the greatest of all wholes, Germany.

The ideologies of the non-Nazi parties limited each to a specific constituency while alienating the rest of the country. The Marxist parties could appeal effectively only to the workers; Marx's version of socialism was feared and hated by the country's property-owners. The standard conservative groups could count only on the supporters of the imperial regime; the conservatives' cry for "German tradition" was regarded, especially by the young and the poor, as nothing but an attempt by the former establishment to regain its special privileges. The Center party by its nature could have only a sectarian (Catholic) appeal. And, as to the middle-of-the-road liberal groups, they had trouble holding on to any constituency at all. By 1920, for instance, the Democrats had already shrunk to the status of a splinter party; middle-class voters opposed to Marxism had decided on the evidence that the Democrats were indistinguishable in practice from the Social Democrats.

The Nazis' ideological synthesis, however, stressed the basic principles common to all groups and thus served as entrée to every major segment of the population, reactionary and radical alike. By appropriate shifts in emphasis, such an ideology could be used to placate the devout and intrigue the pagan, soothe the old and intoxicate the young, reassure the "haves" and offer a new day to the "have nots."

Class warfare, inherited from Germany's long feudal-authoritarian past, was an essential fact of the country's life. When the lower classes looked upward, they saw what they hated as rapacious barons of privilege oblivious to justice. When the upper classes looked downward, they saw what they despised as rapacious malcontents eager to overthrow the proper social hierarchy. The bottom wanted the top cut down; the top wanted the bottom put down; the middle were capable of both feelings, depending on the direction in which they were looking.

The Nazis promised everything to everybody.

As to any contradictions that might be involved in this kind of campaign, Hitler was unconcerned about them.

* * *

During the 1920s, the middle class in Germany, especially its lower rungs, was the constituency most ready to be taken over. This group—white-collar workers, small tradesmen, bureaucrats, academics, and the like—had been ravaged by the war, then hit hardest by the inflation. Millions felt themselves crushed between the powerful, government-protected cartels above and the powerful, government-supported unions below. The middle class, too, wanted government protection and government support, but it had no powerful champion in the political process and no effective organization. Hitler began his climb by leaping to fill this void.

In February 1920, the Nazi party, making its first bid for public support, issued the manifesto that was to become one of its most publicized documents, the "Twenty-Five Points."

Although the document was aimed at the country as a whole and demanded special state action in behalf of virtually every group, the middle class was its most obvious target.

We demand that the State shall make it its first duty to promote the industry and livelihood of citizens . . . (Point 7). We demand extensive development of provision for old age (Point 15). We demand creation and maintenance of a healthy middle class, immediate communalization of department stores, and their lease at a cheap rate to small traders . . . (Point 16). We demand development of the gifted children of poor parents, whatever their class or occupation, at the expense of the State (Point 20). The state must see to raising the standard of health in the nation . . . (Point 21).[1]

The middle class in Germany feared communism—and, like the rest of the country, resented big business. Steeped in anticapitalist slogans, the Germans made no distinction between men who had grown rich by means of productive achievement and men who had grown rich by means of political pull. The country saw millions going hungry, while certain firms were making fortunes by the help of government war contracts, inflation profiteering, politically dictated wages, prices, subsidies. The Germans did not conclude that government intervention was the cause of the injustice. The rich, they said bitterly, the rich as such, are the enemy.

Hitler daily denounced communism as subversive and un-German. He assured middle-class audiences that he rejected the policy of expropriation, at least in regard to small property-owners. In regard to large property-owners, however, he gave voice to the country's bitterness. We demand "an end to the power of the financial interests" (Point 11). "We demand therefore ruthless confiscation of all war gains" (Point 12). "We demand nationalization of all . . . trusts" (Point 13).

The Nazi party, said Hitler, "is convinced that our nation can only achieve permanent health from within on the principle: *The Common Interest Before Self*" (Point 24). But businessmen, he said, obey the opposite principle; capitalism appeals to selfish, "materialistic" interests, such as industrial production, economic success, the accumulation of wealth.

"Gold or Blood," said the Nazis, "Hucksters or Heroes"—this is the choice Germany must make.[2]

When the time was ripe, the middle class was to become the avant-garde of the Nazi mass base. The rest of the country, however, would not be far behind. Most of the other groups were ready for the same kinds of promises and diatribes, appropriately adapted.

To the debt-laden peasants, who were eager to become independent landowners, the Nazis promised among other things "land reform . . . confiscation without compensation of land for common purposes; abolition of interest on and loans, and prevention of all speculation in land" (Point 17)—while inveighing against the Junker magnates, the big stock and grain dealers, the "urban exploiters."

To the factory workers in the cities, who were the stronghold of the Marxist parties, the Nazis promised profit-sharing in industry (Point 14), employee participation in management, and (in the thirties) an end to unemployment—while unleashing furious denunciations of "greedy finance capital," the "slavery of interest," "international bankers," and the "selfish scoundrel" who "conducts his business in an inhuman, exploiting way, misuses the national labor force and makes millions out of its sweat."[3]

The workers, it should be noted, were never to become a major source of Nazi votes, at least not to the extent of the middle class and the peasantry. The unions were too powerful for that: they effectively controlled the job market and had a monopoly on the unemployment dole. As a result, workers had to join one of the unions and vote for its candidates at election time. The hearts of such men were not in their votes.

We may now consider the "inhuman exploiters" themselves, the hated employers or creditors of all the above groups, i.e., Germany's big businessmen.

Most German industrialists were not pro-Nazi prior to 1933; to them almost any kind of regime, including the Republic, was acceptable. Nor were business contributions to the Nazi cause a significant factor in Hitler's success, which is an ideological, not a financial phenomenon. (Money makes it easy to disseminate propaganda; it cannot define the ideas to be propagated or determine the country's receptivity to them.)[4] There were, however, a number of leading industrialists who did support the Nazi movement, especially near the end of the Republic.

To the wealthy magnates and *in private*, away from the eyes of the press and the country, the Nazis took the line that the party's anti-business drumfire was merely rhetoric designed to wean the radical masses from communism, and that the businessmen should not take any of it seriously.

Some of the powerful magnates who contributed to the party did not believe this bit of "pragmatic truth" or Big Lie; they contributed out of fear of terrorist reprisals, or out of despair (better to take orders from the Nazis than bullets from the Communists), or they were merely playing it safe, paying off several parties at the same time. Some, however, did believe it. Hitler, they said to one another, may be unmannerly, but he will look out for our interests; he is a friend of capitalism.

The profit motive, in Germany, had never been regarded "as either desirable or honorable. The tone was set by the bureaucracy and the army; in their opinion the profit motive was something rather contemptible. The capitalist bourgeoisie regarded the way of life of the nonbusiness strata of society as an ideal to which they tried to conform."[5] Such "capitalists" had little concept of private property or of a free market, and no desire for either. Property to them did not mean possession *by right*, but by government permission; capitalism to them did not mean laissez-faire, but government control of the economy, the traditional, imperial kind of control, control mediated by behind-the-scenes deals between politicians and property-holders. Accepting such premises, many businessmen were prepared to grant that a totalitarian could be a defender of capitalism. Theirs was the mentality of a mixed-economy pressure group, trained in "social service" and deaf to principles or ideology, choosing a despot who promised to be benevolent.

One British writer describes these big bankers and industrialists, who prided themselves on their "practicality" in backing Hitler, as "too innocent for politics." William Shirer says that they were "politically childish." In fact, their "innocence" was anti-intellectuality, and their "political childishness" was (in effect) philosophical pragmatism.[6]

At various times prior to 1933, the Nazis offered private deals and/or public promises to virtually every significant group in Germany, including the Junkers, the army, the war veterans, the high-school students, the university students, the artists, even the spinsters. ("In the Third Reich," Hitler said in a Berlin speech, "every German girl will have a husband.")[7] And to material promises the Nazi orators added flattery, stressing each group's incomparable achievement or tradition, praising its unique virtue, fanning the passions of class (and race) solidarity—while denouncing class warfare as pernicious Marxism. Your virtue, Hitler told his audiences from the beginning, is your devotion not to personal success or "class greed," but to the nation. The present government, he said, is too corrupt to appreciate your sacrifices; but in the Third Reich you will be abundantly rewarded, because your welfare is essential to the public interest.

How could Hitler say it to so many rival groups and still maintain his credibility with all of them? "The slogan proclaiming the primacy of public interest," explains one historian, was

> sufficiently vague to take in all sorts of economic currents and contradictory interests. . . . [I]t was easy to assert that community interests required such and such a measure. Thus it was possible simultaneously to appeal to the profit interests of the business community and to the utmost radicalism of the laboring masses and the uprooted intellectuals.[8]

In addition, there is the fact that a campaign championing "contradictory interests" is no problem to an electorate which regards consistency as "only logic."

In one respect, however, despite his attacks on logic, Hitler *was* an exponent of consistency and demanded it from his followers. If his promises were to be achieved, he told each group, Germany must repudiate the mixed, Weimar type of system, and accept the supremacy of the whole in *every* area of life. The "Twenty-Five Points" made it clear, in 1920, what kinds of changes this would involve.

The economic points of the document, indicated above, were regarded for the most part as highly moral by socialist-liberal circles and by many nationalist groups; each of these points has a counterpart or base in the Weimar Constitution. The Nazis, however, regarded these points as merely one expression of a wider principle. Sprinkled throughout the manifesto, peacefully coexisting with its economic planks, are some additional demands.

Points 1-6, 8, 19, and 22 are concerned primarily with foreign policy (and with racism), and put forth a variety of nationalist ultimatums, including demands for abolition of the Versailles Treaty, more German land, the exclusion of Jews from citizenship, an end to non-German immigration, and the formation of a "national army" as against a "paid army."

Four further passages deal with another area: they supplement economic statism and foreign-policy nationalism by calling for domestic thought-control. Point 20, dealing with education, demands curriculum revision. "Comprehension of the State idea (civic training)," it says, "must be the school objective, beginning with the first dawn of understanding in the pupil." Point 23 demands the creation of a "German national press" and concludes: "It must be forbidden to publish papers which do not conduce to the national welfare. We demand legal prosecution of all tendencies in art and literature of a kind likely to disintegrate our life as a nation, and the suppression of institutions which militate against the requirements above-mentioned." Point 24 promises liberty to all religions "so far as they are not a danger to, and do not militate against the moral feelings of, the German race."

Point 18, the climax in this area, is a mere two sentences; they reveal what "the public good," once it has consumed property and liberty, demands in regard to life: "We demand a ruthless struggle against those whose activities are injurious to the common interest. Common criminals against the nation, usurers, profiteers, etc., must be punished with death, whatever their creed or race."

A criminal, according to the Nazi philosophy, is not a man who violates individual rights; he is a man who injures "the common interest." For the supreme crime—activities "against the nation"—they believed, such a man must receive the supreme penalty. In a broad, programmatic statement, the Nazis did not find it necessary to specify in detail which activities were to merit this penalty. The general outlines of the answer, they felt, were clear enough, implicit in the commonly accepted code: "usurers, profiteers, *etc.*"

Within twenty-five years, that "etc." was to subsume millions of lives.

The moderates invoked the altruist code loudly, but applied it inconsistently and incompletely, primarily to demand an extension of economic controls. Hitler invoked the same code, but went the whole way with it. He would not hear of limiting self-sacrifice to the realm of material production, while allowing self-assertion to dominate the realm of men's spiritual concerns. *He indignantly dismissed the dichotomy between economic freedom and political freedom;* he was against both equally and for the same reason. Men, he said, must be prepared to give up everything for others: they must give up soul and body; ideas and wealth; life itself.

"I have learned a great deal from Marxism, as I do not hesitate to admit," Hitler told Rauschning.

> The difference between them and myself is that I have really put into practice what these peddlers and pen-pushers have timidly begun. . . . I had only to develop logically what Social Democracy repeatedly failed in be-cause of its attempt to realize its evolution within the framework of democracy. National Socialism is what Marxism might have been if it could have broken its ab-surd and artificial ties with a democratic order.[9]

The Social Democrats and their allies were widely accused, especially in the thirties and by the young, of using noble slo-gans as mere rhetoric to cover up the manipulations of "poli-tics as usual"; the moderates were unable to convince the country that they really meant the slogans. The Nazis' righ-teous consistency on the issue did convince people, though not at first. In the early twenties, the party's uncompromising demands, moral and political, were a liability, and Hitler was not taken seriously by most Germans. The Republic, people still believed, had not yet been given a chance, and tempo-rizing measures within the framework of the new system might be able to work.

Within a decade people were to see the results of such measures.

* * *

In Weimar Germany a political movement without the backing of an armed troop was doomed to impotence. This was evident from the beginning, when the only efficacious forces in the country were the Free Corps soldiers and the Spartacist guerrillas. The two groups were soon imitated by other factions, large and small, all claiming that the solution to Germany's problems lay not in "talk" but in "action," i.e., in physical force.

By the mid-twenties, all the leading political parties were equipped with their own private armies, either officially or by informal alliance. This was true not only of the Communists and the Nationalists, but also of the Social Democrats, who created a uniformed socialist army, the Reichsbanner, consisting of over three million workers.

Hitler did not intend to be left out. In 1921, he began to organize his own army, recruiting its members largely from unemployed former Free Corps fighters. The result was the brownshirted Sturm Abteilungen (the SA or Storm Troopers). In 1925, a special Nazi elite corps was added, the blackshirted Schutz Staffeln or SS.

Some of the recruits to these squads had strong ideological commitments; many did not. "We were young guys without any political ideas," one man recalled. "[W]hy should we bother ourselves with politics? . . . If Hauenstein [a Free Corps leader] was ready to give his support to this man [Hitler] that was good enough for me."[10]

If a German youth firmly endorsed any kind of idea, then, given what he had been taught, the chances are that he was (or soon would be) ready to fight for Hitler. If he brushed aside ideas and lost himself in a group, he was still following the country's dominant principles, and he was even more ready. Either way, through conscious ideology or professed anti-ideology, the result was the same.

The Nazi formations were trained to vent fury and sow terror—to break up meetings of opponents, to administer beatings, provoke street fights, stage riots, mutilate bodies, kick in skulls. These were the methods by which Hitler proposed to make his nationalism, his socialism, and his promises to every group come true.

The method was brute destruction, and from the beginning the Nazis presented it to the country as such, with little attempt at apology or cover-up. In this regard, Hitler himself was the most eloquent party symbol: wild-eyed, gesticulating, raving—contorted by a frenzy to kill and avidly explicit about it.

The Nazis held out to the electorate something besides material support. They promised the Germans the satisfaction of a special kind of lust: the lust to see their enemies, foreign and domestic, torn into bloody pieces. In the emotionalist republic, this kind of lust was a dominant emotion.

The poor hated the rich, the rich hated "the rabble," the left hated the "bourgeoisie," the right hated the foreigners, the traditionalists hated the new, and the young hated everything, the adults, the Allies, the West, the Jews, the cities, the "system."

The Nazis promised every group annihilation, the annihilation of that which it hated. Just as Hitler offered Germany a *synthesis of ideas*, so, appealing to the nationwide, classwide spasm of seething fury, he offered the voters a *synthesis of hatreds*. In the end, this combination was what the voters wanted, and chose.

10

The Culture of Hatred

An historic group of intellectuals in Weimar Germany—including theorists in the humanities, scientists, novelists, social commentators, journalists, playwrights, artists—professed a deep antipathy to the nation's entrenched dogmas, and undertook to offer their countrymen fresh ideas. On the whole, these men were independent of the political, religious, and educational establishments and beholden to no outside power. They were the "free spirits" of the German Republic.

The product of their activities was that blend of art, theory, values, and manners which observers at the time and ever since have cherished as "Weimar culture."

"Weimar culture," in this sense of the term, does not designate the total of the cultural activities of Weimar Germany, but those highly visible works and trends which rejected the traditional, nineteenth-century approaches, each in its own field, and self-consciously championed the new, the unorthodox, even the revolutionary. For the most part these trends antedated the Republic; despite the vigorous opposition of the imperial regime, Expressionism, for instance, the leading art movement within Weimar culture, had already reached maturity in Germany prior to World War I. After the war, with the conservative forces in disarray, the new trends flourished in every field; although bitterly controversial, they were passionately acclaimed in avant-garde circles, and they set the dominant tone of the Republic's cultural life.

The Weimar vision of the world came to be the pacesetter for the other countries of the West. Weimar Germany, in the words of Walter Laqueur, was "the first truly modern culture."

"Whereas in France," writes Bernard Myers, "the struggle

was far from over and in the United States merely beginning, Germany during the twenties seems to have been a paradise for contemporary painters, sculptors and graphic artists. . . . [P]er capita there was more acceptance of contemporary art in Germany during the pre-Hitler period than anywhere else."

"When we think of Weimar," writes Peter Gay, "we think of modernity in art, literature, and thought. . . ."[1]

This raises the question: what *is* "modernity in art, literature, and thought"?—a question none of these authors discusses. What is the fundamental impulse defining "Weimar culture," the basic principle uniting the work of Kaiser, Kandinsky, and Schoenberg with that of men such as Thomas Mann, Karl Barth, Sigmund Freud, and Werner Heisenberg?

And what does this principle do to the people who have to breathe it in daily? What does it do to their souls, their lungs, their sense of hope, and their capacity for hatred?

*   *   *

If art is the barometer of a culture, literature, the most explicit of the arts, may be taken as the barometer of art.

The two preeminent figures of Weimar literature were Gerhart Hauptmann and Thomas Mann. Both had been famous before the Republic, and both were criticized in certain avant-garde circles as insufficiently modern. Nevertheless the two men are an eloquent indication of the spirit of the new German culture.

Of the two, Hauptmann was the more widely respected at the time. Although his work was not confined to any one artistic school or literary form, his reputation rested on his activity in the German theater of the 1890s. He was the country's outstanding exponent of Naturalism.

Hauptmann was dedicated to portraying "realistic," "human" characters, as dictated by his idea of reality and of human nature. Although his plays typically feature bitter social protest (from a Marxist perspective), the characters are not presented as purposeful men. In this regard, *The Weavers* is representative. Despite their fury at injustice, the weavers are not efficacious proletarian giants. They are, stressedly, pawns determined by economic factors, made wretched by social forces beyond any single man's power to cope with; they are worn, self-effacing "little people," brooding, reckless, weak, given to whining complaints and berserk rages and drink and superstition. There is no outstanding figure among these sufferers, no individual to dominate the action—in fact, no developed characterizations at all. The protagonist of *The Weavers* is not a man but a social class, represented by hordes of interchangeable workers who function only as a mass.

As a social determinist, Hauptmann preached that the individual is a pawn of the group; in his own political behavior, he acted accordingly. He never abandoned his fundamental commitment to collectivism, and he was the perfect German weather vane in regard to the forms of implementing it. In 1914, he wrote poetry defending the war; in 1919, he celebrated the advent of the Republic; in 1933, the "idol of the Socialist masses" voted for Hitler.

In relation to the glowing view of man held by earlier writers such as Schiller (and, in France, Hugo), Hauptmann's late-nineteenth-century Naturalism *is* modern: man the proudly independent being has given way to man the moaning social atom. Hauptmann, however, is not fully representative of the Weimar trend. He is almost an old-fashioned man-glorifier, when compared to the other, much more influential literary leader of the country, Thomas Mann.

Mann, a disciple of Schopenhauer, Nietzsche, and Wagner, began his career as a German chauvinist-authoritarian, explicitly opposed to reason and to the values of Western civilization. Gradually, however, he made his peace with the Republic and became a convert to democratic socialism (he went into exile when Hitler took power).

The essence of the republican Mann's approach to philosophy and to art is eloquently revealed in *The Magic Mountain*, the major philosophical novel to come out of Weimar Germany. According to one observer, the book, published in 1924, "has important symptomatic meaning for Weimar"; according to another, it "may justly be called the saga of the Weimar Republic."[2] These statements are true, though in a different sense than their authors intended. *The Magic Mountain is* an important symptom—of a uniquely twentieth-century condition.

Set in a TB sanatorium in the Alps during the period just before World War I, the novel details seven years' worth of the inner experiences (thoughts, feelings, memories, sensations) of Hans Castorp, a tubercular engineer, presented as a simple, average youth who wishes to discover the meaning of life.

Hans Castorp is an average youth, as such might be conceived by Schopenhauer in a necrophiliac mood. There is nothing distinctive about Castorp, except a penchant for lengthy abstract discussions, and a hypnotic fascination with suffering, disease, and death (his eyes, for instance, glitter with excitement when he hears the coughing of a tubercular patient). ". . . I insist," he says early in the novel, "that a dying man is above any chap that is going about and laughing and earning his living and eating his three meals a day."

The major event in Castorp's life at the sanatorium consists in his falling in love with a young woman, Claudia, who attracts him for a number of reasons—among them, the fact that she is diseased; that her eyes and voice remind Castorp of a boy to whom he had been attracted years earlier in school; and that she slams doors, an act "as intimately bound up with her very being and its state of disease as time is bound up with the motion of bodies in space." After much hesitation and soul-searching, Castorp declares his love to Claudia in pages of (untranslated) French; he explains to her that speaking in French prevents his statements from being fully real to him, thus permitting his declaration to retain the quality of a mere dream. Nothing comes of his dreamlike avowal. The next day Claudia departs from the sanatorium (she later returns as the mistress of a diseased old man and then departs again). Castorp is left, however, with "his keepsake, his treasure," which he carries about with him and often presses to his lips: an X ray of her lungs.[3]

At the end Castorp descends from the mountaintop to fight in the war. We are not told his fate.

These few events (along with a grab bag of Castorp's random experiences) are scattered across hundreds of pages; they are buried under mountains of obsessively detailed trivia (accounts of the weather, the scenery, the meals, the doctors, the entertainments, the treatment of the various patients, etc.), and of similarly detailed conversations and narrative tracts on an assortment of purportedly intellectual subjects (life, nature, physiology, love, art, time, etc.).

During the conversations, two men, presented as the spokesmen of opposite schools of philosophy, fight to win Castorp's intellectual allegiance. One is the "corrosively ugly" Naphta, the defender of death, a passionate, virtually maniacal champion of pain, illness, sacrifice, religious mysticism, the Inquisition, and the dictatorship of the proletariat. The other—presented as the defender of life, health, science, man, happiness, and liberal republicanism—is the freethinker Settembrini.

It has often been said that Settembrini dramatizes Mann's sympathy for the Republic, and that this character, more than any other in the literature of the period, represents the best of the German republican spirit.

Settembrini is described by Mann as having the curling mustache, shabby dress, and general appearance of an Italian "organ-grinder"; the intellectual manner of a posturing "windbag"; and the occupational interests of an unworldly simpleton (to alleviate human misery, e.g., he is working on an "encyclopaedia of suffering"). A self-proclaimed champion of human dignity, Settembrini interrupts a recitation from Latin verse to "smile at and ogle most killingly" a passing village girl, whom he succeeds in embarrassing. An avowed champion of human brotherhood, he has one dominant emotion, mockery; he loves to laugh at the foibles, real or imagined, of others, a practice he defends by warmly endorsing *malice*, which is, he says, "reason's keenest dart against the powers of darkness and ugliness." An avowed champion of this world, he admires the "great Plotinus" for having been ashamed to have a body, and delivers several tirades against physical nature, which he calls a "stupid and evil" power because of its ability to frustrate the intellect (an ability allegedly evidenced in such phenomena as disease and earthquakes). An avowed champion of peace and freedom, he urges Castorp at the novel's end: "Go, then [to the war], it is your blood that calls, go and fight bravely. More than that can no man."[4]

This muck of contradictions and pretentiousness signifies, in the author's opinion, a definite school of philosophy. Mann presents Settembrini, stressedly, as the man of reason and the representative of the era of Enlightenment.

The contest between Naphta and Settembrini for Castorp's soul is resolved not by their interminable arguments or by any existential event, but by a dream which Castorp chances to have, involving an idyllic community of beautiful youths (supposed to represent life), and a temple in which bloody witches dismember a child with their bare hands (death). With no explanations offered, Castorp suddenly intuits the answer to his dilemmas. Unrestricted death-worship, he decides, is wrong, and so is unrestricted life-worship. The truth is the middle of the road, a golden mean as it were between Naphta and Settembrini, "between recklessness and reason . . . between mystic community and windy individualism." "Man," Castorp thinks, "is master of contradictions, they exist through him, and so he is grander than they. Grander than death, too grand for it. . . . Grander than life, too grand for it. . . ." "The recklessness of death," he decides, is inherent in life, but one must award sovereignty in one's thoughts and actions to life—so long as one always remembers to "keep faith with death in [one's] heart. . . ." Settembrini, he decides, is *too rational*. "It is love, not reason, that is stronger than death. Only love, not reason, gives sweet thoughts."[5]

As the caliber of these statements indicates, Mann, despite the abundance of abstract talk in the book, does not take ideas seriously.

In the sequence on Pieter Peeperkorn, he all but says so openly. Peeperkorn is an old Dutchman described as self-indulgent, nonintellectual, and almost completely inarticulate. It is, he tells Castorp, "our sacred duty to feel. . . . For feeling, young man, is godlike." This incoherent creature is presented by Mann as a stammering, often farcical figure and at the same time as a majestic presence, who wins Castorp's admiration, completely overshadowing "pedagogues" like Naphta and Settembrini, because he has a power transcending "the realm of the Great Confusion" (i.e., intellectual debates). "[S]omehow or other," Castorp tells Settembrini, "he has the right to laugh at us all. . . ." He is, Castorp concludes, an example of "the mystery of personality, something above either cleverness or stupidity. . . ."[6]

Thomas Mann, the major philosophical novelist of Weimar Germany, is no thinker. The out-of-focus flow of non-events in the book is matched only by the similar flow of non-thoughts, i.e., of pseudogeneralities purporting to have cosmic significance and amounting only to a high-school bull session with delusions of grandeur.

The key to the meaning of *The Magic Mountain* is that it has no meaning: it commits itself to nothing, neither idea nor value. Mann's method is to present his characters, however "scientific" or maniacal or depraved or pedestrian, with a tolerant detachment overlaid with a furtive mockery; the method is not open satire, but a genteel "irony," a timid, well-mannered sneer directed at man, at aspiration, at ideas, any ideas, including even the idea that ideas are useless. Beneath the surface—beneath the murky half-hints, the numbing details, the indecipherable symbols (which posturing literati have a field day pretending to decode)—the book is a vacuum, which says nothing and stands for nothing.

Except by implication. Implicit in its approach and style—in its well-bred decadence, its sly flirtation with death and disease, its "ironic" cynicism, its logorrheic emptiness, its weary, muted disdain for all viewpoints—is a viewpoint broadcast to the book's readers: the futility of man, of human effort, of human intelligence. To a country and in a decade swept by hysteria, perishing from uncertainty, torn by political crisis, financial collapse, violence in the streets, and terror of the future—to that country, in that decade, its leading philosophical novelist offered as his contribution to sanity and freedom the smiling assurance that there are no answers, no absolutes, no values, no hope.

The message reached its audience. The book was a literary sensation, selling tens of thousands of copies in its first year alone.

Thomas Mann, says Laqueur, was "one of the main pillars of the Republic."[7] If so, anyone could bring the structure crashing down with a single boot.

There were other modern writers in Weimar Germany, each in his own way indicative of the period's trend. The works of this group, which generally reflect the influence of Marx or Freud or James Joyce, are characteristically plotless and structureless. The more avant-garde authors (prominent among the Expressionists in the theater) feature grotesque juxtapositions of deliberately unintelligible events; typically, however, the Weimar moderns, like Thomas Mann, simply discard "stories" as such. Serious literature, these writers held, must transcend "materialism"; its proper subject is not man in action, not man using his mind to pursue values in the world, but man's introspective life, his soul, his feelings (particularly, his fears, his doubts, his alienation, his inner helplessness). "As in the plastic arts," observes Myers, "German literary naturalism does not hold its form very long but soon pours over into the province of symbolism in which the author stresses mood, states of soul and other kinds of feeling wherein intellect as such plays a relatively minor role."[8]

Another example of this development is the leading poet of the period, Rainer Maria Rilke, a Christian mystic widely admired by conservatives and modernists alike. The conservatives, such as the rightist youth groups, praised Rilke as "a unique figure who had conquered and discredited the intellectuality that had dominated the West for a millennium." The modernists at times went even further; the novelist Stefan Zweig, for instance, extolled Rilke's later (virtually unintelligible) work as a form of communion not with human beings but "with the other, with the beyond of things and feelings."[9]

Still another such communer, a leading writer of the time, was Hermann Hesse (later a favorite of New Left college students in America), whose novels shrug off the external world, burrow into the subconscious as viewed through the lens of such theories as Jungian analysis, and reveal the message of salvation through Indian mysticism.

As to the state of man cut off from the intellect, reduced to mood and Jung and "the beyond," Franz Kafka (little known in Germany during his lifetime) was presenting it eloquently. He, too, was immortalizing the "spirit of Weimar," by offering nightmare projections of nameless ciphers paralyzed by a sinister, unknowable reality.

On the whole the academic institutions, strongholds of Prussianism and tradition, were not part of "Weimar culture." Many influential theorists in the humanities and the sciences, however, were part of it. (Although some of these men taught in German universities, most were associated with private groups or institutes, or worked in nearby Switzerland or Austria.)

In academic philosophy, amid a variety of routine movements unknown to the public, one development stands out as both self-consciously new and fairly popular (especially among college students): the Existentialism of Martin Heidegger, whose major work, *Sein und Zeit*, appeared in 1927. Existence, Heidegger declared to his enthusiastic young following, is unintelligible, reason is invalid, and man is a helpless "Dasein"; he is a creature engulfed by "das Nichts" (nothingness), in terror of the supreme fact of his life: death, and doomed by nature to "angst," "care," estrangement, futility.

The novelty of this viewpoint lies, primarily, not in its content—Heidegger traces his root premises back to Kant—but in its blatancy and form (or rather formlessness). Contrary to the major line of nineteenth-century German philosophers, Heidegger does not attempt to offer an objective defense of his ideas; he rejects the traditional demand for logical argument, definition, integration, system-building. As a result, his works, brimming with disdain for the external world (and with unintelligible passages), have been praised by admirers as the intellectual counterpart of modern painting. Heidegger, it is sometimes said, exemplifies "non-representational thinking."

As to human action, according to Heidegger, it must be unreasoned, feeling-dictated, willful. On May 27, 1933, he practiced this idea on a grand scale: in a formal, voluntary proclamation, he declared to the country that the age of science and of academic freedom was over, and that hereafter it was the duty of intellectuals to think in the service of the Nazi state.

Heidegger's philosophy dispensed with God and religion. Many Weimar modernists, however, sought to preserve religious feeling by reconceiving it in appropriately contemporary terms. To define the latter was the special task of the period's avant-garde theologians (among them, Karl Barth, Emil Brunner, Paul Tillich, Martin Buber).

God, these men declared, cannot be reached by the outdated, nineteenth-century method, i.e., by the attempt at a "natural" or "scientific" theology. God, said Barth, is "wholly other"; He is discontinuous with nature, unknowable to the human intellect, alien to human morality. To know God (or acquire true virtue), therefore, man must abandon thought and humbly await the ineffable. On his own, without the benefit of mystical grace, these innovators stressed, man is lost, helpless, wretched; he is tormented by guilt and disfigured by sin—above all, by the sin of pride. "*The* theological problem," writes Brunner, is "to deliver modern man . . . from the illegitimate self-sufficiency of reason and the spirit of autonomy."[10]

Avant-garde religion, in short, consists in ditching one's

mind, prostrating oneself in the muck, and screaming for mercy.

This synthesis of Existentialism and the Dark Ages, which soon ruled "progressive theology" everywhere, did not reach the German public at the time. Its less academic equivalents, however, reflecting the same basic cause and the same spirit, did reach the public.

Weimar Germany was awash with mystic and occult crazes of every kind, including medieval revivals, Orientalist sects, anthroposophy, theosophy, etc. It was also awash with the social concomitants of such crazes. "Certain cultural parallels [between Weimar Germany and America in 1970] are almost uncanny . . . ," observes Laqueur.

> The phenomenal revival of astrology and various quasi-religious cults, the great acclaim given to prophets of doom, the success of highly marketable *Weltschmerz* in literature and philosophy, the spread of pornography and the use of drugs, the appearance of charlatans of every possible description and the enthusiastic audiences welcoming them—all these are common to both periods.[11]

There were also movements which purported to speak to the Germans (and later to the Americans) in the name of *science*. The most widely known, fiercely denounced both by traditionalists and by Communists, was a movement whose world capital in the twenties was Berlin: the psychoanalysis of Sigmund Freud. (Freud's students or admirers in Germany at the time included, among many others of similar prominence today, Karen Horney, Otto Fenichel, Erich Fromm, Herbert Marcuse, Erik Erikson, and Wilhelm Reich.)

In 1922, before a rapt Berlin audience, Freud introduced the theory which many of his followers regarded as *the* intellectual discovery of their era: his tripartite analysis of the human personality.

According to this theory, the prime mover in human nature is an unperceivable entity with a will and purpose of its own, the unconscious—which is basically an "id," i.e., a contradictory, amoral "it" seething with innate, bestial, primevally inherited, imperiously insistent cravings or "instincts." In deadly combat with this element is man's conscience or "superego," which consists essentially, not of reasoned moral convictions, but of primitive, illogical, largely unconscious taboos or categorical imperatives, representing the mores of the child's parents (and ultimately of society), whose random injunctions every individual unquestioningly "introjects" and cowers before. Caught in the middle between these forces—between a psychopathic hippie screaming: satisfaction now! and a jungle chieftain intoning: tribal obedience!—sentenced by nature to ineradicable conflict, guilt, anxiety, and neurosis is man, i.e., man's mind, his reason or "ego," the faculty which is able to grasp reality, and which exists primarily to mediate between the clashing demands of the psyche's two irrational masters.

As this theory makes eloquently clear, Freud's view of reason is fundamentally Kantian. Both men hold that human thought is ultimately governed, not by a man's awareness of external fact, but by inner mental elements independent of such fact. Both see the basic task of the mind not as perception, but as creation, the creation of a subjective world in compliance with the requirements of innate (or "introjected") mental structures. Whereas Kant, however, draws on the concepts of eighteenth-century Enlightenment philosophy to define his "categories" (and strives to defend them as inherent in "pure reason"), Freud derives his key structures from nineteenth-century romanticist philosophy (and flaunts their antirational character). The theory of the "id" is the voluntarist insistence on the primacy of "will." The theory of the "superego" is the Hegelian insistence that the individual, including his moral ideas, is a mere fragment of the group.

In regard to method, the basic novelty of this psychological variant of the Kantian viewpoint lies in the Freudians' claim that their theories are a product, not of a priori philosophizing, but of scientific investigation based on clinical data. Judging by their methodological practice, scientific investigation for the Freudians consists in leaping from random observations to sweeping constructs devoid of evidential justification, rational or empirical; and then in declaring that these constructs are compatible with any factual data of any kind, and are therefore irrefutable. (For example, if one finds no sign of an Oedipus complex, it has, one is told, been "repressed"; if one finds evidence contradicting it, there has been a "reaction formation"; etc.)

This unprecedented approach to scientific inquiry is a corollary of the basic Freudian theory: if man's mind, as Freud says, is ruled by forces indifferent to facts, forces which are "unmoved by logical rebuttal, and unaffected though reality refutes them,"[12] then science in the nineteenth-century sense—science as the rigorous, logical pursuit of objective knowledge—is impossible. The "new science"—like the new philosophy, the new theology, the new art—becomes instead a vehicle of the willful, the arbitrary, the subjective.

Kant had made the attack on the self the essence of virtue. Here, too, Freud is a follower.

The real root of the outrage his own doctrines provoked, Freud says with a certain pride, is their assault on "the self-love of humanity." Whatever the "wounds" that men have suffered from earlier scientific theories, he explains, the "blow" of psychoanalysis "is probably the most wounding." The blow, he states, is the idea that man is not "supreme in his own soul," "that *the ego is not master in its own house.*"[18]

These formulations, while eloquent, are too generalized to capture fully the essence of Freud's "wound": Freud did not originate determinism—or irrationalism, or collectivism, or the theory of Original Sin, or cynicism, or pessimism (or even the idea of the unconscious). What he did originate, relying on all these theories, is a specific, and in its details unprecedented, view of man.

Freud offers to the world not man the dutiful, decorous nonperceiver (as in Kant); not man the defeated plaything of grand-scale forces, such as a malevolent reality or God or society or a "tragic flaw" (as in the works of countless traditional cynics and pessimists); but man the defeated plaything of the gutter; man the smutty pawn shaped by sexual aberrations and toilet training, itching to rape his mother, castrate his father, hoard his excrement; man the sordid cheat who pursues science because he is a frustrated voyeur, practices surgery because he is a sublimating sadist, and creates the *David* because he craves, secretly, to mold his own feces.

Man as a loathsomely small, ordure-strewn pervert: such is the sort of "wound" that Freud inflicted on the being who had once been defined, in a radiantly different age, as the "rational animal."

The expression "beyond freedom and dignity," it has been said, names a distinctively modern view of man. By this standard, Freud is the preeminent modern. In relation to him, B.F. Skinner and the behaviorists, and Heidegger and Barth, and even Thomas Mann, are pikers.

In virtually every important scholarly field, German culture during the twenties was pervaded by new developments—some explicitly disowning the "mechanistic," "bourgeois" nineteenth century, others wearing a fig leaf of traditional elements; some hailed as antiscience, others as new science; some widely known and popular, others academic and cloistered. The educated German could hear the voice of the "Weimar vision" everywhere.

He could hear it from intellectual leaders such as Max Weber, one of the major influences in the popular young field of sociology, who declared that an objective social science can have nothing to do with ethics or with absolutes of any kind, but must be relativist, tentative, "value-free." There were young innovators in the "sociology of knowledge," such as Karl Mannheim, who held that man is moved by class interest and therefore is incapable of objective thought (except for a special elite, the intelligentsia, who transcend this law of human nature). There was the prominent sociologist Werner Sombart, a onetime Marxist who, deciding that values are inescapable and objectivity irrelevant, proceeded to belly flop into the waiting arms of mysticism, "German" socialism, and the Führer.

Political scientists such as Carl Schmitt and Robert Michels "laid bare the irrational basis of political behavior to such an extent as to destroy any possibility for orderly democratic political organization. . . ."[14] The progressive educators were telling German parents that the communication of knowledge is harmful to the process of education, which should focus instead on the child's feelings, fantasies, and social adjustment. The highly reputable art historians associated with the Warburg Institute were pioneering the introduction of new topics into their field, such as the study of magic, astrology, and the occult. The erudite theoreticians and social commentators of the Frankfurt Institute were formulating a new, "Western" Marxism melding the socialism of Marx with the idealism of Hegel and the sex theories of Freud. The logical positivists of the Vienna Circle, in the name of a scientific approach to philosophy, were launching their unprecedented assault against logic, concepts, certainty, metaphysics, ethics, politics, and even philosophy itself.

Meanwhile, the younger physicists—typified by Werner Heisenberg, whose Uncertainty Principle was announced in 1927—were suggesting to the avant-garde that the traditional Newtonian-Einsteinian view of a universe fully accessible to man's mind is outdated, inasmuch as the subatomic realm is ruled not by cause and effect, but ultimately by chance (a viewpoint once confined to the age of pre-physics). Even the professional mathematicians, the onetime guardians of the citadel of certainty and of logical consistency, caught the hang of the modern spirit. In 1931, they were apprised of the latest Viennese development in the field, Kurt Gödel's incompleteness theorem, according to which logical consistency (and therefore certainty) is precisely the attribute that no system of mathematics can ever claim to possess. "There are no guarantees . . . that our cherished edifices of logic and mathematics *are* free of contradiction"—explained *The New York Times* many years later, describing "Gödel's awesome achievement"—"and our daily assumptions to that effect are mere acts of faith."[15]

One American psychologist, summarizing Freudian theory in 1933, makes a statement applicable in principle to all of the above and to many similar developments (most of which arose independently of one another and of any Freudian influence): "The notion of 'reason enthroned' disappears into myth, and the rational man collapses. . . ."[16]

As to the kind of man who is left after this happens, he was free to contemplate everywhere the embodiments of *his* kind of soul: not only the modern novels, but the raving soliloquies of the Expressionists, the "alienated" noise of their music, the piglike snouts of their paintings, the stinking suns of their poems. There were also the semi-Expressionist melanges of the avowedly "anti-Aristotelian" dramatist, Bertolt Brecht, who was urging that playwrights destroy the "theatrical illusion," by such means as intermixing a play's action with the voice of an off-stage narrator, and having the actors step into and out of their roles; and there was the mass of self-consciously ugly images that had swarmed into Germany from abroad, spawned by trends such as Cubism and Surrealism and Italian Futurism. "Logic, order, truth, reason, we consign them all to the oblivion of death," said one Surrealist manifesto. We must "cultivate the hatred of intelligence," said the leader of the Futurists, Filippo Marinetti, an artist hailed by Mussolini as the John the Baptist of Fascism.[17]

There were also the models for many of the above, the ancient models that the new artists, eager for guidance in the new methods, unearthed and strove to emulate. The artists turned not only to the medievals, but also to African primitivism, Bushman paintings, Asian mystery religions, Polynesian witchcraft, the "atavistic clairvoyance" heralded by Rudolf Steiner, and the artifacts of patients locked up in lunatic asylums.

Such is the kind of art, and the kind of cultural-philosophical trend, which, in a spectrum of varying forms and degrees, the new rebels created and spread throughout the country, once they got their foot in the door.

The mind cannot know truth, said the new philosophy. The mind dare not know itself, said the new psychology. The mind cannot understand nature, said the new physics. The mind cannot reach God, said the new theology. The mind is unspiritual and unfeeling, said the new literature. The mind stifles self-expression, said the new education. The mind is banal, said the new art.

The mind is dead, said the new culture. It cannot know reality, it cannot grasp the good, it does not move man.

Man, said the new vision, is guilty, disoriented, futile. He is a being frozen by terror, a cipher, a monster, a filthy little psychopath. The appropriate response to such a being, said the vision's spreaders, is pity or revulsion or an ironic yawn.

This *is* a new culture and a new, modern vision.

There have been mystical cultures in the West prior to our century (in the non-Western world, they have dominated all history). The two most enduring were those of the pre-Greek and the medieval periods. The men of these eras understood, in some terms, how to think, and as a matter of practical necessity they did think to some extent; but they were unable to identify the nature of the process of thought or the principles by which to guide it. The pre-Greek civilizations, never discovering the field of epistemology, had no explicit idea of a cognitive process which is systematic, secular, observation-based, logic-ruled; the medievals for centuries had no access to most of this knowledge. The dominant, mystical ideas of such cultures represent a *non*rational approach to the world, not an *anti*rational approach. In essence, the spokesmen of these earlier times did not know what reason is, or, therefore, what it makes possible in human life.

The Weimar culturati knew it. So do the rest of the moderns.

They know the philosophical discoveries of ancient Greece, they have seen the Renaissance, the Enlightenment, the nineteenth century. They know what had been possible in every field during the more rational eras of the Western past. They know what was possible to Aristotle, to Aquinas, to Michelangelo, to Galileo, to Newton, to Jefferson, to a line of thinkers and creators, to man. The twentieth-century rejection of the mind is not implicit or uninformed; the eyes of the modernists are purposeful and open, wide open in a campaign to close all eyes.

There is a second difference between modern culture and its mystical predecessors. In whatever terms the spokesmen of earlier eras did grasp and then reject the dictates of reason, they did it primarily as a protective measure, to preserve and propagate *ideas,* however otherworldly, ideas which they identified reverently as truth. They sought to protect from question or attack a cosmogonic legend, a cherished theological system, a holy faith revealing to them the nature of the gods or God, of the good and the right, of man's destiny and salvation. When such cultures attacked man, it was on the grounds that he did not measure up to the perfection ascribed to a supernatural realm.

Modern culture is not otherworldly. Among the Weimar intellectuals, organized religion was no longer a living power. Nor did these intellectuals regard secular philosophy as any kind of power or value. The leaders and spokesmen of modern culture, German or otherwise, do not endorse *any* organized set of principles. They do not accept revelation or reason. Whatever their dogmatic subsects, which surface now and then, the modern intellectuals, characteristically and philosophically, are not zealots, but relativists or skeptics. They do not seek salvation, but claim that there is none. Their countenance is not transfigured by an upward glance at truth; it is disfigured by a sneer proclaiming the futility of ideas.

The sneer is expressed by philosophic movements which boastfully offer no message, by educators who deliberately teach no subject matter, by artists whose work eliminates recognizable content, by psychologists who hold that ideas are mere rationalizations, by novelists such as Thomas Mann, and by all the alleged valuers in all these groups, which purport to love Mankind as a whole, a love whose reality may be gauged by a single fact: the same groups extol Mankind, while vilifying men—and man.

The moderns reject reason "disinterestedly," with no explicit idea of anything to put in its place, no alternative means of knowledge, no formal dogma to preserve or protect. And they reject reason passionately, along with every one of its cardinal products and expressions, every achievement it took human thought centuries of struggle to rise to, define, or reach. In form, the modernists' monolithic rejection consists of many mutually contradictory claims; in essence, their line has been consistent and unbreached.

Man's science, they say, requires the dismissal of values (Max Weber), his feelings require the dismissal of science (Heidegger), his society requires the dismissal of the individual (the Frankfurt Institute), his individuality requires liberation from logic (the Bauhaus)—logic is oppression, consistency is an illusion, causality is dated, free will is a myth, morality is a convention, self-esteem is immoral, heroism is laughable, individual achievement is nineteenth-century, personal ambition is selfish, freedom is antisocial, business is exploitation, wealth is swinish, health is pedestrian, happiness is superficial, sexual standards are hypocrisy, machine civilization is an obscenity, grammar is unfair, communication is impossible, law and order are boring, sanity is bourgeois, beauty is a lie, art is shit.

Truth is unknowable, the modern relativists say. And the truth, they say, is the absurdity of life, absurdity and nothingness and crawling human lice. They say it, but they do not believe it in the way that men did once believe its equivalents. When Tertullian said that the Incarnation is an absurdity and therefore certain, it expressed the viewpoint of a religious fanatic, who worshiped what he called absurd. The modern cult of absurdity is different; the Dadaists and their ilk do not worship public urinals or Hamlet slipping on soap or Beethoven symphonies played backwards. When real Oriental mystics proclaim the primacy of Nirvana, their self-flagellating, insect-revering lives are testimony to the fact that in some terms they mean it. When twentieth-century Western

Orientalists say that all is "nothingness," they say it on a full stomach; the zero they preach through the latest microphones does not disturb their routine, their footnotes, their cocktail parties, or their royalties. When the art of savages portrayed man as a cringing monstrosity, it was a terrified attempt to placate the jealous gods of the tribe. When modern savage-emulators portray *their* vision of man, they do not believe the witchcraft they borrow; they do it not in terror, but with a snicker; while their counterparts in the humanities, expressing the same vision, take pride in being "flexible": they are not disturbed if someone denies the Oedipus complex, and substitutes as the key to human nature an inferiority complex or an orgasm complex or a collective unconscious or any equivalent, so long as it *is* an equivalent, which leaves a single constant untouched.

What the moderns actually believe in and seek to accomplish is not the exaltation of an absurdity above the power of science, but the sabotage of science; not the adoration of das Nichts, but the defeat of this world; not human abasement as a desperate plea to the gods, but human abasement for the sake of human abasement.

When the leading voices of the emotionalist Republic championed "feeling," it was not as a source of knowledge or of human happiness, but of freedom: the freedom from objectivity, method, logic, fact. It was feeling not as an alleged means to truth, but as the nullification of thought.

In a masterly essay analyzing the modern sense of life, Ayn Rand points to the pervasive twentieth-century attacks on intelligence, success, achievement, beauty, and identifies the essence and the evil of the spirit they reveal. That essence, she writes, is *"hatred of the good for being the good."*[18]

The modern cultural rebellion is an eloquent testament, on an all-encompassing scale, to the truth of her identification. "Modern culture" is institutionalized hatred of the good. "The good," in this context, includes reason, reality, and man.

This rebellion is not merely skepticism, which is an ancient theory denying that knowledge is possible; or pessimism, which denies that success is possible; or cynicism, which denies that virtue is possible; or decadence, which settles wearily for festering disintegration; or even sadism, which manufactures human pain. The term that captures twentieth-century culture; the term that includes all of these and every similar, value-annulling doctrine and attitude; the term that names the modern soul is: *nihilism*.

"Nihilism" in this context means hatred, the hatred of values and of their root, reason. Hatred is not the same as disapproval, contempt, or anger. Hatred is loathing combined with fear, and with the desire to lash out at the hated object, to wound, to disfigure, to destroy it.

The essence and impelling premise of the nihilist-modern is the quest for destruction, the destruction of all values, of values as such, and of the mind. It is a destruction he seeks for the sake of destruction, not as a means, but as an end.

This is what underlies, generates, and defines "Weimar culture."

Contrary to the cataract of rationalizations spread by their apologists, the Weimar intellectuals were not moved by a feeling of rebellion against the stifling conformity of the German bourgeoisie or the Prussian mindlessness of the imperial establishment. Men do not rebel against mindlessness by urging the abandonment of the mind, and they do not rebel against a specific social class by lashing out at man as such.

The roots of Weimar culture do not lie in the disgust of the younger intellectuals at the senseless slaughter of World War I or the frenzied insanity of the German inflation or any similar "practical" horror. Men do not fight against senselessness by demanding more of it, or against horror by wallowing in it, or against rot by glorifying disease, or against insanity by enshrining lunatics.

The actuating impulse of the Weimar moderns was not passion for innovation. Innovation does not consist in reversion to the prescientific era, or in movements urging "back to Kant" or back to Luther or back to astrology, Bushman paintings, and jungle dance rituals.

The Weimar moderns *were* alienated, as they said, but the cause was not anything so superficial as social institutions or political systems. Their alienation existed on the most profound level men can experience: they were alienated from the basic values human life requires, from the human means of knowledge, from man's essential relation to reality.

A mass revolt against a specific set of fundamental ideas can be explained only by an acceptance of opposite ideas.

The late-nineteenth-century German intellectuals absorbed what all their deepest thinkers had taught them; they caught the essence of the message: reality is out, reason is out, the pursuit of values is out, man is out; and then they looked at the world around them, the Western world still shaped by the premises of the Age of Reason and the Enlightenment. The intellectuals saw pyramiding scientific and technological discoveries. They saw value-glorifying art animated by an inspired vision of man. They saw purposeful innovators in every field creating unprecedented achievements, men who did not find reason impotent, but who were smilingly confident of their power to achieve their goals. They saw the "bourgeoisie" and the workers and every social class, excepting only themselves and the remnants of the feudal aristocracy, reveling in the luxuries of an industrial civilization, producing goods and happiness, seeking more of both, refusing to sacrifice the treasures which, for the first time in history, masses of men were able to acquire.

The intellectuals saw it, and they knew they had to choose. They had to challenge the anti-mind doctrines they had been taught, or the minds of those who had not yet been indoctrinated. Their alternative was to demolish the view of life bred into their feelings, or the glowing aftermath of the world of the Enlightenment, a world which was, to them, an alien planet and a reproach. They chose according to their fundamentals and their guilt. They became nihilists.

Such men could not create an authentically innovative culture, not while believing that reality is unknowable and that man is helpless. All they could do, aside from resurrecting the irrationalism of the past, was to find their "creative" outlet in destroying what they saw around them. Their goal and product was a cultural wasteland, reflecting the kinds of ideas they felt they could live with.

In the case of the leaders of the modern rebellion, many ugly psychological factors were undoubtedly at work, such as self-loathing, and resentment of the success of others, and the lust to be of significance by destroying what one cannot equal. By themselves, however, motives as vicious as these are impotent: they pertain in any age only to a handful of men, and do not explain the world influence of any trend, including the modernist one. The thing that makes the difference between evil private psychology and powerful public movement is: ideas, fundamental ideas, and the science that deals with them.

It is philosophy—a certain kind of philosophy, established on the world scene by means of formal, detailed, multivolumed, universally respected statement—which left certain kinds of men with certain kinds of psychological motives free to bare their souls publicly, and which wiped out the possibility of any effective resistance to these men and motives, first in Germany, the cultural pacesetter, then everywhere else. Just as a few men with Hitler's kind of hatred for the Jews have existed for many centuries, but remained impotent publicly until they heard, voiced on a world scale, the philosophical premises they needed to implement their hatred; just as these men were then free to rationalize their feeling as a crusade for purity or lebensraum, to disarm an entire nation, and to gain mass converts to the cause of mass slaughter; so a few men with the modern intellectuals' hatred for values as such have always existed, but remained impotent publicly until they heard the premises *they* needed. The premises freed them to disarm men on an international scale, to rationalize *their* hatred as "modern culture," and to unleash, on a cowed, bewildered public, a crew of noisy activist-"innovators" dedicated to the cause of mass destruction.

The basic liberator (in both cases) was Kant's philosophy. No earlier system could have done it.

Kant denies this world, not in the name of a glowing super-reality, but, in effect, of nothing, of a realm which is, by his own statement, unknowable to man and inconceivable. He rejects the human mind because of its very nature, while using the same kind of argument against every other possible form of cognition. He regards men, all men, as devoid of worth because they seek values, any values, in any realm.

Kant is the first major philosopher to turn against reality, reason, values, and man as such, not in the name of something allegedly higher, but in the name of pure destruction. He is not an otherworldly thinker, but an antiworldly one. He is the father of nihilism.

The moderate politicians of the Weimar Republic, anxious to combat the irrationalism of the entrenched professorate, created a new university at Hamburg, then elevated to the chair of philosophy Ernst Cassirer, one of the country's top neo-Kantians. This indicates what Germany's leaders grasped about the cause of their plight or about the effects of ideas.

The German intellectuals translated Kant's system into cultural terms in the only way it could be done. They created a culture in which the new consists of negation and obliteration.

Thus the "new" novels, whose newness consists in having no plots and no heroes, novels featuring characters without characterization and written in language without syntax using words without referents; and thus the poems "free" of rhyme, the verse "free" of meter, the plays without action, theater without the "theatrical illusion," education without cognition, physics without law, mathematics without consistency, art without beauty, atonal music, nonobjective painting, unconscious psychology—philosophy without metaphysics, epistemology, ethics, politics, or thought.

And thus, too, the conservative intellectuals of Weimar Germany, who hated the modernists' hatred, and supplied their own brand.

The tone-setters among the conservatives were not nostalgia-craving deadwood, yearning to go back only a few decades or so. They were a new breed, relatively young, highly educated, and more ambitious than that. Such men knew what they thought of thought and of its products, they knew the practical meaning of their crusade against "bourgeois materialism," they knew what the age of pre-industry and pre-science had been, and that it could be again. Thus Spengler, like Sombart, "repudiates even technological progress and labor-saving devices. The fact that they save hard labor and drudgery and open up the possibility of a good life for the workers is reason enough for condemning them. Work and hardship are good in themselves and general education and progress, illusory."[19] And thus in another variant, Ernst Jünger, the fiery conservative youth leader, who hurled anathemas at the bourgeoisie, demanded "heroic" activism, and urged violence, revolution, bloody war—not, he told his eager following, for the sake of ideas or purposes of any kind, but for the sake of violence, revolution, and bloody war.

If "conservatism" means the desire to preserve the traditional forms of a culture, the key to such intellectuals lies in the fact that they were *modern* conservatives, i.e., *conservative nihilists*, who sought to preserve in order to destroy. What they sought to preserve were the most irrational features, social and intellectual, of the German past. What they sought to destroy were any rational, "Western" imports.

The left-moderns claimed to like the West, but hated its distinctive, nineteenth-century culture. The right-moderns liked the nineteenth century—unmechanized nineteenth-century Prussia—and hated the West. The result was, in effect, a division of labor: the left-moderns concentrated on the *intellectual* attainments of the past, on the destruction of art, education, science (while, sometimes, wishing to retain technology); the right-moderns, taking German irrationalism for granted, concentrated on the *material* attainments, on the destruction of the machine age and of industrial civilization.

Such was the kind of choice offered to Germany by its intellectual leaders: the hatred of every human value in the name of avant-garde novelty, or in the name of feudal reaction. The rejection of nature by the Oriental method, or by the medieval method. The denunciation of the mind as an obstacle to "self-expression," or to social obedience. Man as a primordial, Freudian brute versus man as a primordial, Wagnerian brute. Ideas as futile versus the intellect as arid. Life as horror versus life as war. Cynical pessimism on one side versus cynical pessimism on the other side. The open nihilism of Brecht or of Ernst Jünger.

*   *   *

In the orgy which was the cultural atmosphere of the Weimar Republic, the Germans could not work to resolve their differences. Disintegrated by factionalism, traumatized by crisis, and pumped full of the defiant rejection of reason, in every form and from all sides, the Germans felt not calm, but hysteria; not confidence in regard to others, but the inability to communicate with them; not hope, but despair; not the desire for solutions to their problems, but the need for scapegoats; and, as a result, not goodwill, but fury, blind fury at their enemies, real or imagined.

Nihilism in Germany worked to exacerbate economic and political resentments by undermining the only weapon that could have dealt with them. The intellectuals wanted to destroy values; the public shaped by this trend ended up wanting to destroy men.

The social corollary of "Weimar culture" was a country animated, and torn apart, by hatred, seething in groups trained to be impervious to reason.

The political corollary was the same country put back together by Hitler.

For years the Weimar culturati, left and right, dismissed Hitler as a crank who was not to be taken seriously. The leftist intellectuals regarded Nazism as a movement devoid of ideas; Hitler, they said, is merely a vulgar rowdy or a lackey of big business. The rightist intellectuals, as a rule cultured men who were not racists, listened uneasily to Hitler's gutter denunciations of their own favorite targets, such as communism and cultural Bolshevism; the Nazis, they said, are rabble who are debasing the ideal of a reborn Germany. Both these groups found 1933 inexplicable. How, they wondered, as they stumbled dazedly out of the country or into the concentration camps, could a band of near-illiterates have been able to achieve respectability and power on a nationwide scale?

To an extent, the role of the conservative intellectuals in this regard has been recognized. (Their political ideas are so close to those of the Nazis that it is difficult for anyone to miss the connection.) The role of "Weimar culture," however, has not been identified.

Did Freud say, pessimistically, that man is ruled by violent instincts which no rational political arrangements can alter, and that social equilibrium depends on each individual repressing his deepest desires? The Germans heard Hitler say it, too—euphorically. And they heard that, in regard to enforcing such repression, there is an agent more potent than the superego: the SA.

Did the progressive German hear the Existentialists say that one must think with one's will? Did he hear the new theologians say that the "self-sufficiency of reason" is the fundamental sin? He heard the Nazis promise "the triumph of the will" and an end to the age of reason.

Did the concerned citizen hear Hauptmann and Rathenau denounce the evils of machine civilization? Did he hear Max Weber deplore the "loss of magic" inherent in secular, industrial society? He heard the Nazis demand a return to the "purity" of rural communes and to the magic of "blood and soil."

Did the parent hear the new educators say that everything is relative and that feeling or fantasizing supersedes thought? He heard the Nazis say that there is no truth but "myth" and no absolute but the Führer.

Did the art-lover hear all the Kandinskys and Klees curse objectivity and insist that the artist's inspiration is not logic, but the mythological and the occult? It is our inspiration, too, said the Nazi leaders, as they worked to resurrect Wotan, and consulted their astrologers for practical guidance.

Did the theatergoer discover that communication requires delirious raving in "liberated" language? Listen to Hitler, said the Nazis.

Is it good to wipe out the bourgeois world, as the Expressionists said? It is precisely at the task of wiping out that the Nazis promised to be efficient.

Is it daring to turn life into madness, as the Dadaists said? They were village jokers compared to the Nazis.

Is it profound to "keep faith with death in [one's] heart," as Thomas Mann said? It is a faith the Nazis knew how to keep.

The left-moderns miscalculated; if nihilism was the standard, as they made it, then Nazism was unbeatable, because Nazism is the final extreme of nihilism, in a form that was tailored to attract all the major groups in Germany.

Hitler denounced some avant-garde details, he raved against "cultural Bolshevism," but—as he did with Marxism—he unfailingly preached its essence. He differed from the intellectuals only in one (tactical) respect. He stripped the modernist ideas of their world-weary pessimism and made nihilism the basis of a fantasy projection, promising a new order in which men would rise to unprecedented heights, by means of illogic, self-immolation, worldwide destruction, and strict obedience to the Führer.

The intellectuals were spreading the doctrines which, directly or indirectly, produced helplessness, demoralization, despair on a mass scale. Once it was done, it was easy for the right kind of killer to kick the spreaders aside. He had only to announce that *he* was not helpless and would tell men what to do.

In later years, the creators of "Weimar culture," the ones who survived, cursed the German people for not having listened to them.

The tragedy is that the people *had* listened.

II

The Killers Take Over

The Great Depression merely forced the issue, which had been implicit all along in the Germans' philosophy. Economic catastrophe in Germany was an effect, the last link in a long chain of ideas and events—and a catalyst, which gave Hitler a real opportunity for the final cashing in. The catalyst worked because the nation was already ripe for Hitler's kind of cashing in.

If a man long addicted to a toxic drug suffers sudden convulsions and then dies from them, one might validly say that the convulsions were the cause of the death, so long as one remembers the cause of the cause. The same is true of a country addicted to a toxic ideology.

* * *

For several years after the inflationary debacle, the Republic had seemed to return to normal, enjoying its so-called "period of prosperity." It was a shaky, foredoomed prosperity built on credit and quicksands.

In essence, Germany's recovery was the result of a massive inflow of foreign—primarily American—capital, in the form of huge loans along with large purchases of German securities. America was experiencing the artificial boom of the twenties, a pyramid of highly speculative investments and wild spending made possible by a variety of governmental actions—most notably, the action of the Federal Reserve Board in generating a cheap-money policy in the banks. The influx of this capital into Germany, which also lacked the free-market restraints on inordinate speculation and spending, helped to fuel a similar artificial boom.

In particular, the various levels of government in Germany, which had learned nothing and forgotten everything from the inflationary crisis, were once again pouring out money and piling up debts; they were endowing lavish public works, starting a program of unemployment benefits, enlarging the bureaucracy, raising its salaries, and the like. This time, however, the governments were not counting on the printing press to finance their activities, but on the Americans. "I must ask you always to remember," said Gustav Stresemann to his countrymen, "that during the past years we have been living on borrowed money. If a crisis were to arise and the Americans were to call in their short-term loans we should be faced with bankruptcy." He said it to deaf ears, in 1928.[1]

When the New York stock-market crash signaled the collapse of the American boom, the collapse of Germany followed immediately, as a matter of course. For the second time in less than a decade a protracted agony struck the country, this time involving plummeting investment, the crash of famous financial houses, cascading bankruptcies, soaring unemployment, tobogganing farm prices, and widespread destitution.

The mania of the inflation years had been succeeded by a wave of giddy, unreal prosperity. Now the unreal stood revealed as unreal. Giddiness gave way to panic and to black despair.

The unphilosophical majority among men are the ones most helplessly dependent on their era's dominant ideas. In times of crisis, these men need the guidance of some kind of theory; but, being unfamiliar with the field of ideas, they do not know that alternatives to the popular theories are possible. They know only what they have always been taught.

When Hans Fallada in his popular novel of the time asked *Little Man, What Now?* the little men in Germany (and the other kinds, too) knew the answer, which seemed to them self-evident. They turned to the group—to their economic class or trade association—as their only security; each group blamed the others for the crisis; each party demanded action, the kind of action it understood, government action, i.e., more controls.

Man is rotten, the omnipresent chorus of "Weimar culture" was crying, the individual is helpless, freedom has failed.

The Social Democrats, however, playing out to the end

their founding contradiction, were unable to act. One union leader at a party convention indicated the reason eloquently. He asked whether the party at this juncture should strive to preserve the "capitalist" Weimar system or to topple it. Should socialists stand "at the sick-bed of capitalism" as "the doctor who seeks to cure," he wondered, or as "joyous heirs, who can hardly wait for the end and would even like to help it along with poison?" His answer was that the party is "condemned" to play both roles at once, which in fact is what it did, by switching back and forth at random between them.[2]

In the early months of 1930, with the nation desperate for leadership, the party stumbled into its "proletarian" stance: it decided to bring down a coalition government headed by a Social Democratic Chancellor, Hermann Mueller, because of a proposed measure that might have had the effect of reducing unemployment benefits in the future. The Weimar politicians had long been engaged in Kühhandel, as the Germans called it, "cattletrading," and had treated the country to a procession of musical-chair coalitions, sudden governmental collapses, and continual new elections. The spectacle had evoked widespread contempt for popular government even before the depression. After the Mueller cabinet fell on March 27, however—the "black day" of the Republic—no new coalition could be formed; the economic warfare among the parties was too virulent. The Germans' contempt for the Reichstag became disgust. There was only one solution that seemed feasible.

On March 28, 1930, the Reichstag's normal legislative prerogatives were suspended by President Hindenburg. A semi-dictatorial system of government, a system of rule by emergency executive decree, was established under Chancellor Heinrich Brüning, a conservative Centrist. Popular government was abandoned for the duration of the emergency. The dichotomy between political and economic freedom was breaking down by itself, without any help from the Nazis.

In regard to methods, the Brüning government was dictatorial. In regard to policies, however, it was democratic. The program Brüning (and his two short-lived, authoritarian successors in 1932) enacted was an exact reflection of the popular will. These men "did something," in the German sense of the term.

The government issued a torrent of new decrees. It raised

the tariffs, the taxes, the unemployment-insurance premiums; it expanded public works, imposed rigid restrictions on foreign exchange, and introduced a twenty-month "voluntary labor service" for young people; etc. Most important of all, the Reich in this period effectively erased the last significant remnants of private economic power, by turning the banks, the cartels, and the labor unions into mere administrative organs of the state. The Republic, writes Gustav Stolper (a member of the Reichstag at the time), "came close to being a thoroughly developed state socialism. . . . Government was omnipresent, and the individual had become used to turning to it in every need."[3]

The government's policies did not work. Among other things, hyperprotectionism (in Germany and abroad) was strangling the country's vital foreign trade; the cascade of sudden new taxes and emergency decrees was creating a climate of acute business uncertainty, which made impossible any significant recovery of German investment and production; the unions' adamant opposition to further wage cuts was exacerbating the unemployment.

The Germans attempted to assess the situation and determine the cause of the government's failure. "At last," writes Stolper,

> it became common knowledge that all this state interference . . . was of no avail in the most disastrous economic crisis that had befallen Germany in the course of her history. Paradoxically, the system of state interference as such, being far too deeply rooted in the German political and economic tradition, was not blamed by the opposition. On the contrary, the general mood of the public backed the demands that this imperfect and incomplete system of state intervention be superseded by one more perfect and complete. This was the content of the so-called anticapitalistic yearning which, according to a National Socialist slogan of the time, was said to pervade the German nation.[4]

* * *

The harbingers of the era to come were the university students. Well before the rest of the country, these young intellectuals turned for guidance to the self-declared "party of youth," whose leader was promising "a revolt of the coming generation against all that was senile and rotten with decay."[5]

In the student elections of 1929, the Nazis won a majority or plurality of the vote at nineteen universities. Hitler's off-campus support at the time was still insignificant; many Germans were not yet reconciled to the Nazi manners. The students, however, placed content above form, i.e., ideals above social graces. Their ideals were instinct, sacrifice, and hatred, hatred of "the Western enemy" and of "the bourgeois system."

One German observer noted in these youths a "strange connection" between "revolutionary mutiny against authority" and "blind discipline toward the *'Führer.'* "[6] In fact, the students were mutinying against the Republic not because it stood for overbearing authority in their eyes, but because it stood for freedom. They regarded even some shaky fragments of an individualist way of life as selfish materialism. What they wanted was service to a social cause they could accept as noble, and when they found the cause's spokesman they were ready to bow obediently.

As living standards continued to fall, their parents began to mutiny, too. Hitler offered people leadership, an end to class warfare, a "final solution" to the problems of the mixed economy, and, to each group, his special protection. These were the practical inducements. He also offered what had won the campuses: "idealism," as all understood the concept. In the September 1930 Reichstag elections, the first nation-wide result of these promises leaped into view: the Nazi vote increased sevenfold (to about six and one-half million votes), making the party Germany's second largest (after the Social Democrats). According to one study, the party membership in 1930 included among other groups: blue-collar workers, 28.1 percent; white-collar workers, 25.6 percent; self-employed, 20.7 percent; and farmers, 14.0 percent.[7]

If any of these Germans wanted to be moral, he was ready to sacrifice himself for the sake of others, and intrigued by a party that loudly demanded this of him. If he wanted to live, it seemed necessary to sacrifice others to his own group, by joining a party that loudly promised this to him. If he despaired of either course, he was ready to lash out blindly, at fate or at the Jews, and he knew which party felt the same way. The motive might vary, but not the result. It was Hitler for the love in men, and Hitler for the greed, and Hitler for the hatred. "Love" in this context means Christian love; "greed" means the desire to survive in a controlled economy; "hatred" means nihilism.

In 1930-31, pro-Hitler feeling surged higher at the universities. The Nazi totals "rose at the University of Munich from 18.4 to 33.3 percent, at Jena from 30.0 to 66.6, at Erlangen from 51.0 to 76.0 and at Breslau from 25.4 to 70.9." The Nazis were winning something like a fifth of the national vote; the students already "were largely National Socialist in sympathy; perhaps half of them were Nazis. . . ."[8]

Again, as people grew still more desperate, the country moved to catch up. In the March 1932 election for President, Hitler polled more than 11 million votes. In the July 1932 Reichstag elections, the party doubled its 1930 vote. For the first time the Nazis were the largest party in Germany. The hours of Weimar, it was widely said, were numbered.

The Nazis, however, were far from being a majority. Almost 64 percent of the votes in July 1932 were cast for non-Nazi candidates. To some Germans, the action to take seemed obvious: if the other parties would only join forces, they said, Hitler, despite his following, could never gain power.

The other parties were unable to join forces. Each acted according to its nature and its basic premises.

The Nationalists, who had long scorned Hitler as a proletarian rowdy, soon discovered his popular appeal and decided to make use of it. In 1929, Alfred Hugenberg had welcomed Hitler onto a prominent committee he was chairing, designed to fight against the latest reparations plan. For Hitler, writes historian Erich Eyck,

> it was a major triumph to be thus received into proper society. . . . When this mighty leader of the German Nationalists accepted Hitler, the man who had previously been rejected and despised by 'decent' people . . . many Germans felt obliged to take Hitler seriously and to forget his record of misconduct.

Thereafter the Nationalists made money available to Hitler, joined with him in a powerful united front (the Harzburg

Front of October 1931), backed him in a presidential runoff election (April 1932), and, at the end, were eager to serve in the first Nazi cabinet. "We see in National-Socialism the German Liberation Movement," explained one ardent Lutheran pastor, "which we would profess even were it to be led in the name of the Devil."

It would be quite safe, said Hugenberg, to let Hitler become Chancellor, because the cabinet would be filled with traditional conservatives, who would keep him in line. "In this way," said Hugenberg, "we will box Hitler in."[9]

The Communists, too, wanted to use Hitler. Time after time their deputies voted with the Nazis in the Reichstag; they voted against legislation designed to cope with emergencies, against measures designed to curb violence, against the attempt to maintain in office any kind of stable government. The Communists even agreed to cooperate with Nazi thugs. In November 1932, for instance, the two mortal enemies could be observed standing comfortably, shoulder to shoulder, on the streets of Berlin, collecting money to support a violent strike by the city's transportation workers.

When Hitler's fortunes seemed to be faltering for a time in 1932, a stream of anxious Nazis poured into the ranks of the Communists; the Germans watching said that a Nazi is like beefsteak: brown on the outside, red on the inside. Soon, however, the traffic was in the opposite direction. "[T]here is more that binds us to Bolshevism than separates us from it," said Hitler to Rauschning.

> There is, above all, genuine revolutionary feeling, which is alive everywhere in Russia except where there are Jewish Marxists. I have always made allowance for this circumstance, and given orders that former Communists are to be admitted to the party at once. The *petit bourgeois* Social-Democrat and the trade-union boss will never make a National Socialist, but the Communist always will.[10]

In the final months the Communists viewed the growing Nazi strength with equanimity. The triumph of Nazism, they said, has been ordained by the dialectic process; such triumph will lead to the destruction of the republican form of government, which is a necessary stage in the achievement of communism. Afterward, they said, the Nazis will quickly fade and the party of Lenin can take over.

In July 1932, despite the machinations of the Nazi-Nationalist-Communist axis, the two main republican parties, the Centrists and the Social Democrats, were still holding about 40 percent of the electorate. (The Democrats, having lost their following, were virtually extinct. So was the People's party.)

The Centrists during the depression were stressing to the nation's Catholics the urgent need for a moral reawakening, to consist of anti-materialism, social consciousness, faith, and discipline. The party was also seeking an emergency alliance with like-minded groups so as to form a "bloc for public order." In this regard party leaders did not hesitate to be specific. Repeatedly during 1932 they called for a "strong national government in tune with the interests of the people and including the National Socialists."

The responsibilities involved in sharing power, the Centrists said, would "channel" the Nazis into more temperate paths and would "tame" Hitler.[11]

The Social Democrats, meanwhile, were being "tamed" in another way by Chancellor Franz von Papen. In July 1932, using only a token armed force, he ousted them illegally from the government of Prussia. The party leaders understood that this coup, if uncontested, would mean the loss of their last bastion of strength. But they observed the swelling ranks of the Nazis and Communists; the Prussian police and the German army brimming with nationalist militants; the millions of unemployed workers, which made the prospects for a general strike bleak—and they decided to capitulate without a fight, lest they provoke a bloody civil war they had no heart to wage and little chance to win.

There were not many Social Democrats who rose up in fury over the "rape of Prussia." The party had long since lost most of those who take ideas or causes seriously. There was not much youthful ardor to summon to the side of social democracy. "Republik, das ist nicht viel, Sozialismus ist unser Ziel" ("A republic, that is not much, socialism is our goal")—such were the signs carried in parades by young workers of the period.[12]

The republicans from *every* political party and group were in the same position: more and more, the contradictions involved in their views were leaving these men lifeless, and even speechless. They could hardly praise freedom very eloquently, not while they themselves, like everyone else, were insisting on further statist measures to cope with the economic crisis. They could not extol self-government, when the Reichstag had just collapsed. They could not affirm even the principle of statism, while they were struggling to stave off totalitarianism.

To the last-ditch spokesmen of Weimar, from whatever party they hailed, political ideas as such became an embarrassment; theory was not a means of enlisting support or aiding their cause, but a threat to it. The solution of most such men was to counsel "practicality" while dismissing "abstractions," i.e., to turn pragmatist and become enemies of ideology.

We must get away from the "unfruitful controversy over the terms capitalism and socialism," said Chancellor von Papen in a July 1932 radio address designed to rally the country. Instead, he said, Germany should be guided by a moral principle: "general utility comes before individual utility."[13]

The principle is right, answered the Nazis; and it means the end of the Republic.

On December 15, General Kurt von Schleicher, the last pre-Nazi Chancellor, delivered his version of anti-ideology. He explained in a fireside broadcast "that he was a supporter 'neither of capitalism nor of socialism' and that to him 'concepts such as private economy or planned economy have lost their terrors.' His principal task, he said, was to provide work for the unemployed and get the country back on its economic feet."[14]

It is our task, too, answered the Nazis; but a drastic problem requires a drastic solution.

The spokesmen of Weimar had no answers. They could not set aside lesser differences and unite in the name of an overriding political principle; having rejected ideology, they acknowledged no such principle. They could not suggest any alternative to the Nazi plan for a Führer-state; they had no definite idea to communicate, except a gingerly fear of definite ideas.

The totalitarians knew what they stood for. The non-totalitarians stood for nothing, and everyone knew it. "Democracy has no convictions," sneered one of the Nazis. "Genuine convictions, I mean, for which people would be willing to stake their lives."[15]

*   *   *

The symptoms of the end were the messiahs preaching God to wild-eyed mobs; the bookstores flaunting titles such as *The Whip in Sexuality, Massage Institutes, Sappho and Lesbos;* the promiscuity, the nudism, the orgies; the cocaine and opium addiction; the venomous xenophobia and anti-Semitism. Still more eloquent was the collapse of the universities, and its corollary: the murder in the streets.

The Weimar students practiced everything they had learned. Believing that objectivity is impossible, they did not try to reason about political questions. Believing that a man is nothing in the face of the community, they did not concern themselves with an opponent's individual rights. Committed to action based on feeling, they responded to disagreement by unstopping their fury.

The students launched violent mass demonstrations on campus. They invaded the classes of unpopular professors. They gathered in jeering mobs outside lecture halls. They rushed hotly into head-smashing brawls and they coolly instigated bloody riots, both of which soon became routine at the German universities.

When the defenders of one besieged professor appealed to the authorities for help, the Prussian minister of education, a Social Democrat,

> promised that he would not give in, that the professor had the full protection of the government. The excited students committed excesses in the lecture building, prevented students who wanted to attend from coming to classes by bodily force—and got away with it. The professor was given leave of absence for an indefinite time, the students who had wanted to stand up for him were threatened and ill-treated.[16]

The student rebels defended their actions by claiming that the universities must serve the people, and therefore must be transformed into agents of revolution. The rebels dismissed the view that a university should uphold freedom of thought;

they rejected free thought; fundamentally, they rejected it on the grounds that thought as such is a waste of time.

The universities could not survive the assault for long. They bowed to the rebels' demands. They ceased being centers of learning during the Weimar years. The agent of enslavement had not been Hitler, but their own students.

The faculties, the administrations, the authorities, and the press explained to the country that the universities were not enslaved and that the students were victims. "I remember Germany and Austria in the late '20s and early '30s," writes an American who served in the U.S. Embassy in Austria. The "idealistic youth"

> broke up classrooms, invaded university campuses, broke shop windows. The liberals of Berlin and Vienna sprang to the defense of the youth. They labeled any police action against them as 'brutality.' One of the phrases used to describe the idealistic German youth by editorial writers and educators, believe it or not, was 'the culturally deprived.' . . . When they broke windows of Jewish shops, the liberals—even intellectual Jews of Germany and Austria—said: 'how else shall they show their resentment? Most of the shops just happen to be owned by Jews.'[17]

Hitler was soon equipped to show his resentment, too. In 1930 the SA had numbered upwards of 60,000 men. A year later it had grown to about 170,000. By late 1932 it reached at least 400,000.

Increasingly, especially at election times, savage physical battles erupted throughout the country between young Nazis and young Communists. The weapons used ranged from fists and knives to grenades and bombs. The toll of dead and wounded became a commonplace, which was reported by the press in the manner of automobile accidents or the weather.

Many Germans begged the government to restore order. The student rebels and their professorial defenders had, however, been a microcosm. The new youth "are saturated with hatred," Heinrich Mann had observed as early as 1922.

> But the older generation has a bad conscience, and never punishes them. All protests, all threats and actions of the

young are directed against the older generation and its
way of life. The old note all this carefully—and give
them even more freedom of action. If shots are fired,
they frown and wait for the next shooting. They go to
the theater and warmly applaud the plays about the
most popular of subjects—parricide.[18]

The older generation, liberal and conservative alike, was
squirming with guilt. It was disarmed by the fact that, while
it disapproved of the street thugs' actions, it agreed with all
their basic premises and ideals. The Social Democrats had
opposed the Communists in the postwar upheavals, but had
been and still were loath to confront or denounce them. Now
the law-abiding rightists were caught, too. Though they actively disliked the gangs of idle, brawling Storm Troopers,
they were unable to condemn or resist men whom they themselves regarded as idealists.

The antiwar movie *All Quiet on the Western Front* opened
in Berlin in December 1930. The Nazis, making it a test case,
demanded that the movie be withdrawn. Gangs of hoodlums
invaded the theater, set off stink bombs, let mice loose among
the audience, and threatened patrons with bodily harm. The
government decided to restore peace—by banning the movie.

In April 1932, beset by demands that the violence be
stopped, the government imposed a ban on the SA and SS;
but on June 15, after a deal between Chancellor von Papen
and Hitler (who promised his "toleration" of the latest cabinet), the ban was lifted.

A wave of political violence and murder such as even
Germany had not previously seen immediately followed. . . . In Prussia alone between June 1 and 20
there were 461 pitched battles in the streets which cost
eighty-two lives and seriously wounded four hundred
men.[19]

On August 9, 1932, the government decreed the death penalty for those convicted of political murder. The next night a
band of Nazis invaded the home of a Communist worker in
the Silesian village of Potempa and stamped him to death,
kicking his larynx to pieces. When the killers were arrested,
tried, and sentenced in accordance with the new law, Hitler

responded with threats and demonstrations. On September 2, the government gave its answer: the death sentences were commuted to life imprisonment. (The killers were freed by Hitler the next year.)

The civilized men in the country did not know what to do. In the words of one historian, the moderates voiced desperate "appeals to reason. . . . [But] their techniques were distinctly out of tune with the wild emotionalism that seemed to have gripped a large part of the nation."[20]

The civility cherished by the civilized men had finally been defeated by their ideas, although they did not know that this was the cause. After years of preaching contradictions and of evading principles with an anti-ideological shrug, these men were astonished to see the nation conclude that man cannot live by principles, that reason is no guide to action, and that anything goes. After years of institutionalizing interest-group warfare, which they had justified as sacrifice or collective service, these men were astonished to see hostile gangs take to the streets and demand one another's sacrifice. After years of undercutting the mind by preaching the primacy of gentle feeling (whether "progressive" or religious or skeptical), these men were astonished to find that irrational feeling is no counter to "wild emotionalism."

After years of spreading or condoning or subsidizing the cult and culture of nihilism, the civilized men were astonished to find that they had nothing more to say, and that there was no one left to listen.

The moderates were helpless. The authorities were helpless. The killers were taking over.

On January 30, 1933, after due attention to every requirement of German law and of the Weimar Constitution, the Nazi rule was made official.

* * *

The Weimar culturati could not, they said, endure the nineteenth-century world; but they could triumph over it. Within their own sphere, they could act like the god of an ancient legend—in reverse.

When they had extinguished the stars, and the earth was once again without form, and void; when they had remade the living soul of man in *their* image, after *their* likeness; when they had breathed into his nostrils the breath of *anti*-life;

when they saw everything that they had made and, behold, it was ruins—ruins and astrology and word salads and toilet training and diseased lungs—then they knew that their triumph had been completed, and they were prepared to rest from all their work.

When the seventh day came, however, they found that something inexplicable had grown up in their garden of ruins. At first, they could hear only distant howls and approaching steps. It took a while before they were able to see the thing. But at last they recognized the face of Adolf Hitler.

12

Hitler in Power

It took over a century for the ideas of the Kantian axis to be implanted in the German mind. It took fourteen years for Hitler, relying on this preparation, to rise to the position of Chancellor.

It took six months for the new Chancellor to transform the country into a totalitarian state.

The process of transformation consisted in establishing the nation's collectivist premise fully, as the undisputed, uncontradicted law of the land. The method was to wipe out any limitation on the power of the central government.

The first major step was the Decree for the Protection of the People and the State, promulgated (by the aged Hindenburg) on February 28, 1933. This decree abrogated individual rights in Germany.

> Restrictions on personal liberty [the decree stated], on the right of free expression of opinion, including freedom of the press; on the rights of assembly and association; and violations of the privacy of postal, telegraphic and telephonic communications; and warrants for house searchers, orders for confiscations as well as restrictions on property, are also permissible beyond the legal limits otherwise prescribed.[1]

A month later the power of the Reichstag was formally annulled. The Enabling Act of March 23 transferred to Hitler all legislative prerogatives, including the right to deviate from the Constitution at his sole discretion. This act was approved by the Republic's last freely elected Reichstag; that body committed suicide by a vote of 444-94. The Social Democrats

229

cast the negative votes. The Communists had been barred from their seats. All the other parties voted yes.

The non-Nazi parties, including the Nationalists, were then dissolved. The individual states were turned into mere administrative arms of the Reich. The courts leaped to apply the new rule that "the law and the will of the Führer are one." The Officer Corps, still a powerful force in Germany, approved Hitler's policy of rearmament and voiced no opposition to the process of Nazification.

If anyone did voice opposition, he found two new institutions to deal with, both copied from Soviet Russia: the Gestapo and the concentration camps.

Special government bodies were created to control—according to the requirements of "the public interest"—every aspect of literature, music, the fine arts, the theater, the movies, radio, and the press. Hundreds of tons of books were destroyed; the Marxists and the cultural modernists (and several other groups) had done their job; Hitler had no further need for anarchy and subversion of the system. The Churches were not regarded as subversive; though harassed and intimidated, they were allowed to function.

The country's young people were sent to educational institutions, from kindergarten to university, which had been completely "Aryanized." The youngsters joined the Hitler youth at the age of six. "The children declared that they would never speak of 'I' but only of 'we.' "[2]

Through the agency of three new guilds (the Food Estate, the Estate of Trade and Industry, and the Labor Front), the government assumed control of every group of producers and consumers in the country. In accordance with the method of "German socialism," the facade of a market economy was retained. All prices, wages, and interest rates, however, were "fixed by the central authority. They [were] prices, wages, and interest rates in appearance only; in reality they [were] merely determinations of quantity relations in the government's orders. . . . This is socialism in the outward guise of capitalism."

The nation's businessmen retained the responsibility to produce and suffered the losses attendant on failure. The state determined the purpose and conditions of their production, and reaped the benefits; directly or indirectly, it expropriated all profits. "The time is past," explained the Nazi Minister of

Economics, "when the notion of economic self-seeking and unrestricted use of profits made can be allowed to dominate. . . . The economic system must serve the nation."[8]

"What a dummkopf I was!" cried steel baron Fritz Thyssen, an early Nazi supporter, who fled the country.

By ordering a vast series of public works, then a massive rearmament program accompanied by military conscription, the Nazis ended unemployment. Nor did the Germans have to worry about job security any longer. Men were drafted into labor service by the government and attached to their jobs like medieval serfs. The serfs were carefully tended: the state insisted on the beautification of factories, recreational space for the workers, gardens on the factory grounds, better lighting and ventilation, and much more.

The workers' leisure time was taken over. A comprehensive program of government lecture courses, art shows, vacation trips, and the like (the "Strength Through Joy" program) ensured that, even away from their jobs, men never stopped hearing about the need to work and sacrifice for the community.

As to Hitler's pledges to the poorer groups: the Republic's social insurance budgets were greatly increased, and a variety of welfare funds, programs, agencies, and policies were introduced or expanded, including special provisions for such items as unemployment relief, workmen's compensation, health insurance, pensions, Winter Help campaigns for the destitute, the Reich Mothers' Service for indigent mothers and children, and the National Socialist People's Welfare organization.

In regard to fundamentals, Hitler kept his promises to the German people. Everyone, in every class, field, and income bracket, was manacled to the state. The state meant the party.

"The party takes over the function of what has been society—that is what I wanted them to understand," said Hitler to Rauschning.

> The party is all-embracing. It rules our lives in all their breadth and depth. We must therefore develop branches of the party in which the whole of individual life will be reflected. Each activity and each need of the individual will thereby be regulated by the party as the representa-

tive of the general good. There will be no license, no free space, in which the individual belongs to himself. This is Socialism—not such trifles as the private possession of the means of production. Of what importance is that if I range men firmly within a discipline they cannot escape? Let them then own land or factories as much as they please. The decisive factor is that the State, through the party, is supreme over them, regardless whether they are owners or workers. All that, you see, is unessential. Our Socialism goes far deeper. . . .

[T]he people about us are unaware of what is really happening to them. They gaze fascinated at one or two familiar superficialities, such as possessions and income and rank and other outworn conceptions. As long as these are kept intact, they are quite satisfied. But in the meantime they have entered a new relation; a powerful social force has caught them up. They themselves are changed. What are ownership and income to that? Why need we trouble to socialize banks and factories? We socialize human beings.[4]

* * *

Living standards dropped for every major economic group and class. The government continuously seized more of the country's earnings. There was abundance only for the military. "Guns will make us powerful; butter will only make us fat," said Goering.

The Germans had believed that Nazism was a practical solution to the depression. Even before the war they began to find out otherwise; after 1939 they learned still more. But disaster as such does not change a country's mind or its ideas.

No matter how they were exploited or what hardships they suffered, the Germans accepted Hitler's rule. The Nazi reign of terror is merely one part of the reason. The policies and statements of every group still able to speak in the thirties reveal the other part.

The respectable German right rallied behind the swastika from the beginning. The Protestant clergy explained that it saw in the new government the chance for a moral renaissance, which would nourish religious feeling, obedience to authority, and the spirit of sacrifice.

The Centrists protested when the Nazis interfered with

Catholic activities or interests, but conceded Hitler's "achievements," including (in one Bishop's summary) the "defeat of
Communism . . . the introduction of the Führer-principle,
the reinforcement of moral power and the banning of street-
walkers." On June 10, 1933, the Catholic prelates issued a
lengthy Pastoral. They recognized, they said, "that the individual is part of a larger organism and must work, not simply
for himself, but for the common good. Furthermore, just because authority plays such a prominent role in Catholic affairs, they can well understand the emphasis now placed
upon it in relation to the State." The prelates added a reser-
vation: the government, they said, should "not curtail human
freedom more than the general welfare warrants. . . ."[5]

"That many Germans of intellectual as well as of more
simple mentality could at the very same time worship the
'God on the Cross' and idolize the Führer is one of those irrational aberrations of the human spirit that can merely be
described but not intelligently explained," writes Pinson.[6]
Perhaps the fact is not quite so baffling as he suggests.

The country's secular moderates, such as the onetime Democrats, spoke their mind, also. Their reaction to Hitler is epit-
omized by a remark of Hjalmar Schacht, a founder of the
Democratic party who became Nazi Minister of Economics.
"This man," said Dr. Schacht in 1935, "set about first to raise
the moral standard of the nation. That is why I think him a
great man; he has raised the moral standard of the people."[7]

The German left was not free to speak publicly. Many
Communists in particular disappeared in Nazi jails or escaped
abroad. The Marxists who survived, however, did not challenge Hitler's basic viewpoint; the absolute state is right, they
said in effect, but we could have run it better. This kind of
objection posed no threat to the Nazi rule. Nor did it prevent
another disciple of Marx from recognizing a community of
values with Hitler and acting accordingly. In August 1939,
the statesmen of the West, who had long derogated abstract
principles, were struck dumb by the signing of the Hitler-
Stalin pact.

As to the men who ultimately shaped the ideas of the
country's political groups, i.e., the intellectuals: the overwhelming majority forgot their scruples against "rowdiness."
Illustrious, Nobel Prize-winning names eagerly backed the
Nazi cause and flocked to embrace the brutes. Professor Eu-

gen Lüthgen, an authority in philosophy and law at Bonn, named the belief at the root of the embrace, in a statement praising and justifying the bookburning. "The voice of blood," he said, "speaks a louder language than that of the intellect."[8]

The remnants of the Weimar leadership, in every field and almost without exception, rushed to agree with the principles of the Nazis. The rush was often opportunism or appeasement; but the agreement was real. The state which Hitler established did 'in fact embody the fundamental ideas of Germany's political-cultural tradition.

Many Germans still did not like Hitler's personality or associates or tactics. They swallowed their reaction down. They could not challenge the essence and climax of their own long-cherished basic premises.

Did an action of their new rulers make no sense to the Germans? They reminded themselves that reason is nothing and that feeling (or authority) is all. Did men never have a moment to breathe free of a noisy, *heil*ing, swastika-waving mob? They reminded themselves that the individual is nothing and that the Volk is all.

Was every group terrorized, enslaved, and ruthlessly milked dry? The Germans were willing to endure these conditions. "Selflessness in the sense that oneself does not matter, the feeling of being expendable, was no longer the expression of individual idealism but a mass phenomenon," writes Hannah Arendt.[9]

The Germans remembered their age-old vision of national greatness, defined by discipline, obedience, and self-abnegation. They remembered Kant's idea that "the principle of one's own happiness is the most objectionable of all" and that self-love is "the very source of evil." They grasped that now they had their historic chance, the chance to suppress the "evil" and to make the vision a reality—and they seized the chance and they acted on it.

At last, the Germans were practicing in full the philosophy they had been taught.

13

The Concentration Camps

The men, women, and children who were to become the looted corpses or the living skeletons of the Nazi concentration-camp system were seized in Germany, then across Europe, by the hundreds and thousands, then by the millions. They were seized from homes, offices, factories, farms, schools, and even at random from fields and streets.

The transportation of the prisoners to the camps followed a certain pattern. According to Bruno Bettelheim, a survivor of Buchenwald and a brilliant observer of camp life, the nature of the trip was part of a definite plan.

The newly arrested prisoners were taunted, screamed at, slapped, gouged, kicked, whipped, bayoneted, and/or shot. Some were killed immediately. Some were ordered to stare into lights, or to kneel, for hours. Some were forced to hit or beat other prisoners. Some were forced to curse themselves, their loved ones, and their most precious values. Under threat of instant death, none dared utter a murmur of protest or make a gesture of self-defense or move a step to help a wife or husband lying in plain sight, bleeding and dying.

The "tortures became less and less violent," Bettelheim reports, "to the degree that prisoners stopped resisting and complied immediately with any SS order, even the most outrageous." Longtime prisoners, he adds, who often happened to be returning to camp on the same train with newcomers, "were left alone by the SS as soon as they made their status known as prisoners already initiated."[1]

At the end of the trip, the victims were stripped of clothes, hair, name, and—sometimes—left for hours in silence to wait for the unknown.

In other transports there were no SS orders or beatings.

Prisoners were herded into freight cars, crammed naked against one another, driven back and forth senselessly, sometimes for days, then deposited in extermination centers and turned over to trained torturers, or fed directly into gas chambers.

In the camps, prisoners were starved; food became an obsession; a piece of bread or a spoonful of soup was often the difference between life and death. Prisoners were overworked; they often collapsed on the job; rest became an obsession. Men were forced to stand outdoors for hours, with nothing but rags to protect them from freezing cold. They were covered with filth, lacking the facilities even to wash properly. They were ravaged by disease.

They were followed every moment by the threat of beatings, torture, murder. The threat extended even to the latrines. Men were occasionally pushed from their seats into mounds of excrement; some suffocated to death as the guards watched.

Prisoners did not suffer from sexual frustration. Most did not experience the need for sex at all, even in their dreams. Sex is a celebration of life; it is a form of affirmation incompatible with a concentration camp. "After two or three weeks of the regime at Maidanek," a survivor reports, describing an all but universal reaction, "sex problems disappeared. Women lost their periods; men lost their urge."[2]

The prisoners spent their time building installations, making armaments, or turning out, for the private use of the SS, luxuries of every kind, from greeting cards to living-room furniture. The prisoners' output, however, was relatively meager; the conditions were the opposite of what production or even productive slave labor would have required, a fact recognized by the SS and accepted by the party leadership. "[E]conomic considerations," camp officials were told repeatedly, "should fundamentally remain unconsidered. . . ."[3]

Political considerations did not seem to matter, either. The camp population did include political prisoners, as well as criminals, homosexuals, so-called "asocial" types, and others whose arrest was in some way related to their ideas or behavior. But such men were a minority. The great majority of the inmates—including millions of Jews—were apolitical, law-abiding, normal; they were innocent of any opposition to Hitler's government and of any specific crime. According to the Nazi ideology the Jews were guilty by nature. Yet it was a guilt unrelated to their actions: most had planned or done nothing forbidden by or harmful to the Nazis, a fact known to the men who arrested, tortured, and murdered them.

Judging by the long-term trend, the Jews were to be only the beginning. Despite his stress on anti-Semitism, Hitler's agenda of destruction systematically escalated. It soon included the Poles, the Ukrainians, the Russians, and other nationalities. Later, it grew to include even various categories of loyal, racially "pure" Germans, e.g., those with lung or heart disease. (The Soviets, Hannah Arendt points out, have exhibited a similar development in this regard, moving from the destruction of the pre-revolutionary ruling classes, to that of the kulaks, the Russians of Polish origin, and other groups, on through the latest target, Russian Jewry.)[4]

In essence, the Nazis did not care which races inhabited the concentration camps. They imposed no restrictions on admission. What they wanted was not a group of specifically defined victims, but human material as such and in quantity.

Every aspect of the prisoner's life in the camps was controlled by the SS men. Everything was forbidden to him except what was ordered or specially authorized. Any form of independent action was punished. A man needed permission to possess even the most insignificant object (such as a scrap of extra cloth to protect him from the cold). He needed permission to eat, to speak, to wash, to defecate.

Prisoners could grasp no reason for the camp rules. "Warum? [Why?]," a parched prisoner at Auschwitz once asked a guard who had forbidden him to touch an icicle. "Hier ist kein warum [There is no why here]," was the answer.[5]

In place of why, there was whim, the seemingly causeless, inexplicable whim of the SS.

When the prisoners at Buchenwald awoke, they had to rush frantically, often at the price of ignoring urgent bodily needs, to perform the time-consuming, difficult, and utterly pointless task of making their (straw) beds with absolute precision; the mattresses had to be perfectly flat, the sides perfectly rectangular. In addition, "the whole row of beds and mattresses had to be in perfect alignment. Some SS checked with yardsticks and levels to make sure that the beds were built correctly. . . ."[6]

THE OMINOUS PARALLELS

When the prisoners reached the work site, they might be ordered to perform some graspable task, or, without any explanation, to fill a cart with sand without using shovels lying in plain view; or to carry heavy rocks to a certain spot, then back again to the original position; or to build a fence, then destroy it, then rebuild it. When the prisoners lined up for the next in a continual series of roll calls and inspections, they might be inspected, or ignored for hours, or forced to roll through heaps of gravel as "sport," or whipped on the spot, sometimes to the accompaniment of rollicking songs sung under orders by other prisoners.

No one could know what to expect next. Even when men were admitted to the camp hospital, they could not know—it was a matter of caprice—whether their fate was to be medical treatment or drawn-out vivisection or immediate murder. Nothing was certain but inexplicable pain.

The unpredictability was a torture by itself even apart from all the rest. A group of Czechs at one camp were given special privileges and comforts, then thrown into quarries and subjected to the worst living conditions, "then back again into good quarters and easy work, and after a few months back into the quarries with little food, etc. Soon they all died."[7]

The caprice of the Nazis was senseless; it served no existential objective; but it was the law of the realm. Paraphrasing Tertullian, it was the law *because* it was senseless.

The prisoner in the concentration camps soon learned that his function was not compliance with delimited, goal-directed orders, however harsh or brutal. He learned that what his torturers demanded of him was not his achievement of specific objectives, or his understanding, or any kind of initiative, but a single trait: unconditional obedience.

The best theoretical interpreter of the concentration camps is Hannah Arendt. The camps, she states, are the culmination of the central totalitarian motive. Fundamentally, she holds, the camps are "laboratories," laboratories in "total domination."

The camps, Miss Arendt writes,

> serve the ghastly experiment of eliminating, under scientifically controlled conditions, spontaneity itself as an expression of human behavior and of transforming the

human personality into a mere thing, into something that even animals are not. ...

Under normal circumstances this can never be accomplished, because spontaneity can never be entirely eliminated insofar as it is connected not only with human freedom but with life itself, in the sense of simply keeping alive. It is only in the concentration camps that such an experiment is at all possible. ...

The end result of the experiment, she writes, is "ghastly marionettes with human faces, which all behave like the dog in Pavlov's experiments. ..."[8]

The camps, writes Bettelheim, drawing the same kind of conclusion from his own experience, are an "experimental laboratory," designed to "learn the most effective ways of breaking resistance in a defenseless civilian population. ..." "One major goal was to break the prisoners as individuals, and to change them into a docile mass from which no individual or group act of resistance could arise."

"The camps," a recent study sums up in an apt comparison,

> have so far been the closest thing on earth to a perfect Skinner Box. They were a closed, completely regulated environment, a 'total' world in the strict sense. Pain and death were the 'negative reinforcers,' food and life the 'positive reinforcers,' and all these forces were pulling and shoving twenty-four hours a day at the deepest stratum of human need.[9]

In many of the camps, prisoners were interned for lengthy periods; death was put off, perhaps indefinitely. In the special "extermination camps," a brief, violent trauma was inflicted on the prisoners, after which they were slaughtered immediately in vast groups. In either case, the essential goal of the camp system was not death as such; it was not the physical destruction of the victim that the Nazis primarily sought, but his psychological destruction, i.e., the collapse of his capacity to function independently. A man might be allowed to keep his life (for a while), his sanity, and even his physical strength (enough to carry out orders). What he had to give up—what he was methodically "reinforced," processed, conditioned to give up—was that within him which made him an autonomous, self-directed entity.

The young SS men on duty in the camps also received a certain kind of "reinforcement" or processing. They, too, though in somewhat different form, had to be trained to give up their independence and autonomy. *They* had to be turned into creatures who would question nothing and carry out anything, i.e., into the unflinchingly obedient elite corps on which the whole Hitlerite system relied. The camp personnel learned obedience by doing—by doing the kinds of things normal men did not do and could not have conceived.

The prisoners were helpless. The SS had a choice: they could try to escape or at least seek duty outside the camps. Those—the great majority—who did not try it, but merely went along with their assignments, could not be called victims; they were accessories, morally responsible for what they became.

For about a year the camps were run by the thugs of the SA, a group which included many freewheeling sadists, perverts, and psychopaths eager for an orgy of hatred and torture. The SS, who took over the camps after the Röhm purge and the fall of the SA, were a different breed. For the most part the new guards and administrators were ordinary men, at least at the beginning. They did not particularly hate the prisoners or lust after blood; as a rule, they were more interested in time off than in another chance to inflict torture. When the SS took over, writes Miss Arendt,

> the old spontaneous bestiality gave way to an absolutely cold and systematic destruction of human bodies, calculated to destroy human dignity; death was avoided or postponed indefinitely. The camps were no longer amusement parks for beasts in human form, that is, for men who really belonged in mental institutions and prisons; the reverse became true: they were turned into 'drill grounds,' on which perfectly normal men were trained to be full-fledged members of the SS.[10]

Ideological indoctrination alone, it was found, could not create a corps of full-fledged Nazis; but the daily practice of concentration-camp-scale unreason could, and did.

The camps, and all their seemingly inexplicable horrors,

were aimed not only at the victims, but also at the killers. The victims had to become robots, slavishly obedient to the guards; the guards had to become robots, slavishly obedient to the Führer. In both cases, some fundamental element in men had to be destroyed by the camp experience, an element unidentified but taken for granted by most people; it is the element which, in a normal man, underlies and makes possible such attributes as independence, autonomy, self-direction, "spontaneity."

What is this element and by what method did the camps undertake to eradicate it? What specifically did the camp rulers wage war on and seek to destroy in man?

* * *

The process began at the beginning, with the selection of prisoners who had done nothing wrong and who could not understand why they had been arrested.

Hannah Arendt was the first to identify the camps' need of innocent inmates. She explains the policy in sociopolitical terms, as part of a deliberate Nazi (and Soviet) attempt "to kill the juridical person in man," i.e., to destroy the concept of man's rights.

Criminals, Miss Arendt observes, are not proper subjects for a concentration camp. However brutally he is treated by the camp guards, the criminal knows why he is there; he is able to grasp a causal relationship between his actions and his fate. To that extent he retains a certain human dignity. He remains within the normal, pre-totalitarian framework of crime and punishment; he remains within the realm where justice (by some definition) is relevant and where a man's rights are a reality to be respected or at least considered.

If, however, one deliberately arrests men who have done nothing and tortures them methodically for no reason at all, then the normal framework is thrown out, and even the pretense at justice (in *any* definition) disappears. The contemptuous, sweeping rejection of man's rights becomes a principle of the system, and the victim is effectively stripped of human status. Thus the camps' need of innocent inmates. Thus also the fact that those criminals picked for the camps were sent there as a rule only after they had completed their term in prison and were legally free.

"Under no circumstances," Miss Arendt summarizes, "must

the concentration camp become a calculable punishment for definite offenses." If internment were made dependent on *any* definition of crime or heresy, no matter how perverse or tyrannical, the camps would become superfluous: "it would make for a new system of justice, which, given any stability at all, could not fail to produce a new juridical person in man, that would elude the totalitarian domination."[11]

The actual results of the camps' policy in this matter support Miss Arendt's viewpoint. The criminals were the prisoners least devastated by their arrest; they found their internment easiest to endure and became the camp aristocracy everywhere. Conversely, according to Bettelheim, those worst hit psychologically were the law-abiding, apolitical members of the German middle class; these men, many of whom had sympathized with the Hitler regime, had no inkling of any reason (legal, political, or philosophical) to explain their fate, and this was a fact which they could not deal with or bear. "The prisoner," noted the commandant of Auschwitz in his autobiography, "can cope with stern but impartial severity, however harsh it may be, but tyranny and manifestly unjust treatment affect his soul like a blow with a club."[12]

The concept of rights (or of justice) is not a philosophic primary, though Miss Arendt often seems to treat it as such. What she identifies only as the attack on the "juridical person" is, in fact, part of a wider, all-embracing assault. To give a man's soul this kind of blow is one step in the process of plunging him into a certain kind of world. All the other steps continued the process.

The salient feature of the camp world was not merely injustice, or even horror, but horror which was *unintelligible* to the victim.

When they arrived at the camps, many of the prisoners, dazed by their arrest and nightmare transport, did not know what was happening to them or even where they were. As a rule the Nazis told them nothing and answered no questions. The guards' manner was that of a response to the self-evident: they behaved as if the prisoners were creatures with no faculty of intelligence, or as if the prisoners had now entered a realm in which such a faculty was irrelevant.

In the larger society, the Nazis counted heavily on the power of ideology: there is no other way to rule an entire country. The dissemination of ideology, however—any ideology, even the Nazi one—implicitly underscores the importance of ideas, of individual choice and judgment, of the listener's mind. In the camps no such implication was to be permitted.

No attempt was made to present the Nazi viewpoint to the prisoners. There were no self-justifying speeches, no summaries of *Mein Kampf*, no propaganda, no proselytizing. "Education [in the camps]," declared Himmler, "consists of discipline, never of any kind of instruction on an ideological basis."[18]

The SS did not want the prisoners' intellectual acceptance of Nazism and rebuffed any overtures from would-be converts. When certain prisoners sought to make their peace with the Gestapo, Bettelheim reports, the Gestapo's response was to insist that prisoners refrain from expressing any of their feelings, even pro-Nazi ones. "Free consent," observes Miss Arendt, "is as much an obstacle to total domination as free opposition."[14]

The camp rulers would not tolerate a prisoner's concerning himself with ideas of any kind, whether Nazi or otherwise. Ideas are irrelevant to an inmate—this was the guiding idea; in Buchenwald and Auschwitz, thought has no place.

Neither, the inmates soon learned, did individuality have any place. When a prisoner entered the camp, he brought with him the knowledge achieved by civilized Western man: it was self-evident to him that he (like all men) was a separate entity with a unique identity. The camps proceeded methodically to flout this self-evidency.

Characteristically, the guards did not know or seek to know anything about any particular inmate beyond his group membership. Often they failed or deliberately refused to recognize any difference at all between one prisoner and another. An eerie egalitarianism prevailed: to the SS the things being manipulated by screams, kicks, and guns were not separate human entities, each with his own appearance, character, life; they were indistinguishable cells of an undifferentiated mass, faceless units made of agony, filth, and groveling, each equal to and interchangeable with hundreds or millions of other such units.

Personal responsibility was not recognized in the camps. If a prisoner took an action regarded as punishable, he was not treated as the culprit. Instead, so far as possible, every member of the group to which he belonged (including himself) was punished for the action, regardless of any member's own behavior or knowledge of the incident; all were punished equally, ruthlessly, and as a group. (Outside the camps a variant of this method was practiced: the police would intimidate some dissatisfied group—e.g., doctors or lawyers—by arresting a random cross section of its members, without reference to any individual's action, guilt, or innocence.)

Since the prisoners knew that all could be punished for the acts of any one man, they often feared and tried to stop independent action on the part of other inmates, even action aimed at helping prisoners in special need or danger. Thus feats of heroic courage were often condemned by the beneficiaries themselves, and the heroes, in Bettelheim's words, were "kept from rekindling respect for the individual, or from inspiring an appreciation of independence."[15]

Disappear into the mass, the inmate was told repeatedly by the guards: "Don't dare to be noticeable," "Don't dare to come to my attention." The inmates had to obey—e.g., to fight for the least conspicuous spots in roll-call formations; if a man was noticeable, he might be noticed, and not survive it. On pain of instant beating or death, the victim had to shrink out of the Nazis' sight and hearing. He had to try to erase any external signs of individuality and turn himself into the anonymous cell his captors held him to be. In effect he had to absorb the guards' perspective and become, so far as possible, a self-made cipher.

That a specific intention and not merely random cruelty was behind the above is indicated by the policy of the SS toward those prisoners who agreed to serve as their spies. A spy was always vulnerable to reprisals from other prisoners, but the SS would protect a spy only for a limited time, even if he was transmitting desired information; after this time they would kill him (or allow him to be killed). "Under no circumstances," explains Bettelheim, "would they let a prisoner become a person through his own efforts, even if those efforts were useful to the SS."[16]

The prisoner could not become a person—above all, in his own eyes. He had to lose any connection to the realm of human efficacy or human worth. He had to learn to see himself as a cringing, foul-smelling subanimal, a thing capable of nothing but momentary escape from terror and momentary satisfaction of the lowest physical needs.

It was not enough for the prisoners to bury and forget their individuality; as some of the prisoners grasped at the time, it was intended that they become in their own eyes objects of loathing.

> At the outset [writes one survivor] the living places, the ditches, the mud, the piles of excrement behind the blocks, had appalled me with their horrible filth. . . . and then I saw the light! I saw that it was not a question of disorder or lack of organization but that, on the contrary, a very thoroughly considered conscious idea was in the back of the camp's existence. They had condemned us to die in our own filth, to drown in mud, in our own excrement. They wished to abase us, to destroy our human dignity, to efface every vestige of humanity, to return us to the level of wild animals, to fill us with horror and contempt toward ourselves and our fellows.[17]

You cannot understand, because this world cannot *be* understood; such was the first part of the message broadcast to the prisoner by all the man-degrading, soul-destroying conditions he encountered, including the living standards incompatible with life, the rules without cause, the tortures without purpose—the conditions which no mind could take in or grasp, the conditions imposed *because* no mind could grasp them. And: you cannot understand, because *you* are nothing; such was the second part of the message.

To preserve a sense of self-value, some prisoners clung in the privacy of their own mind to the power of moral judgment, fiercely affirming the depravity of their torturers and the righteousness of their own cause: survival. In regard to acting on such judgment these men did what they could. Washing, for instance, was considered by many inmates to be a matter of life-and-death importance. This was not "for purposes of cleanliness and health," a survivor of Auschwitz explains; it was "necessary as an instrument of moral survival," because it expressed "the power to refuse our consent."[18] Washing was a means of defying the Nazi campaign of degradation; it was a daily reaffirmation of one's human status; it was a demonstration in action of that without which men could not survive psychologically: self-assertion, self-protection, self-esteem.

Many prisoners, however, though they may have tended themselves as routine, could not use the weapon of moral judgment. They had succumbed to the camps' war against what Miss Arendt calls "the moral person," i.e., to the SS men's campaign against morality as such.

One method of this campaign was to confront the prisoner with insolvable dilemmas posing unthinkable alternatives, and then demand that he make a choice. A man would have to choose, for instance, whether to betray and thus send to their death his friends, or his wife and children; to make his position still more impossible he would be warned that suicide would lead to his family's murder. Or a mother would be told to pick out which one of her children the Nazis should kill.

It was not enough for the prisoner passively to endure evil; the intention was first to paralyze his moral faculty, then to force him, whatever his choice, to implicate himself in evil. The prisoner becomes, in Miss Arendt's words, a creature who chooses "no longer between good and evil, but between murder and murder"; and he seems to himself to become, however unwillingly, an accessory to the killers. In reason, no man can be held responsible for actions or decisions which have been forced upon him. In many cases, nevertheless, the camp policy did achieve its goal: in the minds of dazed, starving men, it was able to blur the line between victim and killer. The result was to erode the concept of moral responsibility as such, and/or to shift the guilt to the victim.[19]

To institutionalize this kind of result (and also to reduce the camps' need for Nazi manpower), the SS regularly offered to prisoners positions of substantial power in the camp administration. Since the men picked for these jobs effectively controlled most daily operations, they gained a much more secure and tolerable life. These men were in effect allowed to "become a person"; the price was the kind of person they had to become, the kind who demonstrated his loyalty by outdoing the Nazis in harshness.

Some prisoners were tempted by such a prospect. Some gave in, choosing to become torturers rather than objects of torture. Many, writhing under the whip of a brutal "Capo" (prisoner foreman), felt that they did not know any longer whom to hate.

Besides special dilemmas and temptations provided by the SS, there were the choices inherent in camp life itself, the virtue-mocking, conscience-dulling choices which no one could escape. When a man sees that his survival (or that of his wife or child) depends on a neighbor's piece of bread and that the neighbor's survival depends on it, too, the choice is stealing from a starving man or starving. When a council of prisoners meets to discuss an uncontrollably rebellious inmate, whose actions might provoke fatal reprisal against the whole group, the choice is murder of a helpless sufferer or being murdered. Even under such conditions there were men who decided, as conscientiously as they could, on what moral principles they would act and how far they would permit themselves to go. But there were many more who gave in to futility. Those who surrendered came to feel that everyone, themselves included, is irredeemably wrong, or that "right" and "wrong" are terms without meaning.

The base of human knowledge is the evidence provided by the senses, which are man's primary means of contact with reality. The camps did not restrict their concern to the higher reaches of cognition and evaluation; they went all the way, down to the root.

The concomitant of the conditions declaring: "Who are you to understand?" and "Who are you to judge?" was the brazen campaign declaring: "Who are you to *perceive?*"

"Don't dare to notice"—the prisoners were ordered—don't look at what is going on around you, avert your eyes and ears, don't be conscious. To violate this rule, Bettelheim states, was dangerous. "For example, if an SS man was killing off a prisoner and other prisoners dared to look at what was going on in front of their eyes he would instantly go after them, too."

To avoid such reprisals the prisoner had to learn to suppress any outward signs of perceptiveness (as he had to suppress any signs of individuality); or else he had really to comply with the rule, to train himself in the art and practice of *non*perception. Sometimes (if he could not help knowing a forbidden fact) "this passive compliance—not to see or not to know—was not enough; in order to survive one had to actively pretend not to observe, not to know what the SS required one not to know."[20]

Some prisoners concluded that the safest course was to become mentally inert, to deliberately suspend their own consciousness and allow their power of observation to atrophy. The greater a prisoner's intelligence, they felt, the more he grasped or knew, the greater was the threat to his survival. To these men the inversion was complete: in the outside world, perception was a necessity of life; in the camps the two were antonyms. But nonperception did not work, either: to the extent that prisoners succeeded in stifling their power of awareness, they were helpless to protect themselves even from avoidable danger, and they did not last long.

Not infrequently a guard who had forbidden a prisoner to notice a certain action would, a few minutes later, call the same prisoner's attention to the action and even stress it. "This was no contradiction," Bettelheim explains, "it was simply an impressive lesson that said: you may notice only what we wish you to notice, but you invite death if you notice things on your own volition."

The prisoner was expected to give up everything; he was to give up every voluntary trait and function, from thought and values down to the movement of his eyes and the tilt of his head. "But," remarks Bettelheim, "if one gives up observing, reacting, and taking action, one gives up living one's own life. And this is exactly what the SS wanted to happen."[21]

Most of the guards did not know it, but the same type of cause was producing the same type of effect in them, also. The young SS man may have imagined that he was merely doing a job or earning a promotion, but, in fact, he was no longer living *his* own life, either.

The guards were well-clothed, well-fed, and ideologically trained. But they, too, were being processed and shaped. The prisoner was learning to submit to absolute power. The guard (or administrator) was learning to *wield* it, with everything this requires, and destroys, in the wielder.

With every causeless punishment he inflicted, whether in response to an order or on his own initiative, the young guard was negating the idea of man as a sovereign, rights-possessing entity; he was negating it not only in the prisoner's mind, but in his own. With every unthinkable atrocity he committed, the guard was negating his former sense of morality; he was helping to make unreal in his own eyes his pre-camp life, including such non-Nazi values as he had once pursued. With every insane rule and switching contradiction he enforced or invented, the guard was schooling himself in senselessness; he was learning to make the negation of logic into a mental habit, which soon became second nature to him. (The guard experienced all these negations from the receiving end, also: there was no form of punishment or evil or wanton caprice that his superiors did not inflict on *him*, whenever they chose.)

The guards' defiance of all sense created in them a profound feeling of instability and helplessness and, as a result, a profound feeling of dependence on their superiors. Thus obedience in the camps became a self-reinforcing trait: it was gradually stripping the SS of their capacity to judge or to protest. Obedience was turning the young Nazis into monsters, monsters of obedience. According to Bettelheim, the higher a man stood in the hierarchy, the more fully he embodied this state. Bettelheim gives the example of Hoess, the commandant of Auschwitz, who

> so laid aside his personal existence that he ended a mere executor of official demands. While his physical death came later, he became a living corpse from the time he assumed command of Auschwitz. . . . [H]e had to divest himself so entirely of self respect and self love, of feeling and personality, that for all practical purposes he was little more than a machine functioning only as his superiors flicked the buttons of command.[22]

The power-lusters of the death factories did not pursue their quest with impunity. The opponents of man's rights, trampling on the rights of others, were underscoring their own rightlessness. The crusaders against the individual, crushing the "self respect and self love" of their enemies, were losing their own in the process. The authors and rulers of a brain-wrecking dimension, learning to accept and adapt to it, were making *themselves* brainless.

No one, neither prisoners nor guards, could stand it or even fully believe it.

The prisoners could not believe a world in which the whim of the SS set all the terms of human existence, replacing reality as the basic absolute and frame of reference. They could not believe a world which seemed, in Miss Arendt's words, "to give permanence to the process of dying itself," as if "some evil spirit gone mad were amusing himself by stopping them for a while between life and death. . . ." They had to struggle even to take in the kind of events they witnessed or heard about, such as major surgery being performed on prisoners by trained doctors, "without the slightest reason," a survivor writes, and without anesthesia; or, as another reports, an inmate being thrown for punishment into "a large kettle of boiling water, intended for preparing coffee for the camp. The [victim] was scalded to death, but the coffee was prepared from the water all the same"; or youngsters being picked out at random, "seized by their feet and dashed against tree trunks"; or flames "leaping up from a ditch, gigantic flames. [The Nazis] were burning something. A lorry drew up at the pit and delivered its load—little children. Babies! Yes, I saw it—saw it with my own eyes. . . . Was I awake? I could not believe it."

"It seemed to me, I'm in another world. . . . It was so unbelievable that many of the prisoners had hallucinations . . ." (survivor of Auschwitz). "I lived as in a dream, waiting for someone to awaken me" (survivor of Auschwitz). "This can't be true; such things just don't happen" (prisoners at Buchenwald, according to Bettelheim).[23]

Aside from the actual murders, this was the most lethal feature of the camps: that most prisoners could not accept the reality of what they saw, they could not reconcile the horror with life as they had once known it, and yet they could not deny the evidence of their senses. To such men, the camps lost all connection to life on earth and acquired a kind of metaphysical aura, the aura of being not human institutions in Europe, but "another world," an impossible world, like a second, supernatural dimension of existence inconceivable in itself yet wiping out the first. The concentration camp seemed to its inmates to be a dimension which is at the same time a foolish nightmare and true reality; a dimension which cannot be, yet cannot be escaped; a dimension which *is not*, but which also, terrifyingly, *is*. It was a world of *A and non-A*.

By the nature of what went on behind the barbed-wire fences, the concentration camps to most inmates represented in essence, a universe which violates the basic law of exis tence, the Law of Identity.

Most prisoners could have coped somehow with privation

or with pain, or even (up to a point) with purposeful torture in a knowable world. They were helpless to deal with *metaphysical disorientation*. They could not cope with the eerie feeling that the solid objects and facts of the past have vanished; that there is no difference any longer between truth and raving; that the universe itself, the realm and sum of that which is, has gone crazy. The concomitant of such a feeling is a state of paralysis.

Some prisoners were able to hold on to their knowledge of reality even during the camp experience. They were able to defeat the eerie "other world" around them by clinging to some kind of consistent convictions of their own, on the implicit premise that, the camps to the contrary notwithstanding, things *are* what they are. Many prisoners, however, had no lead to explain any part of what they saw, and they succumbed to the metaphysical pressure.

The most widely known of the latter cases are the columns of prisoners who marched to certain death with no attempt to put up a fight, despite the fact that they vastly outnumbered the guards. This phenomenon, often taken as a sign of cowardice, has nothing to do with the concepts of courage or cowardice, which are inapplicable in this context. These prisoners did know the fate in store for them—they had heard about it from others, or they saw the smoke coming from the crematoria, or they smelled the burning flesh—but most of them could not believe or deal with a universe where such a fate, on such a scale and without any reason, was possible. The result was inertia, vagueness, mental drifting, and obedience. (Some undoubtedly were not disoriented, but chose passivity deliberately, as a form of suicide.)

What disarmed the death-marchers was the converse of the Big Lie: the Incredible Truth,[24] which cannot be accepted and which acts to annul the victim's grasp of reality as such.

The final product of the camps, one which the Nazis carefully shaped, was death. What the SS shaped was mass death without a murmur of protest; death accepted placidly by victims and killers alike; death carried out not as any kind of exception, not as an act of purposeful vengeance or hatred, but as casual, smiling, even homey routine, often against a background of colorful flower beds and to the accompaniment of lilting operetta music. It was to be death as a confirmation of all that had preceded it, death as a last demonstration of absolute power and absolute unreason, death as the final triumph of Nazism over man and over the human spirit.

But the killers, too, were human, at least biologically, and even with all their training could hardly stomach such a triumph. Most could not face what they were doing and tried not to know whatever they did not have to know. Like the prisoners, the SS, too, ended up in effect practicing the art of "not noticing." The prisoner's "noticing" was to be knocked out of him by terror; for itself the SS found another method: drink.

Most of the guards were drunk so often that sobriety became noteworthy: "In his report of a mass execution by the SS," Miss Arendt writes, "a [Nazi] eyewitness gives high praise to this troop which had been so 'idealistic' that it was able to bear 'the entire extermination without the help of liquor.' "[25]

The partisans of Adolf Hitler were forbidding their enemies to perceive reality, and were struggling to induce a similar nullity within their own skulls. The opponents of consciousness were fighting to extinguish it in their victims and in themselves.

It was the final victory of a bleary, vacant, mindless stare—and of the profession which had unleashed it on a civilized world.

*   *   *

The concentration camps were a major factor fueling the Nazis' nationwide reign of terror, a reign which in some form has proved indispensable to every dictatorship in history. All details of camp life were kept hidden from the Germans by strict government edict; but the existence of the camps, together with the threat they represented to anyone guilty of disobedience, was noisily publicized.

As a total phenomenon, however, the camps transcend this explanation; they transcend economic issues, political calculation, historical precedent, and *any* "practical" need or concern, including even the elementary requirements of the regime's own survival, a fact eloquently illustrated by the actions of the camp leadership during the last part of the war. Confronted by an ominous military situation, these men commandeered desperately needed rolling stock to transport camp victims, built huge extermination plants despite an acute shortage of construction materials, and undermined critical armament projects by arresting and deporting the workers en masse. "In the eyes of a strictly utilitarian [i.e., practical] world," remarks Hannah Arendt, "the obvious contradiction between these acts and military expediency gave the whole enterprise an air of mad unreality."[26]

There is only one fundamental explanation of the concentration camps.

The camps *are* "experiments" in power; but they are experiments of a unique kind, with a specific inspiration and method, and with specific findings, which have yet to be fully identified. The inspiration is implicit in the nature and practices of camp life itself.

The Nazis preached a certain philosophy—and they carried it out in action.

They preached authority above rights, the group above the individual, sacrifice above happiness, nihilism above morality, feelings above facts, pliability above absolutes, obedience above logic, the Führer above the self—and they applied it.

They waged a campaign against all the principles that keep man free, which is what enabled them to rise to power. Then they put the campaign into practice, transposing every essential of their viewpoint from the realm of ideology to that of bloody, daily, moment-by-moment existence.

To the extent possible, they did it first outside the camps, creating a society of rightless creatures plunged in a flux made of shifting party lines, switching Big Lies, nonobjective laws, contradictory policies, and incomprehensible arrests.

In the outside world, however, there were limits to the process. Some degree of intelligibility and of individual self-sufficiency was necessary to the continued functioning of the nation. In the camps, there was no need to limit human destruction, and no need for any cooperation from the victim.

The essence of the camp method was the attempt to achieve the effects of a certain theoretical viewpoint without mentioning the viewpoint or any other abstraction. It was the attempt to bypass the process of persuasion: not to urge men to suspend their faculties and have to depend on the victims' voluntary agreement, but to suspend their faculties by oneself, by one's own action. The action was: not to preach the ideology of irrationalism, but to make it come true in real life, and thus to paralyze men at the root, no matter what their choice or the content of their thought.

The camp rulers no longer needed to batter men with denials of the physical world. The rulers made reality unintelligible, and thereby annulled the concept as a guiding factor in human life. They no longer derogated human intelligence in words. They made it helpless in fact and thereby choked it off. They did not condemn self-concern or self-esteem as a moral betrayal. They degraded the prisoner so profoundly that in the end any vestige of either was to become impossible to him.

The specific element in man which the camps attacked was *the conditions of the mind's ability to function.* The target was not primarily the physical conditions, but the root of man's capacity of independence, i.e., the mind's essential *inner* conditions: its grasp of existence, its confidence in reason, its commitment to values and to its *own* value.

The Nazis in the camps were not attacking ideas explicitly, but they *were* attacking ideas. They were attacking the essence of what men need and get from three sciences, as these had developed in a more rational age: metaphysics, epistemology, ethics. They were using fists, guns, and the instruments of brute physical torture in order to frustrate man's most abstract, delicate, spiritual requirements: his *philosophical* requirements.

The concentration camps are an unprecedented testament to the need of theory, a certain kind of theory, in human life. They are a testament that works in reverse; they reveal the need by means of starving it.

The experimental findings of the Nazi "laboratories" can be reduced to a single statement: total domination over man requires philosophical disarmament—after which, nothing much, and little human, is left of the victim.

In the ultimate stage of the lust for power, domination must really be total, i.e., it must seem to be metaphysical. No entity or law of any kind can be allowed to stand in the way of any of the ruler's whims, however casual or contradictory. The prisoner's absolute obedience is used to satisfy this wider demand, also. The victim's fawning compliance with orders which defy every conceivable fact of nature is taken as the defeat not only of human independence, but also of nature as such. The victim's submission to utter senselessness becomes the defeat of sense. His obeisance to absurdity becomes the refutation of logic. His acceptance of lies becomes the overthrow of truth. His surrender of all his values, including his life, becomes the smashing of values and of life itself.

In essence, what the Nazis wanted for themselves from the camps was the same unlimited unreason that they imposed on the prisoners. They expected it to wreck the prisoners, while making the rulers omnipotent. For both purposes, what they needed was a certain kind of universe: a universe of nonfact, non-thing, *non-identity*.

It was the universe that had been hinted at, elaborated, cherished, fought for, and made respectable by a long line of champions. It was the theory and the dream created by all the anti-Aristotelians of Western history.

The philosophers had only been fantasizing their noumenal dimension. The Nazis took it straight and tried to make it come true, here, in Europe, on earth.

*   *   *

Hitler's philosophical experiment failed. Nature could not be defeated. Human nature could not be changed.

Man is a rational being. He cannot survive without a mind and without values. He can be tortured, mutilated, paralyzed, destroyed, but, so long as he exists and acts at all, his identity, including the requirements of his survival, is an absolute. The Nazis did not want man to exist. They wanted men-as-robots, men without thought, purpose, passion, or self.

The robots could not be created, no matter what the Nazi struggle. The moment the victim reached a condition of perfect obedience was the moment he collapsed and started to die.

The fundamental enemy of Nazism is a fact: that man is man—and a wider fact, the one which makes the first an absolute: the fact that facts are what they are, that reality is not malleable to human whim, that A is A, no matter what the dictator's screams, guns, or squads of killers.

This is the actual answer to Auschwitz.

We are told insistently to remember the Holocaust. Eloquent, horrifying books describe the facts to us in every detail. The truth about a monstrous, historic evil virtually screams out from hundreds of thousands of pages. But few, including the authors, seem to hear the scream.

The commentators do not say that the camps are the final, perfect embodiment of all the fundamental ideas which made Hitler possible, and that the way to avenge the victims is to fight those ideas. Most commentators do not know the category of issues necessary to reach or even consider such a conclusion.

One writer (Terrence Des Pres) accounts for the camp survivors by postulating an undefined "biosocial instinct" which guided their actions, but does not discuss why this instinct failed to work for the nonsurvivors. Bruno Bettelheim, despite many brilliant insights, interprets the camps from the perspective of the standard Freudian categories, which explain nothing (the inmates' preoccupation with food and elimination indicates regression; the marchers to the crematoria "had permitted their death tendencies to flood them"; etc.).[27]

Hannah Arendt, the best and most philosophically inclined of the commentators, is also, in regard to her ultimate conclusions, the worst, i.e., the most perversely wrong-headed. In a final warning, she singles out for special attack the attitude which she regards as a major source of the Nazis' evil and of their success: an unswerving commitment to *logic*. The Nazis, she says, and the masses attracted to them, were "too consistent" in pursuing the implications of a basic premise (which she identifies as racism); they gave up the freedom of thought for "the strait jacket of logic" or "the tyranny of logicality"; they did not admit that complete consistency "exists nowhere in the realm of reality," which is pervaded instead by "fortuitousness."[28]

Like the other commentators but even more so, Miss Arendt moves in the modern intellectual mainstream, accepting without challenge all its basic ideas, including the conventional derogation of logic. Thus she can fail to see what her own book makes all but inescapable: that the essence of Hitler's theories was not consistency, but unreason; that "fortuitousness" is a property not of reality, but of Nazism; and that "logicality" is not tyranny, but the weapon against it.

It is a sin to study the agony of a continent of victims and end up offering as explanation the intellectual equivalent of a drugstore nostrum, or worse: end up preaching, as antidote, an essential tenet of the murderers. It is a sin and a portent. The battle against Nazism has not yet been won.

It is true that we must remember the Holocaust. But what we must remember above everything else, and eradicate, is its cause.

We owe this to the past, to the memory of those men, women, and children who died in a German nightmare, with no answer to the "Why?" burning and fading out in their eyes. We owe it to the present, to those who are suffering a similar fate today in the Communist world. And we owe it to the future.

14

America Reverses Direction

"He who thinks not of himself primarily, but of his race, and of its future, is the new patriot." (Charles R. Van Hise, president of the University of Wisconsin and a spokesman of the Progressive movement, 1910)

"We are turning away from the entrusting of crucial decisions . . . to individuals who are motivated by private interests." (Rexford G. Tugwell, New Deal Brain Truster, 1935)

"My fellow Americans, ask not what your country can do for you, ask what you can do for your country." (President John F. Kennedy, 1961)

"We think that . . . the duties of a revolutionary transcend his individual wants. That's why in our collectives we fight individualism at every point." (Mark Rudd, New Left student leader, 1970)

"Self-government, the basic principle of this republic, is inexorably being eroded in favor of self-seeking, self-indulgence, and just plain aggressive selfishness." (Irving Kristol, neo-conservative intellectual, 1972)[1]

* * *

America, as conceived by the Founding Fathers, lasted about a century.

There were contradictions—government controls of various kinds—from the beginning; but for a century the controls were a marginal element. The dominant policy, endorsed by most of the country's thinkers, was individualism and economic laissez-faire.

The turning point was the massive importation of German philosophy in the period after the Civil War. The first consequence, increasingly manifest in the postwar decades, was the proliferation of statist movements in this country. The new statists included economists who adopted the "organic" collectivism of the German historical school, sociologists and historians who interpreted Darwin according to the social ideas of Hegel (the "reform" Darwinists), clergymen who interpreted Jesus according to the moral ideas of Kant (the Social Gospelers), single-taxers who followed Henry George, Utopians who followed Edward Bellamy, revolutionaries who followed Marx and Engels, "humanitarians" who followed Comte and the later John Stuart Mill, pragmatists who followed William James and the early John Dewey.

In essence, it was a single, growing trend, which by the turn of the century had mushroomed into a national crusade of the avant-garde intellectuals. The American system, the crusaders said, is morally wrong; it must be "reformed" in accordance with a nobler vision of life. Novelist William Dean Howells offered a name for the new vision. "Altruria," he called the ideal society in his Utopian novel of 1894—the land of altruism.

The first target of the reformists' campaign was business, which, it was claimed, had too much power. The authors of this claim made no attempt to discover what part of such power derived from the operation of free-market factors, and what part from the growing policy of special government favors to certain business interests (favors such as subsidies, protective tariffs, and monopolistic franchises). The reformists did not believe that any such analysis was necessary. They knew what was right and wrong, and that business by its nature was wrong; they knew it from God or from feeling. "Christianity means co-operation and the uplifting of the lowliest," stated one Social Gospeler; "business means competition and the survival of the strongest." The reformists also knew that there was only one sure method by which to implement their code of right and wrong. "Private self-interest," explained the new economists, "is too powerful, or too ignorant, or too immoral to promote the common good without compulsion."[2]

The philosophical pragmatists in the 1880s and '90s were pioneering the method of eroding the nation's founding ideas under cover of verbal fealty to them. The reformists followed this lead. Legislation controlling big business, they told the public, would represent not an attack on the American system, but a means of preserving individualism, freedom, and real competition. It is true, economist Richard Ely admitted, that more state action might "lessen the amount of theoretical liberty"; but, he added, it would "promote the growth of practical liberty." As this remark suggests, Richard Ely was a follower of Hegel. He was also a teacher of Woodrow Wilson.[8]

The businessmen and their intellectual defenders tried to stave off the assault. Businessmen, they declared, must be left free of government controls in order to be able to function successfully, and thus achieve their proper end: serving the public welfare. The view that unrestricted freedom is necessary to business functioning provoked heated debate among economists; the debate was technical and largely unheeded by the public. The view that businessmen are social servants provoked no debate; on this point, everyone was in agreement. The rich man should administer his "surplus revenues" so as "to produce the most beneficial results for the community—the man of wealth thus becoming the mere agent and trustee for his poorer brethren," declared multimillionaire industrialist Andrew Carnegie, an enthusiastic follower of Herbert Spencer, in 1889. Someday, Carnegie said in a subsequent letter, an "ideal Commonwealth" may emerge and "deal with the *prevention* of immense fortunes . . . when the masses become truly educated and the few become less selfish. . . ."[4]

Contrary to the Marxist theory, big business has been one of the least influential groups in American history. Most businessmen brushed aside the realm of ideas or echoed passively the ideas of their own worst enemies. Carnegie and his fellow industrialists were struggling to save a political system opposed to the West's new ideological trend, while part-evading, part-appeasing that trend. With each moral pronouncement they issued, these men were strengthening the power of their adversaries.

From the outset, the result of this kind of contest between reformists and conservatives was no contest. In 1887, the Interstate Commerce Commission Act established the first Federal regulatory body (to supervise railroad rates). This was the prelude to the top legislative triumph of the nineteenth-century reformists: the Sherman Antitrust Act of 1890. The latter made a sweeping grant of power to the national authorities to punish a newly proclaimed economic crime indicated only in vague, undefined language ("restraint of trade"). In principle, the Sherman Act represents the landmark beginning of government control over the economy in America (in practice, such control was minimal until after the turn of the century).

Henry Demarest Lloyd, a leader of the antitrust movement, named the base of the new approach to government. The principle of self-interest, he said, is "one of the historic mistakes of humanity"; what America needs, he said, is a system "in which no man will have a right to do with his own what he will, but only a right to do what is right." A century earlier, the country's leaders had fought a war against England on the premise that individual rights are "what is right." In 1883, sociologist Lester F. Ward, a reform Darwinist, gave the modern intellectuals' answer to Thomas Jefferson. "The individual," Ward said, "has reigned long enough."[5]

The antitrust act was passed by a conservative Republican Congress. Many members supported the measure as a political gesture, a device to quiet popular concern (which had been aroused by the reformist campaign). Congress must pass the law, Sherman predicted direly (and without foundation), "or be ready for the socialist, the communist, and the nihilist." "[N]othing in the debates on the Sherman Act," observes one historian, "suggests that Congress anticipated its vigorous enforcement."[6]

The factors involved in the passage of the early regulatory acts indicate the pattern operative in all the turning points of the subsequent decades. Insistent, philosophically generated pressure from the left inaugurates each new development. Popular confusion permits the antistatist nation of the Enlightenment to accept new increments of state power, one at a time, without any idea of the trend's intellectual sources or meaning. Conservative default, moral and political, leaves the public permanently disarmed.

In the 1890s the main source of the pressure on a national scale was the Populist party, a group of discontented farmers who took up the ideas of several radical reformists. The party, which demanded such policies as deliberate inflation, a graduated income tax, and full government control of the railroads and trusts, was only slightly ahead of its time. From 1900 to 1917, its heir and successor dominated the nation's top leadership, intellectual and political, Democratic and Republican. The heir was the Progressive movement.

For the most part, the leading spirits of the Progressive era were men who had been students here or abroad in the 1880s or '90s. They were the voices of the first American generation to be reared in college on the new collectivist theories; they were men trained to the conviction that an increase in the power of the state is the solution to most of mankind's problems. These men turned the ideas of their avant-garde professors into an enduring American orthodoxy. In this endeavor, jurists, historians, economists, and bestselling novelists fought side by side, along with Settlement House social workers who deplored mass "poverty," muckraking journalists who denounced the profit motive, Presidents who denounced "malefactors of great wealth" (Theodore Roosevelt), and Progressive educators who denounced the mind.

All these men and movements preached the prerogatives of the poor and the weak, whom they described as the victims of big business; they demanded a new approach to social questions, an approach eloquently characterized by Herbert Croly. Croly was an editor and co-founder of *The New Republic* and an adviser to Theodore Roosevelt.

> The Promise of American Life [Croly wrote in an influential work] is to be fulfilled—not merely by a maximum amount of economic freedom, but by a certain measure of discipline; not merely by the abundant satisfaction of individual desires, but by a large measure of individual subordination and self-denial.

Herbert Croly was the son of a leading American disciple of Auguste Comte's positivism; he was also a philosophy student at Harvard under the Hegelian Josiah Royce. Positivism, Comte had explained, places itself "at the social point of view," and therefore "cannot tolerate the notion of *rights*, for such notion rests on individualism." Individualism, Royce was teaching his students, is "the sin against the Holy Ghost."

"The National Government must step in and discriminate," Croly wrote; "but it must discriminate, not on behalf of liberty and the special individual, but on behalf of equality and the average man."[7]

The average man at the time was struggling to enter this

country in order to find sanctuary from governments around the globe eager to "step in and discriminate"; he was struggling to enter the fabled land of abundance, where all men, including the poorest, were enjoying a standard of living surpassing that of their counterparts anywhere in the world. But the Progressives were not a movement of average men; they had a different view of life. By himself—declared Frank Norris and Theodore Dreiser and the other Naturalists of the period—man has no choice and no chance; he is a helpless social product doomed to poverty and despair; his only hope is the government.

Organized labor was not making radical demands. In contrast to European workers, who were in the vanguard of a class struggle and of the socialist movement, American workers, like the American people, continued to reflect the influence of the Enlightenment. American labor leaders upheld labor's independence and resisted any form of paternalism. The Progressives were undeterred. "The program of a government of freedom," said President Woodrow Wilson, "must in these days be positive, not negative merely." "Freedom to-day," he said, "is something more than being let alone."[8]

Laissez-faire is not an absolute, explained Oliver Wendell Holmes, and it is not inherent in the Constitution; "social needs" must be supreme over all laws and abstract principles, however venerable. The Constitution is not sacrosanct anyway, added historian Charles Beard; it merely reflects the selfish desire of the Founding Fathers to protect their own property holdings. Reality is a social product, said the pragmatists; logic itself is in continual flux; why should politics be any different?

Let us not hesitate, but "experiment" now, said all these voices; the essence of man is not primarily intellect, but action.

The Progressives did not hesitate to name the model of their action. The model was the mother country of the leading Progressive state, Wisconsin. Wisconsin was described at the time as being "fundamentally a German state," which was "doing for America what Germany is doing for the world." "In Germany, perhaps more than anywhere else," said the New England humanitarian Jane Addams, "the government has come to concern itself with the primitive essential needs of its working people." "Shall a democracy," she asked, "be slower. . . ?"[9]

The result of the Progressives' ideas was a wave of new measures and policies in this country, including labor laws which specified working conditions and maximum hours; a compulsory system of workmen's compensation; the regular use of the Sherman Act to prosecute businessmen; legislation forbidding "unfair" competition (the Clayton Act); a major new regulatory agency (the Federal Trade Commission); and government entry on an unprecedented scale into such fields as finance (the Federal Reserve Act), conservation, food and drugs. To administer and pay for the foregoing, two additional factors, long familiar in Europe, appeared here for the first time: a large, entrenched civil service and, after 1913, a graduated income tax.

In Europe, the statist intellectuals, in harmony with the continent's basic philosophic tradition, could afford to be ideologically outspoken. In America, their counterparts could not afford it. Characteristically, following the pragmatists, they preached Progressive ideas, and then presented each new governmental measure as a product not of ideology, but of limited, "practical" factors without wider implications. At the same time they continued to offer ideological reassurances to the nation. There must be a "partial substitution of collectivism for individualism," said Theodore Roosevelt in 1913, "not to destroy, but to save individualism."[10]

In Europe, the rise of statism had been accompanied by the rise of an aggressive nationalism. The same combination of policies was evident in the American reformist movement. (The best-known example is Theodore Roosevelt, the first major opponent of capitalism to occupy the Presidency, who united zeal for trust-busting with ardent militarism.) The two policies were complementary: each involved a major growth in the power of the central government, and each rested on appeals to the ethics of social service (at home, to the poor; abroad, to the "backward peoples"). "The spirit of imperialism," observes American historian R.E. Osgood, "was an exaltation of duty above rights, of collective welfare above individual self-interest. . . ."

Imperialism in the new world had further, deeper roots. It was difficult to defend such a policy by reference to reason; it was easy by reference to "will." American imperialism, adds

Osgood—like its European model—also exalted "the heroic values as opposed to materialism, action instead of logic, the natural impulse rather than the pallid intellect."[11]

When 1914 came, the country did not wish to pursue "the heroic values as opposed to materialism." But a group of determined intellectuals, religious leaders, and politicians did wish it. This group, which prevailed over an antiwar public, included in time almost all the leading Progressives. President Wilson, in his war message to Congress, observed that the United States had "no selfish ends to serve" in entering the war. Herbert Croly said that entering the war would provide America with "the tonic of a serious moral adventure." He warned his countrymen of the "real danger of national disintegration," if the average man should elevate "having his own way" above "national service."[12]

After the war the Progressive movement faded. Its political legacy, however, which included many wartime controls never repealed despite the armistice, endured. The Progressives had started America moving in a new direction: they had taken the first major steps toward the establishment of a welfare state.

Culturally and politically, World War I was the turning point. It marked the end of the individualist era throughout the West. Although Americans yearned in 1920 to go "back to normalcy," there was to be no normalcy again. "Normalcy" to them meant a civilized world which respected man's rights, and its consequences: international harmony, lasting peace, a continuously rising standard of living, unobstructed freedom, cheerful self-confidence, hope for the future. Instead, the country faced the aftermath of global breakdown, the mushrooming of European dictatorships, the growing fear that the selfless crusade of 1917 had been a senseless slaughter, the growing claims of men's duty to their neighbors, and the newer claim of America's duty to the world. The response to all of it was a binge of giddy, gin-soaked escapism.

The last of the nineteenth-century defenders of laissez-faire were gone. The schools and colleges were not turning out replacements. Although Progressivism had faded, its major cultural ally was flourishing: the twenties marked the emergence of Progressive education as a national force. For the first time, the ideas of the new educators gained a mass base, spreading beyond a comparatively small vanguard to engulf the children of the middle class. Increasingly, the children were hearing more about feelings and less about objective reality; they were also hearing more about social responsibility and less about the country's past. A generation was losing the knowledge of what the American system had originally been.

At the same time, the avant-garde, led by a group of expatriates, was introducing a similar perspective into the arts; it was presiding over the first major eruption in America of the modernist revolt against objectivity and the nineteenth century. Obediently imitating their old-world mentors, fawning over Continental decadence while cursing the "philistine Americans," the Pound-Eliot-Stein axis and its equivalents in the other arts were turning out free verse, stream-of-consciousness novels, expressionist plays, "abstract" paintings, nonintelligible forms, nongraspable symbols, obscurity as a means of "bourgeoisie"-baiting, obscurity offered as spirituality, obscurity for its own sake. The artists said they were bored by life in the United States; they found European manifestations they could admire. The work of Paul Klee, boasted the newly founded Museum of Modern Art during the painter's American debut in 1930, "makes the flesh creep by creating a spectre fresh from a nightmare."[18]

America was still decades away from the cultural condition of Germany. At one time, however, the distance between them would have had to be measured in light years.

The conservative Republicans in the twenties made their own contributions to the trend. Harding, Coolidge, and Hoover, whom people took to be advocates of capitalism, accepted without challenge and thus effectively removed from the field of controversy all the precedent-setting controls of the Progressive era. In addition, while continuing the longtime practice of dispensing Federal favors to business, they gradually introduced new statist measures of their own. As early as 1919, Herbert Hoover, for instance, rejected laissez-faire in favor of an undefined "progressive middle way" between socialism and anarchism. As Secretary of Commerce under Harding and Coolidge, Hoover supported several regulatory innovations, including government agencies to control the air transport and radio industries. Hoover at the time also backed compulsory unionization for railway labor, and recommended that American business organize itself into industry-wide, cartel-like trade associations. "We are passing," he said, "from a period of extremely individualistic action into a period of associational activities."[14]

When the disaster struck in 1929 the country was intellectually disarmed. There were no prominent voices to name the disaster's cause.

The Great Depression was not the result of a free market, but of controls; the economic dislocations which led to the collapse were a product of the government intervention of the preceding decades. A few men in the thirties, speaking for the remnant of the classical tradition, tried to point this out. They did not, however, offer any comprehensive or philosophic approach to the issues; they were concerned mostly with the details of current legislation—and their viewpoint was thoroughly ignored. The disaster created by controls was widely ascribed to the free market. On this point the Hoover Republicans and the liberal intellectuals were in agreement.

President Hoover responded to the crisis by preaching individualism, while at the same time clinging to the earlier controls and urging more government action, including massive public works, welfare programs at the state and local levels, farm price supports, and emergency loans to business. Hoover's policy was historic; it defined a new role for the government, which has been accurately described by Walter Lippmann. "It was Mr. Hoover," he noted, "who abandoned the principles of *laissez faire* in relation to the business cycle [and] established the conviction that prosperity and depression can be publicly controlled by political action. . . ."[15]

Hoover's policy, like Brüning's in Germany, did not work. The soup kitchens and the desperation spread.

The intellectuals stated their conclusions. The cause of the misery, declared Charles Beard, is "the individualist creed. . . . The task before us, then, is not to furbish up an old slogan, but to get rid of it. . . ." The intellectuals had long condemned the American system and the ideas on which it was based. They had their own creed, their own, "antimaterialistic" ideals, and their own ambitions. To such men, the Great Depression was a godsend. To the writers and artists

who had grown up in the Big Business era and had always resented its barbarism, its crowding-out of everything they cared about, these years were not depressing but stimulating [writes Edmund Wilson]. One couldn't help being exhilarated at the sudden unexpected collapse of that stupid gigantic fraud. It gave us a new sense of freedom; and it gave us a new sense of power.[16]

In 1933 a voice congenial to the writers and artists took over. Franklin Delano Roosevelt, invoking an old ethics, offered the country a New Deal. The nation, declared Roosevelt in his first Inaugural Address, must act "as a trained and loyal army willing to sacrifice for the good of a common discipline."

As a result of the statist foundation and the economic catastrophe they inherited, the New Dealers could afford to be more explicit than their predecessors in the reformist movement. "[W]hether we like it or not," sociologist Henry Pratt Fairchild wrote, "modern life has become so highly integrated, so inextricably socialized, so definitely organic, that the very concept of the individual is becoming obsolete."[17]

It seemed at the time to be unanimous. The Progressive educators abruptly shifted their emphasis from the earlier "child-centered" orientation to a "community-centered" version. The fiction writers wrote *U.S.A.* or *The Grapes of Wrath* or *Waiting for Lefty* (as the curtain comes down, furious workers, learning that the bosses' police have murdered a union leader, howl repeatedly "Strike, strike, strike!"). The churches—according to a group representing the major Protestant denominations—"protest against the selfish desire for wealth as the principal motive of industry," seek "a social order which shall be based upon Jesus' principles of love and brotherhood," and therefore offer "hearty support of a planned economic system." Even the skeptics joined in. There is nothing "peculiarly sacred" about American "folklore," such as capitalism or the Constitution, said Thurman Arnold, a Yale law professor who typifies the increasingly pragmatist approach of the later New Deal. We need not "rush to theories and principles as guides," said Arnold, who soon moved to Washington to serve as head of the Antitrust Division of the Justice Department.[18]

The absolutists knew what was absolute; the relativists knew what to dispense with. Some were dogmatists and some were pragmatists; but all were working toward the same kind of end.

The New Dealers did not lavish praise on Germany. They were warmer to Mussolini's Italy. For most of them, however, the real beacon was elsewhere. "The future," said Rexford Tugwell, "is becoming visible in Russia; the present is bitterly in contrast."[19]

The thirties have been described correctly as America's Red Decade; the Communist influence on the country's intellectuals and on the New Deal was palpable. Communism, however, was not the decisive causal factor. It was merely one fashionable expression of the ideas advocated by every major group.

If Americans were to "reconstruct" society properly, wrote John Dewey at the start of the Depression, it "would signify that we had entered constructively and voluntarily upon the road which Soviet Russia is traveling with so much attendant destruction and coercion." Dewey was not a Marxist; he described himself as a liberal democrat; he disagreed with the Bolsheviks on the method of travel—but not on the road or direction.

Dewey did not fear that the end of that road would have to be the same in America as in Russia. There are no absolutes, he said; reality is inherently "unfinished." We can know where a course will take us, he said, only "after we have acted."[20]

The political program of the New Deal centered on a goal that had been endorsed but not stressed by the Progressives. The Democrats demanded Federal action to achieve equality, "equality of opportunity." Besides the traditional Constitutional rights, which were political in nature, they said, men also have economic rights.

The Founding Fathers had conceived "rights" as entitlements to act and to keep the products of one's actions, not as claims to the actions or products of others. "Equality," in the original American view, meant the right of every man to independence—to make his way and sustain his life by his own effort; "opportunity" meant freedom. The New Dealers rejected this approach as unfeeling and cruel. "A hungry man," they said, "is not free"; and anyway, they said, freedom is not enough. "Talk of liberty in reform circles now was likely to produce a yawn, if not a scowl," writes one historian; "opportunity . . . was the point."

"Every man has a right to life," said President Roosevelt, "and this means that he has also a right to make a comfortable living." The government, therefore, must provide the citizens with appropriate jobs: it "owes to everyone an avenue to possess himself of a portion of [the American] plenty sufficient for his needs, through his own work." As to the men whose thought and action had made the plenty possible: "in the future," said Roosevelt, "we are going to think less about the producer and more about the consumer." It was safe to say it. The mind, Dewey had taught a generation, is not a private possession, but a social asset.[21]

The New Dealers never offered a fixed definition of "opportunity" as they conceived the term. From their actions, however, it was apparent that the word could be extended beyond the issue of jobs, to cover a series of "economic rights" and of government powers which never stopped growing. Two swelling streams poured out of Washington: the stream of Federal favors and the stream of Federal controls.

The "experimenting fingers of the New Deal" (in one admirer's phrase)[22] were everywhere, providing funds or programs for every major group, including the unemployed, the young, the writers and artists, the workers, the businessmen, the farmers. The biggest beneficiaries were the unions; as a result of laws such as the Wagner Act, organized labor was converted from the status of voluntary association to that of quasi-official, government-mandated spokesman and bargaining agent for the worker.

The "experimenting fingers" also repudiated the gold standard, moved to regiment agriculture, imposed new controls on the banks, created a commission to supervise the stock market, pressed a more vigorous antitrust policy, and tried to force businessmen into a system of industry-wide, government-regulated cartels (the National Industrial Recovery Act). The NRA was the New Deal's attempt to bring to America the substance of Mussolini's corporativism.

Some of the New Deal measures, such as the NRA, did not last; the essential policies underlying the measures, however, did last. With the passage of the Social Security Act, which provided for compulsory old-age and unemployment insurance, the United States caught up with Europe: by

1935, five decades after Bismarck had inaugurated the idea, America, too, had become a welfare state.

The New Deal measures had to be conceived, guided through Congress, rammed through the courts, administered, enforced, financed. Thus the appearance of some corollaries of Bismarckianism: the leap in executive power, the growth of the bureaucracy, the mounting debt, the skyrocketing taxes. Since each group's benefits required some other group's sacrifice, there was a further corollary: the rise of nationwide pressure-group warfare.

To compare the New Deal with any European version of statism, its champions said at the time, is ridiculous. This administration, they said, is not wedded to a particular ideology; Roosevelt's concentration of power in government hands is not doctrinaire, but pragmatic. Such concentration, they added, is no threat to liberty, because the government here is using its power to cut down "economic royalists" and thus promote the welfare of the common man. In fact, said President Roosevelt in the 1932 campaign, the purpose of government restrictions is "not to hamper individualism but to protect it."

"It was this administration," the President told a Chicago audience in 1936, "which saved the system of private profit and free enterprise. . . ."[23]

The conservatives of the period, furiously opposed to Roosevelt, attacked every feature of the New Deal, except its ideological essence. They decried its breach with tradition, the tradition of Herbert Hoover. They denounced it as unconstitutional, but stopped short of offering any defense of the Constitution's principles or philosophic base. Some denounced the Democratic innovations as a product of science or the sin of pride, while affirming that the foundation of America was faith and the virtue of humility. All of them attacked Roosevelt as a menace to individual liberty, while stressing that their own ideal was the Christian ethics of service and duty to those in need. It was a spectacle of rage laced with appeasement, a combination not calculated to swell the conservative ranks.

[E]very person who lives by any useful work, should be habituated to regard himself not as an individual working for his private benefit, but as a public function-

ary; and his wages, of whatever sort, not as the remuner-
ation or purchase-money of his labour, which should be
given freely, but as the provision made by society to enable him to carry it on. . . .

The author of this statement—more extreme a collectivist utterance than any Democratic politician would permit himself
in public—was not a New Dealer. It was John Stuart Mill, a
philosophic hero of the conservatives of the time.[24] As in the
1890s, so in the 1930s: both sides in the political battle held
the same *basic* ideas; and so the conservatives were helpless.

By the later thirties the conservative attacks on Roosevelt
began to peter out, and the debate, such as it had been, was
over. The Republican leadership, bowing to the trend, adopted a permanent policy of "me-too'ing" the Democrats.

Judged by the standard its leaders publicly set themselves—the restoration of employment and prosperity—the
New Deal was a failure. At the end of the thirties there were
still ten million people unemployed, about two-thirds of the
number without jobs in 1932. The problem was not solved
until the excess manpower was sent to die on foreign battle-
fields.

Once again, a period of rising statism in the West was cli-
maxed by a world war. Once again, the American public,
which was strongly "isolationist," was manipulated by a pro-
war administration into joining an "idealistic" crusade. (On
November 27, 1941, ten days before Pearl Harbor, writes
John T. Flynn, "the President told Secretary Stimson, who
wrote it in his diary, that our course was to maneuver the
Japanese into attacking us. This would put us into the war
and solve his problem.")[25]

The result of the first crusade had not been a "world safe
for democracy," but the emergence of modern totalitarianism. The result of the second crusade was not the attainment
of "four freedoms," but the surrender of half of Europe to
Soviet Russia.

From the founding of the United States through the 1920s,
the "private sector," as it is now called, was the nation's dominant element; the state and the principle of statism were always encroaching, but always peripheral. The New Deal,
including its progeny of wartime controls and its Fair Deal
successor, ended this historical relationship.

After the two Roosevelts, America was no longer an essentially capitalist country with a sprinkling of controls. Nor was it a socialist country. It was, and still is, a modern "mixed economy," with the philosophic base and the political future that this implies. In a mixed economy, one of the two elements gradually withers away. That element is not the state.

America had beaten the Fascists. It had stamped out Hitler. But it was turning into the Weimar Republic.

15

Convulsion and Paralysis

Since World War II, America has been following a course of passive drifting. It has drifted from crisis to crisis, at home and abroad, without policy, leadership, or any large-scale political initiative. For decades now, despite the public's growing restiveness, the United States has moved but not acted. It has moved by the power of inertia and in the direction of disintegration.

A country's action is directed by its intellectuals. The cause of its inaction (when it has the material means to work its will) is the collapse of its intellectuals—their abandonment of ideals, ideas, programs, and hope. This collapse is the central fact in recent American history. It is the fundamental development of the present era throughout the West.

Three generations of crusaders, moved by the power of German philosophy, had fought to refashion America's political institutions in the image of Europe's. By the end of World War II, it seemed that the reformists were on the verge of achieving their goal. At this point the crusade petered out.

When the liberals saw the results of their ideas in worldwide practice, the conviction and the moral zeal went out of the reformist cause.

During and after the war, the intellectuals of the West saw the meaning of a "planned society." They saw it in Germany, in Russia, in Britain, in variants around the globe. They saw that the consequences of collectivism ranged from impoverishment to starvation to mass slaughter, with the degree of a country's agony a function of the degree of its collectivization. The result, in the minds of the more honest observers, was the death of socialism.

If World War I marked the close of the individualist era,

World War II marked the end of collectivism, not as the West's dominant practice, but as its leaders' social ideal.

The collectivist practice continued by default, as the lobbyists endemic to a mixed economy continued routinely to demand more controls. This routine was not disturbed by the intellectuals, whose policy was not to consider any alternative to their onetime ideal. The ethics of altruism, which they still accepted, eliminated in their eyes the possibility of a political direction which was *not* collectivist.

Unable to choose or approve any direction, the intellectuals chose to turn away from principles as such. They decided to dismiss long-range programs and confine themselves to dealing piecemeal with the problems of the moment.

It is *The End of Ideology*, said sociologist Daniel Bell in his 1961 book, accurately subtitled *On the Exhaustion of Political Ideas in the Fifties*. Ideology, Bell said, "which once was a road to action, has come to be a dead end." As a result of "[s]uch calamities as the Moscow Trials, the Nazi-Soviet pact, the concentration camps, the suppression of the Hungarian workers," the ideologies which ruled the first half of the twentieth century "have lost their 'truth' and their power to persuade. Few serious minds believe any longer that one can set down 'blueprints' and through 'social engineering' bring about a new utopia of social harmony."[1]

Like "philosophy," the term "ideology" is a broad abstraction, which subsumes many different concretes; it designates any set of principles underlying a social or political institution or movement; in effect, it means social or political philosophy (as a rule in simplified form). The modern liberals, however, equated the abstraction with a specific movement, i.e., with a single one of the possible concretes, and the calamities Bell cites indicate which one: communism. The failure of communism, therefore, led the liberals to reject the entire field of social thought. The failure of "blueprints"—which means: of totalitarian planning—led to the downfall in their eyes not of statism, but of political philosophy as such.

The liberals did not understand what had gone wrong. They did not know why, by its essence and moral base, communism had to fail. They knew only that it had failed and that they did not intend to get caught a second time. They resolved never to crusade again for an ideal society. "What is

left for the critic," said Bell, "is the hardness of alienation
. . . which guards one against being submerged in any
cause. . . ."[2]

The alienation of the postwar years pervaded every area of
American culture. In art and science as in politics, the new
trend was weariness, skepticism, and a vacuum.

Naturalism in America had reached its climax in the so-
cial-protest literature and painting of the Depression years.
Thereafter, drained of its crusading passion, the school began
to fade. About a generation later the same fate befell its Kantian successor: by the fifties the modernist movement, too,
was starting to run down.

When the message of apocalypse had become routine,
there was not much left for the horror-mongers to say. When
the essentials of every art form had been destroyed, there was
not much left for the nihilists to do (except to carry the job
of destruction out to the end). Even the movement's rationalizations were crumbling. After decades of rehashing European rehashes of primitivism and the like, it was difficult for
the avant-garde to go on claiming "innovation." After years
of being safely entrenched in the universities, the museums,
the theaters, the press, and the government funding offices, it
was impossible to claim "revolt against the establishment." In
the arts the modernists had become the establishment, a tired
establishment that was losing its power to shock and therefore
its lease on life. But, as in politics, no new movement arose
to challenge or replace it.

Science, by its nature, is an undertaking based on reason,
and therefore on a rational epistemology. This is why modern
science arose in an Aristotelian period. It is why scientists
have relied (in their professional work) on the remnants of
Aristotelianism for a longer time than men in areas such as
art or politics. And it is why, when those remnants dwindle
past a certain point, the spirit of a scientific method begins to
disintegrate.

Decades ago, the exponents of purposefully guided, objective cognition—which is what scientists had once been—began
yielding to two newer breeds: the narrow technicians and the
punch-drunk theoreticians. The former are intent on amassing
disconnected bits of experimental data, with no clear idea of
context, wider meaning, or overall cognitive goal. The latter—trained in a Kantian skepticism by Dewey, Carnap, Hei-

senberg, Gödel, and many others—turn out increasingly
arbitrary speculations while stressing the power of physical
theory; not its power to advance man's confidence or make
reality intelligible, but to achieve the opposite results. Quan-
tum mechanics, the theoreticians started to say, refutes
causality, light waves refute logic, relativity refutes common
sense, thermodynamics refutes hope, scientific law is old-fashioned, explanation is impossible, electrons are a myth, mathematics is a game, the difference between physics and religion
is only a matter of taste. If all of it is true, what is the future
of science?

In February 1950, P.W. Bridgman, an influential physicist
at Harvard, gave the avant-garde answer. Writing in the *Bulletin of the American Academy of Arts and Sciences*, he declared:

> We are now approaching a bound beyond which we are
> forever stopped from pushing our inquiries. . . . The
> very concept of existence becomes meaningless. It is
> literally true that the only way of reacting to this is to
> shut up. We are confronted with something truly ineffa-
> ble. We have reached the limit of the vision of the great
> pioneers of science, the vision, namely, that we live in a
> sympathetic world, in that it is comprehensible by our
> minds.[3]

Most philosophers at the time were not available to com-
ment on any of the above developments. The leading movements were writing the obituary of academic philosophy.
They were agreeing that "system-building" (i.e., a comprehensive view of existence) is outdated, that the questions of the
past have no rational answers, that broad abstractions are
irrelevant to art, science, or politics, and that philosophers
are irrelevant to life.

The neo-Kantians who reached these conclusions proceeded to hold a series of meetings in order to discuss a
new problem: they did not know what to do with their time.
They did not know what issues, if any, their profession
should be dealing with. "[P]erhaps," one such thinker said
recently, "there are *no* central or foundational questions in
philosophy. There may remain only philosophy as kibitz-
ing. . . ."[4]

The Kantian spirit had ruled Western culture and politics increasingly since the late nineteenth century. By the 1950s, that spirit had been given every major form of expression, theoretical and existential. In every field the result was destruction and a dead end, a state of affairs soon widely acknowledged, even by those who had no idea of its cause or significance.

The disillusionment of the modern intellectuals is usually described as a reaction to this century's numbing progression of wars, economic disasters, and the like. But this is not a full explanation; such events are not primaries; they are the products of certain ideas.

The deeper meaning of the widespread disillusionment of our time is philosophical. It indicates the drawn-out ending of an historical development—*the exhaustion of the Kantian tradition*. Adapting a line from Victor Hugo, Kant's is a philosophy whose time has gone. Men had tried it, they had staked their souls and their rights on it, and they were not able to live, or think, with the results. But they had no other philosophy to guide their actions.

The result has been gradual, protracted disintegration, across a span of bankrupt decades that seems to go on without end. In broad, historical perspective, these decades are a transition period (to whatever comes next). The sounds of the period have been only the sighs, then the screams, that signify the smashup of an era.

The Eisenhower Administration was an eloquent symbol of the start of this period. Although the intellectuals rejected Eisenhower, his Presidency in fact was a monument to their growing belief that thought is futile, and to the consequences of this belief: uncertainty, lifeless routine, drift.

The screams were the next phase. If thought is futile, one began to hear, then a replacement is necessary. If concepts lead to paralysis, there is another source of knowledge: passion. If the mind of the West has failed, there is a superior guide: the religions of the East. The quiet voices of the more civilized skeptics had prepared the way. They began to be drowned out by their natural successors.

The successors included the Existentialists, the Zen Buddhists, and a number of figures inspired by Weimar Germany's Frankfurt Institute, who sought to fuse Hegel, Marx, and Freud. Typically, the fusers affirmed a nonmaterial dimension, denounced Aristotelian logic, and upheld the cognitive powers of an emotion-oriented faculty, such as "phantasy." *Time* magazine summarized the trend among American intellectuals eloquently, in a 1972 essay titled "The New Cult of Madness: Thinking as a Bad Habit." " 'Reason' and 'logic,' " the essayist reported, "have, in fact, become dirty words—death words. They have been replaced by the life words 'feeling' and 'impulse.' "[5]

When Kant concluded that reality was unknowable to the mind, the historical sequel was the open irrationalism of the romanticist movement. For generations, the main line of American thinkers had denied the necessity of this kind of sequel. From Emerson to Dewey and even later, they had sought to accept the conclusions of Kant while continuing to advocate such ideals as science, intelligence, enlightenment, progress. They had observed the rising Continental schools of will-and-doom preachers, and they had said: "It won't happen here." In the end, however, the same cause led to the same effect: worn down by successive defeats, the American intellectuals conceded their contradiction and went the way of their European mentors. They began to drop the made-in-America masks. What showed up was the made-in-Germany essence.

It was a recapitulation in the New World of the history of nineteenth-century European philosophy. The standard textbook progression was reenacted, in mini-terms. "From Kant to Schopenhauer and Nietzsche" became "from Dewey to Norman O. Brown and Herbert Marcuse."

The men and women growing up in the 1920s and '30s, the first large-scale group of Americans to be reared in Progressive schools, had been rendered incapable of offering their future children any intellectual guidance. As it happened, their children, growing up in the postwar years, were the first generation to be exposed to the new irrationalist trend. These children became the rebels of the sixties.

Brought up in an age when the masks were being dropped, the rebels denounced the traditional hypocrisies and cover-ups. For the first time in a century of American history, ideas—the ideas that had been increasingly in the ascendancy among the intellectuals since the Civil War—did not remain discreetly semihidden in the background of events, but moved forthrightly onto center stage.

The cultural manifestations which resulted could not be dismissed as the theoretical projection of an alarmist; they were actually happening. They could not be dismissed as an old-world nightmare; they were happening here. They could not be dismissed as the accidental product of a single clique, political or otherwise; they were obviously the expressions of a philosophy, because they were showing up in every area—in the art galleries, the theaters, the elementary schools, the research laboratories, the colleges, the streets. In every area, with the clarity of a textbook, one impulse stood out to define the goal of the new spirit.

In the visual arts, according to critic Harold Rosenberg, an admirer of the trend, the

> revolutionary phrase of 'doing away with' was heard with the frequency and authority of a slogan. The total elimination of identifiable subject matter was the first in a series of moves—then came doing away with drawing, with composition, with color, with texture; later with the flat surface, with art materials. . . . In a fervor of subtraction art was taken apart element by element and the parts thrown away.[6]

The "theatrical principles" of Absurdist drama, explains a guide written for college students,

> are primarily reductive (not only anti-Aristotelian like Brecht but anti-play): characters are reduced almost to non-entities . . . plot is minimal if there is any, place and time are often reduced to any place and any time, language or dialogue is minimized, made absurd, close to being eliminated. . . .

The new playwrights, said the Dean of the Yale School of Drama approvingly, "have been attempting to repeal the fundamental law of cause-and-effect which had been an unquestioned statute at least since the Enlightenment—the law that rules the linear, logical, rationalistic world of literature. . . ."[7]

The new educators attempted a similar repeal. Completing the work of their Progressive predecessors, they dispensed in their "open classrooms" with tests, grades, dress rules, spell-

ing, grammar, arithmetic, student attendance, teacher "interference" and/or any organized subject matter—which left
their students free to choose, for credit, from an array of
"relevant" offerings, including (these are actual examples)
Hip Lit, Things Russian, Ecology, Weaving, and Treasonable
Activities. Parents in one New York school protested that
their children would not learn to read or write under the new
policies; "[t]he teachers," says Charles Silberman, author of
Crisis in the Classroom, "gave them a lecture on not being so
uptight about basic skills, told them the kids' feelings were all
that mattered."8

"[N]othing less is required," wrote a professorial admirer
of the new attitude, "than the subversion of the scientific
world view, with its entrenched commitment to an egocentric
and cerebral mode of consciousness."

The avant-garde scientists did not need further subversion.
"We will study physics as an example of many of the contradictions of life," said an announcement put out by the Department of Physics of New York University, describing a
course to be taught by a Ph.D. in physics from Columbia.

"What the hell are you studying anyhow?" an interviewer
asked a junior at Harvard, who had just declared his belief in
astrology, tarot cards, and the *I Ching*. "Physics," replied the
student. "You're kidding!" "I'm not kidding. I'm studying
physics, and there's a lot in elemental particles that's weirder
than astrology." Judging by recent developments in particle
physics the student's last statement is true; what it indicates,
however, is not the nature of the universe, but of the
student's teachers, and of the theoreticians who taught them.9

There was also the new trend of the period in the study of
man and society. "Subjective Sí! Objective No!" the *Times*
titled a piece by Robert Nisbet, a sociologist alarmed by "the
very recently begun, fast-accumulating nihilistic repudiation
in the social sciences of the ancient Western ideal of dispassionate reason, of objective inquiry. . . ." (Among other
symptoms, Nisbet cited the growing belief by younger social
scientists in "*the necessary ethnic roots of science*," a belief
which he compared, correctly, to the theory of "Aryan
science.")10 And there was the new journalism, which deliberately blurred the distinction between reporting and fiction; the
new music, which was atonal and arrhythmic; the new dance,
which dispensed with meaning, music, and even movement;

the serious novels, which dispensed with seriousness or values, specializing instead in "put-ons" and "black humor"; and the modern movies, which offered spectacles of Satanic cults or obsessive gore-spilling or wriggling genitalia or the deliberately unintelligible or filthy language spewed by ratlike actors scratching themselves lazily and urinating onscreen.

If all of it made anybody sick he could consult the new therapists, who promised people inner harmony to be achieved by such techniques as "primal" screaming or Indian meditation or going to "encounter" group-gropes in Southern California or going to bed with the therapist or going mad.

There was also the political expression of all the above, the heirs of generations of liberal reformists, the new advocates of "love" and of "the people": the college students of the New Left; the students who blew their noses in the American flag or wore it to patch the seat of their pants, while acclaiming Oriental gurus, French criminals, Russian anarchists, and Cuban killers; the students who rejected physical reality in favor of a superior world to be reached by "tripping out" or parapsychology or UFO's or witchcraft; the students who demanded, here on earth, the end of the influence of the past: the end of the selfish "performance principle" (i.e., of the need to work for a living), the end of man's conquest of nature, the end of the Industrial Revolution, the end of the last remnants of "the system," the *American* system with everything it implies.

What kind of society was to replace the American system? What positive goal justified all the negative demands? What was the rebels' program? "We haven't any," declared youth leader Tom Hayden in 1968. "First we will make the revolution, and *then* we will find out what for."[11]

Some observers at the time criticized the "excesses" of the New Left, if not its principles. They were answered by the head of the English Department of Columbia University. "At this moment in American history," he wrote in 1970, "the praise of moderation, even of 'liberal humaneness and rational discourse,' is just a bit priggish and is a form of aggression against the young."[12]

In every area—from paintings of Brillo boxes to actors stuffing their heads into toilet bowls onstage, to "dances" performed by thalidomide victims, to bloody campus riots, to scholars kissing thugs—the "spirit of the sixties" was a culmination, which had been made possible by earlier trends. It was the consistent, full-fledged expression of the impulse that defines "cultural modernism." It was "Weimar culture" replayed fifty years later, stripped of any nineteenth-century vestiges and therefore incalculably more degraded in form, with nothing to conceal the hatred at its root or the lust for destruction. It was the field day of nihilism in the New World.

"From my own very extensive investigations," writes a Michigan historian, comparing the American youth-culture of the sixties to the German youth movement before 1933, "I can categorically assert that there is not one value, not a single slogan, not a posture or costume, not a technique or political or cultural position which was not manifested in that earlier movement."[13]

In Germany, the nihilist impulse had been unleashed, nourished, and protected by a line of intellectuals and philosophers, a line resting ultimately on the ideas of one figure. Was it the same in America? Here are some voices relevant to the answer.

The theater of the past, said Absurdist director Julian Beck in New York City in 1967, "is a theater whose presentation and appeal is intellectual." But the intellect, he went on, is inherently twisted and unreliable: "our thinking, conditioned by our already conditioned minds, is so corrupt that it is not to be trusted."

"No serious thinker any longer believes in a verifiable, objective reality," an Arizona newsman told a meeting of the American Society of Newspaper Editors in 1971. "In epistemology and natural science," he said, "it's been pretty well proven that there's no such thing as objectivity. There are only different patterns of subjectivity. . . ."

What the "counter culture" undertakes, wrote a historian defending the new youth, "is to attack men at the very core of their security by denying the validity of everything they mean when they utter the most precious word in their vocabulary: the word 'I.' "[14]

It is Kant, above all others, who taught that the mind by its nature is "conditioned" and that thinking, therefore, is untrustworthy. It is Kant's epistemology which replaced objectivity with "patterns of subjectivity." It is Kant's ethics which made the attack on the "I" the essence of the good.

Here is another voice to consider. "Well, he's [R.D. Laing] one of the only ones in psychiatry that makes fantasy legitimate," said a Radcliffe girl approvingly, referring to a British champion of insanity as liberation. "He's not always knocking you over the head with reality."[15]

"I have therefore found it necessary to deny *knowledge*," said the Preface to the *Critique of Pure Reason*, "in order to make room for *faith*."

Here is another voice.

> Why is the cult of irrationality, the rejection of all traditional norms, strongest precisely in the best universities? [asked a college professor in 1970, writing in *The New York Times*]. Why are the students readiest for an apocalyptic leap into an inconceivable and unlikely future those who are now most immediately involved in the study of the humanities? . . . The answer is not simple. . . .[16]

The answer is virtually contained in the question. It is what those universities in their humanities departments are teaching the students. The answer is as simple as the fact that the leading Harvard philosopher is Willard V. Quine, who—quietly and for decades—has taught his classes that physical objects are "comparable, epistemologically, to the gods of Homer. . . . [T]he physical objects and the gods differ only in degree and not in kind."[17] Once one knows that a generation has been subjected from the start to a culture shaped in every decisive area by this kind of teacher, with almost no voices left to offer an alternative, little else is needed to explain a "cult of irrationality" on campus.

The men who made it possible for Professor Quine and the rest to take over were William James and John Dewey. Behind them stood Hegel. Behind him stood Kant.

In every area, the rebels of the sixties accepted and then carried out consistently the philosophic fundamentals of the establishment they cursed. The "spirit of the sixties" was at root the spirit of the eighties—the 1780s, the decade of the Kantian *Critiques* and of everything they unleashed on an unsuspecting world.

It was the climax of the Kantian influence in the United

States, and, simultaneously, it was the Kantian movement's
death throes.

The death of a philosophy does not necessarily mean the
immediate fading of its spokesmen or slogans, which may
continue to rule a culture and exact the consequences for
many years. The death of a philosophy means its withdrawal
from the realms that in the long run determine the course of
human existence: the realm of cognition and the realm of
values. In this regard, what Ayn Rand has observed about the
collectivist movement in politics applies equally to the whole
Kantian tradition: it "lost the two crucial weapons that raised
it to world power and made all of its victories possible: intellectuality and idealism, or reason and morality. It had to lose
precisely at the height of its success, since its claim to both
was a fraud. . . ."[18]

When a tradition which began as an alleged expression of
"pure reason" and stern morality ends up fooling with LSD,
"Saint Genet," and "polymorphous perverse sexuality," its
breach with cognition and with values is complete. The
growing disillusionment of the early postwar years marked
the beginning of the Kantian end. The convulsion of the sixties was the next step: the declaration of bankruptcy.

Most Americans (like men everywhere) do not know
formal philosophy or even the name of Kant. In some terms
during the sixties, however, the majority did grasp—for the
first time—that an alien element had entered their culture,
that the basic principles of the nation were under attack, that
something fundamental was wrong with America's course.

Within the limits of their power, people acted on this
knowledge. They rebelled against the new breed of rebels,
smashing the political hopes of the New Left along with the
Presidential candidacy of its fellow traveler, George McGov-
ern. Some, including thousands of New York City construction workers and longshoremen, even took to the streets to
break up mobs of unruly student protesters.

Support came in "from all over the country" and "from all
walks of life," said the head of New York City's building
trades unions in the spring of 1970, citing calls and letters
running twenty to one in favor of the workers' actions. "I
don't care if a person stands on a street corner and tells everybody 'I don't like the [Vietnam] war,' I don't like it either," said an elevator constructor from Brooklyn, explaining

why he was taking part in the workers' demonstrations. "But when they try to ruin the country and desecrate the flag, I can't stand it."

"Communism must be fought every place," said a black worker from the Bronx. "A stop should be put to all this violence by kids."

"I'm scared," said a college freshman and would-be rebel, eyeing a group of flag-waving workers. "If this is what the class struggle is all about, there's something wrong somewhere."[19]

The student's teachers had miscalculated. They did not know why the country was shoving them and their disciples into the discard heap of history. They did not understand that the American people are not a Marxist proletariat, but the last heirs of the era of Enlightenment left on earth.

Eager to find a new direction, the people turned to the political right.

There was no one there. All they found was Richard Nixon and Ronald Reagan.

* * *

The American people may oppose the nation's present course, but by themselves the people cannot change it. They may oppose the taxes and the bureaucrats, but these are merely consequences, which cannot be significantly cut back so long as their source is untouched. The people may curse "big government" in general—but to no avail if the pressure groups among them, following the logic of a mixed economy, continue to be fruitful and to multiply. The people may "swing to the right," but it is futile, if the leaders of the right are swinging to their own (religious) brand of statism. The country may throw the rascals out, but it means nothing if the next administration is made of neo-rascals from the other party.

To change a nation's basic course requires more than a mood of popular discontent. It requires the definition of a new direction for the country to take. Above all, it requires a theoretical justification for this direction, one which would convince people that the proposed course is practical *and* moral. Moral considerations alone might not be sufficient to move men, if they believe the course being urged is impractical; practical considerations alone will not move men, if they believe the course is immoral. The union of the two, however, is irresistible.

By its nature, changing the course of a nation is a task that can be achieved only by men who deal with the field of ideas. In the long run the people of a country have no alternative: they end up following the lead of the intellectuals.

The intellectuals cannot escape ideas, either. They may become anti-ideological skeptics, who offer the country for guidance only subjective feelings and short-range pragmatism; but it is the ideas—ultimately, the basic ideas—they still accept, explicitly or otherwise, which determine the content of their feelings and of their pragmatism. In the long run the intellectuals, too, have no alternative: *they* end up following the lead of the philosophers.

If there is no new philosophy to guide and rally the better men among them, the intellectuals will follow one that is old and bankrupt. If there are no living ideas, they will follow dying ones and take the country with them. The shambles of the Kantian movement, therefore, does not necessarily mean an early end to its stranglehold over the nation's life and institutions. In the absence of any principled opposition, the Kantian ideas by default will continue to rule, and to move us further down the road on which, for so many years, we have been traveling.

The more brazen elements of the sixties are long gone now. What has endured and become still clearer is the nature of that road.

As government controls and the power of political pull have soared, many Americans have come to feel—some reluctantly, others righteously—that survival requires identification with a group, which can serve as one's refuge in an uncertain world, one's protector from the other groups, and one's lobbyist in Washington. The easiest group to form or to join is one defined by race.

Thus the fading of the New World's legendary "melting pot," which had once demonstrated that men from around the globe could live together in harmony; the harmony had followed from the principle that group ties did not have to matter, because in America self-reliance was possible and individual accomplishment was the source of rewards. Instead, we see the oldest kind of social splintering and sectarian hatred. We see the "unmeltable ethnics," the "hyphenated-

Americans," the "roots"-seekers through genealogy, and all the others eager to define their identity in terms of ancestral tradition and/or brute physiology, i.e., blood.

This is the emergence in the United States of the most primitive form of collectivism, the form endemic to backward cultures (and to controlled economies): tribal racism. Racism is what takes over anywhere—wherever the knowledge of the nature and possibilities of man, man the individual, has not yet been grasped, or is being battered into oblivion.

The batterers state their viewpoint clearly.

> There is not now, there never was, there never will be, a solitary autonomous self, apart from society [writes an intellectual defending the ethnic movement]. The human being is a social network, necessarily dependent and psychically interrelated, a social organism, a political animal. The self is not an 'I' but a 'we.'

(The author of the above, Michael Novak, is not a Communist or a political radical, but a Catholic and a moderate.)[20]

If some voices today urge a return to tribalism, others are working to ensure that the tribes subsist on an appropriate level. These voices demand that material progress be limited, that economic growth be ended, that living standards be lowered, that the unprecedented achievements of Western technology be fought, cut back, swept aside.

This is the phenomenon that first erupted in the romanticist circles of nineteenth-century Europe: the war against the Industrial Revolution. The war has the same underlying motor here. Industrial wealth is a product of human ingenuity, of painstaking thought, of the faculty of reason dedicated to the improvement of man's life. The attack on such a product has only one meaning: the attack on its source, i.e., on man's mind.

The European romanticists identified their theoretical base openly. Today's ecologists and environmentalists are less philosophical; acting apparently on the idea that the public in an age of uncertainty will accept anything, they claim to speak in the name of science. If one can judge by their cognitive practices, "science" to them means the methodology of the punch-drunk modernists; it means unanalyzed statistics and undigested data dressed in Rube Goldberg formulae, spun into arbitrary projections, and culminating in a series of contradictory "scenarios" predicting the end of the fish, of the balance of nature, or of the world.

What *moral* theory underlies the fight to return whole nations to the agony and the life expectancy of subsistence in raw nature? "It is hard to even begin to gauge how much a complication of possessions, the notions of 'my and mine,' stand between us and a true, clear, liberated way of seeing the world," says a member of the Berkeley Ecology Center.

We must transcend the selfishness inherent in "making man the center of attention," according to a professorial nature-champion at Claremont; the West has gone too far in upholding "the absolute value of every human individual." "As Christians we need to develop a new asceticism based not on economics but on ecology."[21]

For generations, American statists had insisted that they were the defenders of science and technology, which, they said, require socialism. Now, in a historic reversal, many are admitting the opposite. They are explaining that what their viewpoint requires is the rejection of science and technology.

When cultural trends reach so extreme a stage, corollary signs appear. Increasingly, people shrug off as irrelevant to their lives not only science and secular philosophy, but even theology, the subject that attempts to give order and definition to the tenets of supernaturalism. Instead, men start to turn to mankind's primordial source of guidance: religion. They turn not to a sophisticated religion such as Roman Catholicism, or to any definite, structured creed, but to plain religion, i.e., an inarticulate, pre-philosophical mix of myth, ritual, freewheeling mysticism, and uncomplaining obedience, without concern for definition, consistency, or understanding. Thus, among middle-class American youth, such portents as the Jesus freaks or the Moonies or the chanting, skull-shaven, glassy-eyed Hare Krishnas. Thus also, in the larger society, the spread of the oldtime Fundamentalist and evangelical and Pentecostal movements, with their hot-eyed converts eager to speak in tongues or hurrying to be "born again"—while Billy Graham (or his equivalent) admonishes them "to oppose self, to abase self . . . . Smash pride, step on it, crush it, mash it, break it . . . break down and thresh out and destroy every mountain of self. . . . Deny yourself. . . . To deny self is to disown self."[22]

There have been mystic revivals before in the United States, as there have been racial antagonisms and back-to-nature movements. But in earlier years these were comparatively isolated manifestations, cut off from the nation's intellectual leadership, in conflict with the country's dominant trend. Such is not the case today.

Today the religious cultists are at one with the intellectual vanguard in assaulting the essence of the American view of life. They are counting on and working to intensify the feeling of human helplessness. Many of them, who describe themselves as conservative, enthusiastically promote such statist policies as mandatory prayer, censorship, and anti-abortion. The nature-lobbyists are even more explicit. "Coercion is a dirty word to most liberals now," writes one ecologist (Garrett Hardin), "but it need not forever be so. As with the four-letter words, its dirtiness can be cleansed away by exposure to the light, by saying it over and over without apology or embarrassment."

Today's statists are not apologizing, but businessmen are eagerly continuing their century-long policy of appeasement. "Free private responsible enterprise?" asked the banner headline of a Mobil ad in *The New York Times*, with the first two words slashed out. Business freedom and privacy, the text explained, are no longer fully possible or desirable, but this is no cause for corporate concern: "we try to be responsible. . . . Doing this leaves us no time to fret about being 'free' or 'private.' "[23]

Marx was wrong: businessmen will not fight to the end to save their property. But Hitler was right: if men have enough "idealism," he said, they will submit voluntarily, they will beat the dictator to the punch and turn themselves into "dust particles" before he can get around to it.

Few men in America preach the totalitarian state. What today's voices, right and left, are fighting for is gradual, successive steps in its direction.

Germany Puts the Clock Back, says the title of an anti-Nazi book by E.A. Mowrer published in 1933, one of the earliest books to indicate the self-destructive course of the Weimar Republic. We, too, are putting the clock back; back before the era of individualism, before the Industrial Revolution, before the discovery of secular philosophy; and back before freedom.

One recent development, however, is still worse. The *egalitarian* movement does not represent a throwback. It represents a demand, mediated by an ethical code that has now reached its climax, for conditions under which men cannot survive at all.

There must be a new kind of equality in the country, the egalitarians say; not the Founding Fathers' equality of individual rights, or even the older reformists' undefined "equality of opportunity," but a militantly specific "equality of results"; the "results" must be equal for all, regardless of any man's or group's efforts, virtues, or merits. Men must be equal in goods and services, regardless of ability to pay. They must be equal in jobs and promotions, regardless of qualifications or performance (e.g., the quota system). They must be equal in college training regardless of academic preparation (open admissions); in cultural prestige regardless of talent (minority-group art subsidies); in authority regardless of knowledge (Student Power); in moral respectability regardless of behavior (Gay Lib); in credit for achievement regardless of achievement (Women's Lib).

A new, modern kind of pressure group is now active in America, defined not by economic function or even by blood, but by a negative, by impotence, inability, deficiency of some kind. We see men who expect special consideration merely because they are minorities, i.e., *not* numerous or powerful. There are feminist handout-seekers who count on the fact that women are generally thought to be the weaker sex. There are poverty activists, not the poor and the halt of Christian tradition, who asked humbly for alms, but a new breed of militants, who boast that they are *not* well off and who puff up with resentment that this claim has been ignored. There are homosexual activists who feel righteous because their constituency is *not* normal, youth activists who feel it because theirs is *not* mature, old-age activists who feel it because theirs is *no longer* strong.

To sacrifice is to renounce or annul a value. Carried out consistently, therefore, the Kantian advocacy of sacrifice had to lead eventually to rule by the losers—by those who, for whatever reason, cannot or choose not to achieve values on their own, but depend instead on the work and effort of others. In a philosophy of sacrifice, the top duty is the negating of values; the top virtue, their *nonpossession*. Hence the new social conclusion: values properly belong to those who have reached the eminence of *not* having achieved them.

As to the non-losers, the men of ability, who do achieve values, such men have no moral claims and deserve nothing, says Harvard philosopher John Rawls, the leading American theorist of egalitarianism. The able, he says, are merely lucky, having been blessed at birth by a desirable social environment and/or by superior natural attributes, such as talent or brainpower. (Rawls, an implicit determinist, does not believe that a man deserves any reward for choosing to exercise his brain; man, he holds, is merely a passive reactor without the faculty of choice.)

"Earning" a value, in the egalitarian view, does not mean creating a product by one's thought and action. Rawls requires that a man create the circumstances of his entry into the world, and the organs of his own body, including his brain. He requires that a man create *the attributes he possesses at birth*—which a man could do only before he had any attributes, i.e., before he was anything, i.e., before he existed. Since no one can do it, Rawls concludes, there is no such thing as "earning" values, and no injustice in draining the producers.

The fact which Rawls uses to invalidate the claims of the producers, ultimately, is the fundamental law of reality: the Law of Identity. Because man has a nature, because he does not emerge from the womb as a zero, the producers have no rights and are relegated to the status of permanent serfs. This is not merely a political but a metaphysical attack on the men of ability: it disqualifies them from moral standing, not because they allegedly exploit the proletariat, not because they have money or power or any tangible asset, but because man has identity.

Kant described his denial of reason as a defense of "pure reason." Rawls, who is a follower of Kant, calls *his* viewpoint "a theory of justice."[24]

To a casual observer, the "humanitarian" worship of weakness might appear to be the opposite of the Nazi worship of muscles. In fact, these are two superficially varied manifestations of the same philosophical essence, leading to the same political result.

The immediate victims of today's trend—business, labor, and the other productive groups—have never known the philosophical issues at stake and have no answers to offer. Neither do the liberal intellectuals and politicians, purged of ideas, shaken by the sixties, and reduced to the status of short-range, gingerly lobbyists for the poor. Neither do the so-called "neo-conservatives," who urge a return somehow to the allegedly more civilized statism of the New Deal era. Neither do the traditional conservatives, who seem to be abandoning the last vestiges of Americanism in its original sense, and who are becoming in effect lobbyists for the churches. All these groups know that something is fundamentally wrong with the world, but none knows what it is, and all are pursuing a weary quest to find some piecemeal action or remedy that "works." The quest is weary because, as a British editor has observed in another context: "Now nobody believes anything will work."[25]

Pragmatists not out of rebellion or reformism, but out of exhaustion; pragmatists not at the beginning of an era, but at its dead end; pragmatists who believe that nothing will work—such is the shape of today's leadership and of today's paralysis.

In October 1976, three hundred philosophers met in New York City to participate in a Bicentennial symposium on the topic: "Philosophy in the Life of a Nation." According to *The New York Times*, their consensus was that philosophy is a technical subject of no practical significance. "Wasn't it extraordinary, [one professor] suggested, for philosophers to convene and solemnly discuss 'Philosophy in the Life of a Nation' when 'they have nothing to do with that life. . . .' "[26]

The profession most responsible for today's collapse knows nothing about any part of it, including its cause.

* * *

Here are the ominous parallels.

Our universities are strongholds of German philosophy disseminating every key idea of the post-Kantian axis, down by now to old-world racism and romanticist technology-hatred. Our culture is modernism worn-out but recycled, with heavy infusions of such Weimarian blends as astrology and Marx, or Freud and Dada, or "humanitarianism" and horror-worship, along with five decades of corruption built on this kind of base. Our youth activists, those reared on the latest viewpoints at the best universities, are the pre-Hitler youth movement resurrected (this time mostly on the political left and addicted to drugs).

Our political parties are the Weimar coalition over again, offering the same pressure-group pragmatism, and the same kind of contradiction between their Enlightenment antecedents and their statist commitments. The liberals, more anti-ideological than the moderate German left, have given up even talking about long-range plans and demand more controls as a matter of routine, on a purely *ad hoc* basis. The conservatives, much less confident than the nationalist German right, are conniving at this routine and apologizing for the remnants of their own tradition, capitalism (because of its clash with the altruist ethics)—while demanding government intervention in or control over the realms of morality, religion, sex, literature, education, science.

Each of these groups, observing the authoritarian element in the other, accuses it of Fascist tendencies; the charge is true on both sides. Each group, like its Weimar counterpart, is contributing to the same result: the atmosphere of chronic crisis, and the kinds of controls, inherent in an advanced mixed economy. The result of this result, as in Germany, is the growth of national bewilderment or despair, and of the governmental apparatus necessary for dictatorship.

In America, the idea of public ownership of the means of production is a dead issue. Our intellectual and political leaders are content to retain the forms of private property, with public control over its use and disposal. This means: in regard to economic issues, the country's leadership is working to achieve not the communist version of dictatorship, but the Nazi version.

Throughout its history, in every important cultural and political area, the United States, thanks to its distinctive base, always lagged behind the destructive trends of Germany and of the rest of the modern world. We are catching up now.

We are still the freest country on earth. There is no totalitarian (or even openly socialist) party of any size here, no avowed candidate for the office of Führer, no economic or political catastrophe sufficient to make such a party or man possible—so far—and few zealots of collectivism left to urge an ever faster pursuit of national suicide.

We are drifting to the future, not moving purposefully. But we are drifting as Germany moved, in the same direction, for the same kind of reason.

"A Republic—If You Can Keep It"

There are essential differences between the United States and Germany.

The hope of the United States lies in *the philosophical breach between the American people and the intellectuals*.

By the "intellectuals" in this context I mean those whose professional field is the humanities, the social sciences, education, or the arts, i.e., the study and/or evaluation of man and his actions. By the "people" I mean the rest of the country, including physical scientists and businessmen.

The German intellectuals and the German people—in the empire, in the Republic, under the Nazis—shared the same view of the world, the same fundamental values, the same political goals. Hence the staunchly pro-German attitude of the great majority of the German intellectuals (including most of the Weimar Communists and even many of the dissident culturati): the intellectuals felt philosophically at home in Germany; they were proud to embrace a heritage, a Fatherland, and finally a Führer that embodied all of their essential ideas.

The same ideas which led the intellectuals in Germany to chauvinism have led their counterparts in the United States to *anti*-patriotism, i.e., to anti-Americanism. In the nation of the Enlightenment, the irrationalist intellectuals are and know themselves to be displaced persons, alienated by the basic premises of the country, hostile to the essential character of its institutions, its tradition, and its people.

The American people do not accept (or often even know) the ideas of the Enlightenment in explicit terms; but they do accept a significant philosophic remnant from the American past. They accept it largely by implication, in unidentified form; as a result they are often inconsistent, inadvertently contradicting their own deepest beliefs. And there are many groups today, especially among the affluent young, the college educated, and some of the newer immigrants, who have openly rejected or never discovered the American legacy; such groups are indistinguishable from the kind of malleable, favor-craving, state-worshiping masses one sees in Europe or elsewhere around the globe.

There is still, however, an implicit *American* view of man and life, embodied in the character and fundamental attitudes of most of the people, a view which sets Americans to this day apart from other nations, and on a collision course with their country's intellectual leadership.

The people, as a rule, respect common sense, think that science can solve men's problems, and believe that answers to basic questions can be found. The intellectual leadership regards these attitudes as superficial, naive, and "simplistic."

The people admire material wealth, practical success, technological innovation. The intellectuals dismiss such values as "middle-class" and say that machines are destroying the globe. The people admire self-reliance, productiveness, and the other virtues of the so-called "work ethic." The intellectuals say that these virtues are impossible, unnecessary, antisocial, and/or "Puritan compulsiveness." The people feel goodwill toward the human race, believe that men can achieve their goals on earth, and hold that happiness is possible. The intellectuals regard this as self-deception, as a refusal to face the impotence or ugliness of man and the "tragic" nature of life.

The people approve of personal ambition, are eager to pursue their *own* happiness, think that a man should not live on handouts but should earn what he gets, and reject the insistent demands for self-immolation. The intellectuals denounce this—every element of it—as selfish and therefore vicious.

The people, despite some increasing lip service to religion, are still fundamentally secular in their ideas and concerns. The intellectuals either describe this as "vulgar American materialism," or claim that unthinking, "Bible-belt" mentalities are the real indicator of the nation's essence. The people reject the Marxist view of life and do not spend their time cursing "class enemies." The intellectuals regard the people (including organized labor) as exploiters of a neo-proletariat: "the young, the poor, the black, and the women." The people (like all people on earth) reject "modern culture." The intellectuals explain this as "philistinism" and "tradition-worship."

The people hotly reject the proliferating manifestations of the welfare state, from soaring welfare rolls to forced busing to sexual quotas. The intellectuals condemn this as unfeeling, racist, "sexist." The people respect the Founding Fathers and want less government interference in their lives. The intellectuals dismiss this as an anachronism, while explaining that the Founding Fathers were really religious mystics at heart (the conservative interpretation) or "communitarians" who valued society above liberty (a recent "revisionist" viewpoint).[1] The people love the United States, are proud of its historic achievements, and insist that the country be able to defend itself against Communist aggression. The intellectuals equate American patriotism with sordid nationalism, American history with "imperialistic greed," and American self-defense with "paranoia" and/or with warmongering militarism.

The Germans of the Weimar period were increasingly frustrated, angry, disgusted with "the system," and ready for change. So are Americans. The Germans, following their intellectuals, were disgusted with what they regarded as reason and freedom, and they were ready for Hitler. The Americans are disgusted with unreason and statism; but they are directionless. Without intellectual guidance, they do not know what went wrong with their system or how to prevent the country's disintegration and collapse.

Thus, by default—despite the profound difference between Americans and the pre-Hitler Germans—the similarities between the two nations, the similarities between their intellectuals and the social trends they shape, are growing.

The most ominous aspect of the trend is that, if it is not reversed, it will ultimately change the character of the American people. It has already begun to do so.

The philosophy that shapes a nation's culture and institutions tends, other things being equal, to become a self-fulfilling prophecy: by creating the conditions and setting the requirements of men's daily life, it increasingly establishes itself as an unquestioned frame of reference in most people's minds. A society shaped by altruism, for instance—a society of chronic, politically enforced man-eat-man policies in the name of "the public welfare"—leads many of its victims to feel that safety lies in flaunting public service, that selfishness (the "selfishness" of others, who are draining *them*) is a threat, and that the solution is to urge and practice greater selflessness. A society shaped by collectivism, in which the only effective means of survival is the group or the state, leads many to feel that the ideas and the personal independence appropriate to an individualist era are no longer possible or relevant. A society shaped by irrationalism—a society dominated by incomprehensible crisis and inexplicable injustice and the constant eruptions of a senseless, nihilist culture—leads many to feel that the world cannot be understood, i.e., that their own mind is inadequate, and that they need guidance from some higher power.

Thus corrupt ideas, once institutionalized, tend to be continually reinforced (the same would hold true of rational ideas); and unphilosophical men, however decent their own unidentified premises might be, eventually succumb. Across a span of generations they gradually relinquish any better heritage. In part, they are yielding to the explicit ideological promptings of their teachers and their universities. In part, they are adapting resignedly to what they have come to accept from their own experience as the facts or necessities of life.

The American spirit has not yet been destroyed, but it cannot withstand this kind of undermining indefinitely.

If the United States continues to go the way of all Europe, the people's rebellion against the present intellectual leadership will be perverted, and rechanneled into an opposite course.

Nonintellectual rebels cannot challenge the fundamental ideas they have been taught. All they can do by way of rebellion is to accept a series of false alternatives urged by their teachers, and then defiantly choose what they regard as the anti-establishment side. Thus the proliferation of groups that uphold anti-intellectuality as the only alternative to today's intellectuals; mindless activism as the alternative to vacillating "moderation"; Christian faith as the alternative to nihilism; female inferiority as the alternative to Women's Lib; racism as the alternative to egalitarianism; sacrifice in behalf of a united nation, as the alternative to sacrifice in behalf of warring pressure groups; and government controls for the sake of the middle class, as the alternative to government controls for the sake of the rich or the poor.

The type of mentality produced by these choices—activist, religionist, racist, nationalist, authoritarian—would have been familiar in the Weimar Republic.

If it happens here, the primary responsibility will not belong to the people, who still reject such a mentality and are groping for a better kind of answer. The responsibility will belong to those who banished from the schools all knowledge of the original American system, and who would have finally convinced the nation that men's only choice is a choice of dictatorships.

No one can predict the form or timing of the catastrophe that will befall this country if our direction is not changed. No one can know what concatenation of crises, in what progression of steps and across what interval of years, would finally break the nation's spirit and system of government. No one can know whether such a breakdown would lead to an American dictatorship directly—or indirectly, after a civil war and/or a foreign war and/or a protracted Dark Ages of primitive roving gangs.

What one can know is only this much: the end result of the country's present course is some kind of dictatorship; and the cultural-political signs for many years now have been pointing increasingly to one kind in particular. The signs have been pointing to an American form of Nazism.

If the political trend of the world remains unchanged, the same fate—collapse and ultimate dictatorship—is in store for the countries of Western Europe, which are farther along the statist road than America is, and which are now obviously in process of decline or disintegration. (The Communist countries and the so-called "third world" have long since fallen, or never risen to anything.) A European dictatorship need not be identical to an American one; dictatorships can vary widely in form, according to a given people's special history, traditions, and crises; in form, but not in essence.

Most of the East is gone. The West is going.

The following statement was made by a German intellectual after the Nazis fell from power. In the early days of Hitler's regime, he recalled, anyone troubled by the Nazi practices and concerned about Germany's future was shrugged off as an alarmist.

And you *are* an alarmist. You are saying that *this* must

lead to *this*, and you can't prove it. These are the beginnings, yes; but how do you know for sure when you
don't know the end, and how do you know, or even surmise, the end? On the one hand, your enemies, the law,
the regime, the Party, intimidate you. On the other, your
colleagues pooh-pooh you as pessimistic or even neur-
otic.[2]

One can "know, or surmise, the end" by knowing what
cause produces what effect, i.e., what factor determines the
fate of nations.

Today, the only nation still capable of saving itself, and
thereby the world, is the United States. It can do so by only
one means.

The Constitution cannot stop the trend. A constitution,
however noble, cannot withstand the death or eclipse of its
animating principle.

Religion cannot stop the trend. It helped to cause it.

The demonstrated practicality of the original American
system cannot stop the trend. Practicality as such does not
move nations.

The profound differences between America and Germany—the differences in history, institutions, heroes, national
character, starting premises—cannot stop the trend. After a
century, a crucial similarity began to develop between the
two countries, the similarity of basic ideas; and this one similarity is gradually overriding, subverting, or negating the differences, and consigning their remnants to the dead end of
the unappreciated, the undefended, the historically impotent.

There is only one antidote to today's trend: a new, pro-reason philosophy. Such a philosophy would have to offer the
nation for the first time a full statement and an unbreached
defense of the fundamental ideas of America.

"Most of us," said the German intellectual quoted above,
looking back at the Hitler years,

did not want to think about fundamental things and
never had. There was no need to. Nazism gave us some
dreadful, fundamental things to think about—we were
decent people—and kept us so busy with continuous
changes and "crises" and so fascinated, yes, fascinated,
by the machinations of the "national enemies," without

and within, that we had no time to think about these dreadful things that were growing, little by little, all around us. Unconsciously, I suppose, we were grateful. Who wants to think?[3]

Do *you* want to think about "fundamental things"? In America, there is still time.

*   *   *

What fundamental truths did the Nazis and the American collectivists and all their sources in the history of philosophy struggle to evade and annihilate?

The answer is contained in two concepts, with everything they include, lead to, and presuppose: *reason* and *egoism*. These two, properly understood and accepted, are the immovable barrier to any attempt to establish totalitarian rule.

Obedience is the precondition of totalitarianism. The preconditions of obedience are fear and guilt; not merely the existential fear created by terroristic policies, but the deeper, metaphysical fear created by inner helplessness, the fear of a living creature deprived of any means to deal with reality; not merely the guilt of committing some specific crime, but the deeper, metaphysical guilt of feeling that one is innately unworthy and immoral.

Reason destroys fear; egoism destroys guilt. More precisely: reason does not permit man to feel metaphysically helpless; egoism does not permit him to accept unearned guilt or to regard himself as a sacrificial animal. But a man indoctrinated with the notion that reason is impotent and self-sacrifice is his moral duty, will obey anyone and anything.

If sacrifice is equated with virtue, there is no stopping the advance of the totalitarian state. "It goes on and will go on," said Howard Roark, the hero of *The Fountainhead*, "so long as men believe that an action is good if it is unselfish. That permits the altruist to act and forces his victims to bear it."

"The world," said Roark, "is perishing from an orgy of self-sacrificing." It was true in 1943, when *The Fountainhead* was published. It is just as true and much more obvious today.[4]

A full system of philosophy advocating reason and egoism has been defined in our time by Ayn Rand. It is the philosophy of Objectivism, presented in detail in *Atlas Shrugged, In-*

troduction to Objectivist Epistemology, and *The Virtue of Selfishness*. It is the antidote to the present state of the world. (All further quotations, unless otherwise identified, are from the works of Ayn Rand.)[5]

Most philosophers have left their starting points to unnamed implication. The base of Objectivism is explicit:

"Existence exists—and the act of grasping that statement implies two corollary axioms: that something exists which one perceives and that one exists possessing consciousness, consciousness being the faculty of perceiving that which exists."[6]

Existence and consciousness are facts implicit in every perception. They are the base of all knowledge (and the precondition of proof): knowledge presupposes something to know and someone to know it. They are absolutes which cannot be questioned or escaped: every human utterance, including the denial of these axioms, implies their use and acceptance.

The third axiom at the base of knowledge—an axiom true, in Aristotle's words, of "being qua being"—is the Law of Identity. This law defines the essence of existence: to be is to be something, a thing is what it is; and leads to the fundamental principle of all action, the law of causality. The law of causality states that a thing's actions are determined not by chance, but by its nature, i.e., by what it is.

It is important to observe the interrelation of these three axioms. Existence is the first axiom. *The universe exists independent of consciousness.* Man is able to adapt his background to his own requirements, but "Nature, to be commanded, must be obeyed" (Francis Bacon). There is no mental process that can change the laws of nature or erase facts. The function of consciousness is not to create reality, but to apprehend it. "Existence is Identity, Consciousness is Identification."[7]

The philosophic source of this viewpoint and its major advocate in the history of philosophy is Aristotle. Its opponents are all the other major traditions, including Platonism, Christianity, and German idealism. Directly or indirectly, these traditions uphold the notion that consciousness is the creator of reality. The essence of this notion is the denial of the axiom that existence exists.

In the religious version, the deniers advocate a consciousness "above" nature, i.e., superior, and contradictory, to existence; in the social version, they melt nature into an indeterminate blur given transient semi-shape by human desire. The first school denies reality by upholding two of them. The second school dispenses with the concept of reality as such. The first rejects science, law, causality, identity, claiming that anything is possible to the omnipotent, miracle-working will of the Lord. The second states the religionists' rejection in secular terms, claiming that anything is possible to the will of "the people."

Neither school can claim a basis in objective evidence. There is no way to reason from nature to its negation, or from facts to their subversion, or from any premise to the obliteration of argument as such, i.e., of its foundation: the axioms of existence and identity.

Metaphysics and epistemology are closely interrelated; together they form a philosophy's foundation. In the history of philosophy, the rejection of reality and the rejection of reason have been corollaries. Similarly, as Aristotle's example indicates, a pro-reality metaphysics implies and requires a pro-reason epistemology.

Reason is defined by Ayn Rand as "the faculty that identifies and integrates the material provided by man's senses."[8]

Reason performs this function by means of concepts, and the validity of reason rests on the validity of concepts. But the nature and origin of concepts is a major philosophic problem. If concepts refer to facts, then knowledge has a base in reality, and one can define objective principles to guide man's process of cognition. If concepts are cut off from reality, then so is all human knowledge, and man is helplessly blind.

This is the "problem of universals," on which Western philosophy has foundered.

Plato claimed to find the referent of concepts not in this world, but in a supernatural dimension of essences. The Kantians regard concepts (some or all) as devoid of referents, i.e., as subjective creations of the human mind independent of external facts. Both approaches and all of their variants in the history of philosophy lead to the same essential consequence: the severing of man's tools of cognition from reality, and therefore the undercutting of man's mind. (Although Aristotle's epistemology is far superior, his theory of concepts is intermingled with remnants of Platonism and is untenable.)

Recent philosophers have given up the problem and, as a result, have given up philosophy as such.

Ayn Rand challenges and sweeps aside the main bulwark of the anti-mind axis. Her historic feat is to tie man's distinctive form of cognition to reality, i.e., to validate man's reason.

According to Objectivism, concepts *are* derived from and *do* refer to the facts of reality.

The mind at birth (as Aristotle first stated) is *tabula rasa*; there are no innate ideas. The senses are man's primary means of contact with reality; they give him the precondition of all subsequent knowledge, the evidence that something *is*. What the something is he discovers on the conceptual level of awareness.

Conceptualization is man's method of organizing sensory material. To form a concept, one isolates two or more similar concretes from the rest of one's perceptual field, and integrates them into a single mental unit, symbolized by a word. A concept subsumes an unlimited number of instances: the concretes one isolated, and all others (past, present, and future) which are similar to them.

Similarity is the key to this process. The mind can retain the characteristics of similar concretes *without specifying their measurements,* which vary from case to case. "A concept is a mental integration of two or more units possessing the same distinguishing characteristic(s), with their particular measurements omitted."

> The basic principle of concept-formation (which states that the omitted measurements must exist in *some* quantity, but may exist in *any* quantity) is the equivalent of the basic principle of algebra, which states that algebraic symbols must be given *some* numerical value, but may be given *any* value. In this sense and respect, perceptual awareness is the arithmetic, but *conceptual awareness is the algebra of cognition.*[9]

Concepts are neither supernatural nor subjective: they refer to facts of this world, as processed by man's means of cognition. (The foregoing is a brief indication; for a full discussion see *Introduction to Objectivist Epistemology.*)

The senses, concepts, logic: these are the elements of man's rational faculty—its start, its form, its method. In essence, "follow reason" means: base knowledge on observation; form concepts according to the actual (measurable) relationships among concretes; use concepts according to the rules of logic (ultimately, the Law of Identity). Since each of these elements is based on the facts of reality, the conclusions reached by a process of reason are *objective*.

The alternative to reason is some form of mysticism or skepticism.

The mystic seeks supernatural knowledge; the skeptic denies the possibility of any knowledge. The mystic claims that man's means of cognition are inadequate and that true knowledge requires illumination from God; the skeptic agrees, then throws out God. The mystic upholds absolutes, which he defends by an appeal to faith; the skeptic answers that he has no faith. The mystic's faith, ultimately, is in his feelings, which he regards as a pipeline to the beyond; the skeptic drops the beyond, then follows *his* feelings, which, he says, are the only basis of action in an unknowable world.

Feelings are products of men's ideas and value-judgments, held consciously or subconsciously. Feelings are not tools of cognition or a guide to action.

The old-fashioned religionists condemned human reason on the grounds that it is limited, finite, earthbound, as against the perfect but ineffable mind of God. This implies an attack on identity (as does any rejection of the finite); but it does so under cover of affirming a consciousness with an allegedly greater, supernatural identity. The modern nihilists are more explicit: they campaign, not for the infinite, but for a zero. Just as in metaphysics they reject the concept of reality, so in epistemology they reject the possibility of consciousness.

Man, say the Kantians, cannot know "things as they are," because his knowledge is acquired by human senses, human concepts, human logic, i.e., by the human means of knowledge.

The same type of argument would apply to any consciousness—human, animal, or divine (assuming the latter existed): if it is something, if it is limited to some, *any*, means of knowledge, then by the same reasoning it would not know "things as they are," but only "things as they appear" to that kind of consciousness.

Kant objects to the fact that man's mind has a nature. His theory is: identity—the essence of existence—invalidates consciousness. Or: a means of knowledge makes knowledge impossible. As Ayn Rand points out, this theory implies that "man is blind, because he has eyes—deaf, because he has ears—deluded, because he has a mind—and the things he perceives do not exist, *because* he perceives them."[10]

Just as Kant's epistemological nihilism sweeps cognition away from identity, so his ethical nihilism sweeps morality— the field of *values*—away from any enjoyment of life.

The Objectivist ethics is the opposite of Kant's.

The Objectivist ethics begins with a fundamental question: why is ethics necessary?

The answer lies in man's nature as a living organism. A living organism has to act in the face of a constant alternative: life or death. Life is conditional; it can be sustained only by a specific course of action performed by the living organism, such as the actions of obtaining food. In this regard plants and animals have no choice: within the limits of their powers, they take automatically the actions their life requires. Man does have a choice. He does not know automatically what actions will sustain him; if he is to survive he must discover, then practice by choice, a code of values and virtues, the specific code which human life requires. The purpose of ethics is to define such a code.

Objectivism is the first philosophy to identify the relationship between life and moral values. "Ethics," writes Ayn Rand, "is an *objective, metaphysical necessity of man's survival*—not by the grace of the supernatural nor of your neighbors nor of your whims, but by the grace of reality and the nature of life."

The standard of ethics, required by the nature of reality and the nature of man, is Man's Life. "All that which is proper to the life of a rational being is the good; all that which destroys it is the evil."

"Man's mind," states John Galt, the protagonist of *Atlas Shrugged,*

> is his basic tool of survival. Life is given to him, survival is not. His body is given to him, its sustenance is not. His mind is given to him, its content is not. To remain

alive, he must act, and before he can act he must know the nature and purpose of his action. He cannot obtain his food without a knowledge of food and of the way to obtain it. He cannot dig a ditch—or build a cyclotron—without a knowledge of his aim and of the means to achieve it. To remain alive, he must think.[11]

Thinking is not an automatic process. A man can choose to think or to let his mind stagnate, or he can choose actively to turn against his intelligence, to evade his knowledge, to subvert his reason. If he refuses to think, he courts disaster: he cannot with impunity reject his means of perceiving reality.

Thinking is a delicate, difficult process, which man cannot perform unless knowledge is his goal, logic is his method, and the judgment of *his* mind is his guiding absolute. Thought requires *selfishness*, the fundamental selfishness of a rational faculty that places nothing above the integrity of its own function.

A man cannot think if he places something—anything—above his perception of reality. He cannot follow the evidence unswervingly or uphold his conclusions intransigently, while regarding compliance with other men as his moral imperative, self-abasement as his highest virtue, and sacrifice as his primary duty. He cannot use his brain while surrendering his sovereignty over it, i.e., while accepting his neighbors as its owner and term-setter.

Men learn from others, they build on the work of their predecessors, they achieve by cooperation feats that would be impossible on a desert island. But all such social relationships require the exercise of the human faculty of cognition; they depend on the solitary individual, "solitary" in the primary, inner sense of the term, the sense of a man facing reality firsthand, seeking not to crucify himself on the cross of others or to accept their word as an act of faith, but to understand, to connect, to know.

Man's mind requires selfishness, and so does his life in every aspect: a living organism has to be the beneficiary of its own actions. It has to pursue specific objects—for itself, for its own sake and survival. Life requires the gaining of values, not their loss; achievement, not renunciation; self-preservation, not self-sacrifice. Man *can* choose to value and pursue self-immolation, but he cannot survive or prosper by such a method.

Moral selfishness does not mean a license to do whatever one pleases, guided by whims. It means the exacting discipline of defining and pursuing one's *rational* self-interest. A code of rational self-interest rejects every form of human sacrifice, whether of oneself to others or of others to oneself. The ethics of rational self-interest upholds the exercise of one's mind in the service of one's life, and all of the specific value-choices and character attributes which such exercise entails. It upholds the virtues of rationality, independence, integrity, honesty, justice, productiveness, pride. It does not advocate "survival at any price."

> Man's life, as required by his nature, is not the life of a mindless brute, of a looting thug or a mooching mystic, but the life of a thinking being—not life by means of force or fraud, but life by means of achievement—not survival at any price, since there's only one price that pays for man's survival: reason.[12]

Reason is an attribute of the individual. Thought is a process performed not by men, but by man—in the singular. No society, committee, or "organic" group can do it. What a group can do in this regard is only: to leave the individual free to function, or to stop him.

The basic *political* requirement of Man's Life is freedom.

"Freedom" in this context means the power to act without coercion by others. It means an individual's power to act according to his own judgment, while respecting the same right in others. In a free society, men renounce a lethal method of dealing with disagreements: the initiation of physical force.

Force is the antonym and negation of thought. Understanding is not produced by a punch in the face; intellectual clarity does not flow from the muzzle of a gun; the weighing of evidence is not mediated by spasms of terror. The mind is a cognitive faculty; it cannot achieve knowledge or conviction apart from or against its perception of reality; it cannot be forced.

The proper political system, in essence—the system which

guards the freedom of man's mind—is the original American
system, based on the concept of inalienable individual rights.
"[T]he source of man's rights is not divine law or congressional law, but the law of identity. A is A—and Man is
Man. *Rights* are conditions of existence required by man's
nature for his proper survival."[18]

The Founding Fathers were right about the fact that rights
are political, not economic, i.e., that they are sanctions to act
and to keep the products of one's action, not unearned claims
to the actions or products of others. And they were right
about the fact that the proper function of government is the
protection of man's rights.

Man's rights, Ayn Rand observes, can be violated only by
physical force (fraud is an indirect form of force). A political system based on the recognition of rights is one that
guards man against violence. Men therefore deal with one another not as potential killers, but as sovereign traders, according to their own independent judgment and voluntary
consent. This kind of system represents the methodical protection of man's mind and of his self-interest, i.e., of the
function and purpose on which human life depends.

Government is the agency that holds a monopoly on the legal use of physical force. In a free society the government
uses force only in retaliation, against those who start its use.
This involves three main functions: the police; the military;
and the courts (which provide the means of resolving disputes peacefully, according to objective rules).

The government of a free society is prohibited from emu-
lating the criminals it is created to apprehend. It is prohibited
from initiating force against innocent men. It cannot inject
the power of physical destruction into the lives of peaceful
citizens, not for any purpose or in any realm of endeavor, including the realm of production and trade.

This means the rejection of any dichotomy between political and economic freedom. It means the separation of state
and economics. It means the only alternative to tyranny that
has ever been discovered: laissez-faire capitalism.

Historically, capitalism worked brilliantly, and it is the
only system that will work. Socialism in every variant has led
to disaster and will again whenever it is tried. Yet socialism is
admired by mankind's teachers, while capitalism is damned.

The source of this inversion is the fact that freedom is selfish, rights are selfish, capitalism is selfish.

It is true that freedom, rights, and capitalism are selfish. It is also true that selfishness, properly defined, is the good.

There is no future for the world except through a rebirth of the Aristotelian approach to philosophy. This would require an Aristotelian affirmation of the reality of existence, of the sovereignty of reason, of life on earth—and of the splendor of man.

Aristotle and Objectivism agree on fundamentals and, as a result, on this last point, also. Both hold that man *can* deal with reality, can achieve values, can live *non*-tragically. Neither believes in man the worm or man the monster; each upholds man the thinker and therefore man the hero. Aristotle calls him "the great-souled man." Ayn Rand calls him Howard Roark, or John Galt.

In every era, by their nature, men must struggle: they must work, knowingly or not, to actualize some vision of the human potential, whether consistent or contradictory, exalted or debased. They must, ultimately, make a fundamental choice, which determines their other choices and their fate. The fundamental choice, which is always the same, is the epistemological choice: reason or non-reason.

Since men's grasp of reason and their versions of non-reason differ from era to era, according to the extent of their knowledge and their virtue, so does the specific form of the choice, and its specific result.

In the ancient world, after centuries of a gradual decline, the choice was the ideas of classical civilization or the ideas of Christianity. Men chose Christianity. The result was the Dark Ages.

In the medieval world, a thousand years later, the choice was Augustine or Aquinas. Men chose Aquinas. The result was the Renaissance.

In the Enlightenment world, four centuries later, the founders of America struggled to reaffirm the choice of their Renaissance ancestors, but they could not make it stick historically. The result was a magnificent new country, with a built-in self-destructor.

Today, in the United States, the choice is the Founding Fathers and the foundation they never had, or Kant and destruction. The result is still open.

*   *   *

"Various approaches," writes a contemporary historian, have been made to the "problem of the rise of National Socialism in Germany."

> Political and constitutional historians have sought the solution in the weaknesses of the Weimar Constitution, in its party structure and in its political leadership. Others urge the importance of economic factors and find the answer to the rise of Hitler in the inflation of the early twenties, or in the long German tradition of state socialism. Intellectual historians have pointed to the peculiar nature of the German mind and the continuity of a stream which has had many sources: Luther, Fichte, Hegel, von Treitschke, Nietzsche, Spengler, and Moeller van den Bruck. More recently, social psychologists— amateur and professional—have discovered that National Socialism is explicable only in psychopathological terms. Thus the Germans have become, variously: sadomasochists, paranoids, the victims of a big brother fixation, or the inevitable consequence of forced toilet training.
>
> I have no serious quarrel with any of these major interpretations, provided that they are all brought into focus. For I am persuaded that here, as elsewhere in history, no one-line interpretation can give an adequate explanation of so complex a social phenomenon. Confronted by such a barrage of evidence from so many different sides, I am perfectly willing to fall back to the safety of a badly worn but well-tested cliché: it was a little of all of these things.[14]

The above explains why Nazism has not been explained. Today's intellectuals are, in effect, as unaware of the science of philosophy as were their ancestors in the era before Thales.

The quote implies that Nazism is a product of chance—of the accidental conjunction of a grab bag of concrete, dis-

connected evils. But the evils do have a connection, an attribute in common. There is a human discipline that can explain
all of them. There is a reason why all those Hitler-inviting
concretes occurred in the same country at the same time; it is
the same reason why none was present in the United States
during the Enlightenment.

The reason lies in the discipline concerned with fundamentals, because these subsume all derivatives and all social concretes. Philosophy is the factor that moves a nation, shaping
every realm and aspect of men's existence, including their
values, their psychology, and, in the end, the headlines of
their daily newspapers.

Most people regard the social system under which they live
as a given not open to question or challenge. Then, unwittingly, step by step, they carry the system to its logical conclusion—which they regard as a product not of abstract
theory, but of practical necessity.

The men moved by "practicality" as against "theory" are
still moved by theory, but it is theory they have not learned
to acknowledge, theory in the form of the social facts, problems, crises, trends, to which that theory has given birth and
reality.

The direct source of a nation's economic trends is its political trends. The source of its political trends is its cultural
trends. The source of the source of all the sources and all the
trends is: metaphysics, epistemology, ethics.

The faculty of reason makes philosophy possible, but the
converse is also true: philosophy is the implementation of
reason, which makes its application and triumph in every
area of human existence possible, or impossible. Philosophy is
that which ultimately creates the creators among men, with
their shining, life-giving achievements, or which unleashes the
destroyers, who wreck it all. Philosophy is that which explains why one society adopts a weak constitution and another a strong one; why one reaches bankruptcy and another
abundance; why one is aroused by Moeller van den Bruck
and another by Thomas Jefferson; why one embraces
"paranoia" or concentration camps, and another the rights of
man.

The complexity of a human society does not make it unintelligible, not even when it is a society torn by contradictions

and in process of collapse—unless one views the collapse without benefit of philosophy. Such a procedure means: viewing the symptoms of a disease without knowing that they *are* symptoms, or that they have a unifying cause.

No doctor would ascribe a case of bubonic plague to the accidental onset at the same time of fever, chills, prostration, swellings in the groin, etc. None would say that, given "such a barrage of evidence from so many different sides," no "one-line interpretation" can be adequate. If any doctor did say it, he would not be entrusted for long with the care of men's bodies.

In the humanities and social science departments of our universities, the counterparts of such a doctor are being paid to shape men's minds.

The intellectuals are ignorant of philosophy's role in history—because of philosophy. Having been taught by philosophers for generations that reason is impotent to guide action, they regard the mind and its conclusions as irrelevant to life. Having been taught that philosophy is a game, with no answers to offer, they do not look to it for answers. Having been taught that there is no system to connect ideas and no causality to connect events, they do not look for system or causality, but treat social developments as random, unrelated occurrences. Having been taught that abstractions have no basis in reality, they brush them aside and focus only on concretes, whether of the moment or of the century.

Men who hold such ideas are unable to take ideas seriously. They cannot believe that ideas are the motor of history.

They do ascribe some influence to political ideas, such as racist preachments; but they do not understand the nature or source of this influence, because they treat politics as a self-contained subject, without reference to the rest of philosophy. What they do not grasp is the power of wider abstractions in man's life, such as men's view of reality, of knowledge, of values. Thus the omission from the above quote, which in this regard is standard, of the philosopher most responsible for the condition of modern Germany and of the modern world.

Those who do not grasp the *essence* of historical events cannot discover their relationship to similar but superficially varied events in other nations or eras. If a man sees only disconnected concretes in pre-Hitler Germany, he can see no more than that in America today.

A dictator is not a self-confident person. He preys on weakness, uncertainty, fear. He has no chance among men of self-esteem. But in an age of self-doubt, he rises to the top: men who do not know their own course or value have no means to resist his promises and demands.

Men cannot know their course or value without the guidance of principles. A nation does not learn from disaster—only from discovering its cause.

The solution is the rebirth of the great science discovered by the Greeks. What it would lead to is the rebirth of the great country founded on that science.

A country with a philosophic base, freed of fundamental uncertainty and guilt, would not tolerate leaders who evade every choice, crawl down the middle of every road, and wait for the deluge. It would not tolerate any deluge by the waves of self-righteous, man-hating evil, foreign or domestic. It would not apologize for its greatness to the worshipers of weakness. It would not watch in despair while its youth turned in despair to cults, communes, and cocaine.

A country with a philosophic base would know its ideas and its direction: conviction would replace paralysis. It would know its values: moral judgment would replace appeasement, and the passion for justice would stamp out the haters. It would know what to say to its youth: it would tell them the source of human joy, and the meaning of their nation in history, and the standard to which the wise and honest can always repair, the *human* standard, reason.

Then the kind of man who loves his life—the kind who still feels hope and pride—the man who loves this country, would teach it to love itself.

And then the country, and the world, would be safe.

According to the Greek legend, as the spirit of Narcissus crosses the river leading to the land of the dead, he leans over the boat's edge to look in the waters, in order to gain a last glimpse of his own beauty.

For the spirit of man, it does not have to be a last glimpse—not if men can discover once more the land of the living.

In 1787, one of the members of the Constitutional convention, asked by a bystander what kind of government the framers were giving to the new nation, answered: "A republic—if you can keep it."[15]

He was not asked what is required to keep it, but the answer to that now would be: "A philosophy—if you can get one."

References

Chapter One

1. Hitler at Bückeburg, Oct. 7, 1933; *cf. The Speeches of Adolf Hitler*, 1922-39, ed. N.H. Baynes (2 vols., Oxford, 1942), I, 871-72; I owe this translation, and several later ones, to Professor George Reisman. *Mein Kampf*, trans. R. Manheim (Boston, Houghton Mifflin, 1943), p. 298.
2. William Shirer, *The Rise and Fall of the Third Reich* (New York, Simon & Schuster, 1960), pp. 969-70.
3. *National Socialism*, prepared by Raymond E. Murphy *et al*; quoting Huber, *Verfassungsrecht des grossdeutschen Reiches* (Hamburg, 1939); reprinted in *Readings on Fascism and National Socialism*, selected by Dept. of Philosophy, U. of Colorado (Denver, Alan Swallow, n.d.), pp. 77, 90.
4. *The Mind and Face of Nazi Germany*, ed. N. Gangulee (London, John Murray, 1942), p. 26; quoting Sieburg, *Germany: My Country*. Ley's statement was made in Munich in 1938.
5. "The Political Doctrine of Fascism" (address delivered at Perugia, Aug. 30, 1925); reprinted in *Readings on Fascism and National Socialism*, pp. 34-35.
6. Hitler at Bückeburg; *cf.* Baynes, *op. cit.*, I, 872 (trans. G. Reisman). Gregor Ziemer, *Education for Death* (London, Oxford U.P., 1941), p. 20; quoting Bernhard Rust, *Erziehung und Unterricht* (1938). Murphy *et al.*, *op. cit.*, p. 65; quoting Gottfried Neesse, *Die Nationalsozialistische Deutsche Arbeiterpartei—Versuch einer Rechtsdeutung* (1935). *Ibid.*, p. 90; quoting Huber.
7. *Ibid.*, p. 91.
8. *Op. cit.*, p. 262.
9. Erich Fromm, *Escape from Freedom* (New York, Farrar, 1941), p. 233; quoting Goebbels, *Michael*.

10. Fred M. Hechinger, "Educators Seek to Teach Context of the Holocaust," May 15, 1979.

Chapter Two

1. *Dialogues*, trans. B. Jowett (2 vols., New York, Random House, 1937), *Laws* 739C-D. *Republic*, trans. F.M. Cornford (New York, Oxford U.P., 1945), 462C.
2. *From Shakespeare to Existentialism* (Garden City, N.Y., Doubleday, 1960), p. 105. Rosenberg's statement is from *Der Mythus des Zwanzigsten Jahrhunderts* (Munich, 1935).
3. *Works*, ed. W.D. Ross (12 vols., London, Oxford U.P., 1910-52), *Ethica Nicomachea* 1124a1-2.
4. *Critique of Pure Reason*, trans. N. Kemp Smith (New York, St. Martin's, 1956), p. 29.
5. *Philosophy of Right*, trans. T.M. Knox (London, Oxford U.P., 1967), p. 241.
6. *The Philosophy of History*, trans. J. Sibree (rev. ed., New York, Colonial Press, 1900), p. 39.
7. *Ibid. Philosophy of Right*, pp. 279, 156.
8. "The Doctrine of Fascism" (*Enciclopedia Italiana*, vol. xiv, 1932); trans. M. Oakeshott, Cambridge U.P., 1939; reprinted in William Ebenstein, *Great Political Thinkers* (New York, Rinehart, 1951), p. 590.
9. *Cf.* Walter T. Stace, *The Philosophy of Hegel* (New York, Dover, 1955), p. 406.
10. *Philosophy of Right*, p. 196.
11. "The Doctrine of Fascism," trans. I.S. Munro, Maclehose, 1933; reprinted in *Readings on Fascism and National Socialism*, p. 10. Gangulee, *op. cit.*, p. 114; quoting Dietrich at the University of Berlin, 1937. Murphy *et al., op. cit.*, p. 74.
12. *The Philosophy of History*, pp. 31, 30, 66-67.
13. Hitler at Würzburg, June 27, 1937; Baynes, *op. cit.*, I, 411.
14. *Philosophy of Right*, pp. 217-18.
15. *Omnipotent Government* (New Haven, Yale U.P., 1944), p. 132.
16. *Mein Kampf*, pp. 290, 324.
17. Ernst Nolte, *Three Faces of Fascism*, trans. L. Vennewitz

(New York, Holt, Rinehart & Winston, 1966), pp. 280-81; quoting *L'Aryen, son rôle social* (1st ed., Paris, 1899).

18. *The Open Society and its Enemies* (4th ed., 2 vols., New York, Harper & Row, 1963), II, 61-62.
19. Quoted in Walter Kaufmann, *Existentialism from Dostoevsky to Sartre* (New York, Meridian, 1957), p. 18. Hartmann Grisar, *Luther*, trans. E.M. Lamond, ed. L. Cappadelta (London, Kegan Paul, 1916); *On the Jews and their Lies*, V, 405. Luther Hess Waring, *The Political Theories of Martin Luther* (New York, Putnam's, 1910), p. 104; quoting a sermon on "Tribute to Caesar."
20. *The Characteristics of the Present Age*, trans. W. Smith (2nd ed., London, John Chapman, 1859), p. 36. *Addresses to the German Nation*, ed. G.A. Kelly, trans. R.F. Jones & G.H. Turnbull (New York, Harper & Row, 1968), p. 177.
21. *Economic and Philosophical Manuscripts*, trans. T.B. Bottomore; reprinted in Erich Fromm, *Marx's Concept of Man* (New York, Ungar, 1966), pp. 78, 130. *Critique of the Gotha Programme*; quoted (by Lenin) in *Modern Political Thought*, ed. W. Ebenstein (2nd ed., N.Y., Holt, Rinehart & Winston, 1960), p. 431.
22. *Works*, ed. O. Levy (18 vols., New York, Russell & Russell, 1964); *The Genealogy of Morals*, First Essay, XIII, 40.
23. Von Treitschke, *Politics*, trans. B. Dugdale and T. deBille (2 vols., London, Constable, 1916), I, 66. Peter Viereck, *Metapolitics* (New York, Capricorn, 1965), p. 105; quoting aphorisms "from Wagner's various works during 1847-51." Moeller quoted by Walter Laqueur, *Weimar: A Cultural History 1918–1933* (New York, Putnam's, 1974), p. 96.

Chapter Three

1. Rauschning, *The Voice of Destruction* (New York, Putnam's, 1940), p. 222. Melvin Rader, *No Compromise* (New York, Macmillan, 1939), pp. 25-26; quoting Rosenberg, *Mythus. The Nazi Years*, ed. J. Remak (Englewood Cliffs, N.J., Prentice-Hall, 1969), p. 41; quoting

Neesse, *Brevier eines jungen Nationalsozialisten* (Olden-
burg, 1933).

2. Rauschning, *op. cit.*, pp. 224, 184, 212, 210-11.
3. Rauschning, *The Revolution of Nihilism*, trans. E.W.
   Dickes (New York, Longmans, Green, 1939), pp. 49-50.
   Rader, *op. cit.*, p. 43; quoting *Mythus*. Johst quoted in
   Viereck, *op. cit.*, p. 255.
4. Rauschning, *The Voice of Destruction*, p. 224.
5. *Mein Kampf*, p. 408. George L. Mosse, *Nazi Culture*,
   trans. S. Attanasio *et al.* (New York, Grosset & Dunlap,
   1968), pp. 282-83; quoting *Hans Schemm spricht*, ed. G.
   Kahl-Furthmann (Bayerische Ostmark, 1935). *The
   Great Quotations*, ed. G. Seldes (New York, Lyle Stuart,
   1960), p. 321; taken from John Gunther, *The Nation*
   (n.d.).
6. *Mein Kampf*, p. 233. Sombart, *A New Social Philosophy*
   (Princeton, Princeton U.P., 1937), p. 10.
7. George L. Mosse, *The Crisis of German Ideology* (New
   York, Grosset & Dunlap, 1964), p. 15.
8. *The Portable Nietzsche*, ed. W. Kaufmann (New York,
   Viking, 1954); *Thus Spake Zarathustra*, Second Part, p.
   238.
9. *Romanticism*, ed. J.B. Halsted (New York, Harper &
   Row, 1969), p. 26. *Ibid.*, p. 237; from "The Revolution,"
   in *Richard Wagner's Prose Works*, trans. W.A. Ellis
   (London, 1899-1900).
10. Viereck, *op. cit.*, p. 7; quoting Ernst Troeltsch. *Deutscher
    Geist und Westeuropa* (Tübingen, 1925).
11. Koppel S. Pinson, *Modern Germany* (New York,
    Macmillan, 1954), p. 272; quoting Rathenau, "Zur
    Mechanik des Geistes" (1912).
12. *Mein Kampf*, pp. 337-38.
13. *Ibid.*, pp. 267, 459. Rauschning, *The Voice of Destruc-
    tion*, pp. 239-40.
14. Rader, *op. cit.*, pp. 191-92; quoting Goering, *Germany
    Reborn* (London, 1934).
15. Viereck, *op. cit.*, p. 289; quoting from Eugene Lyons,
    "Dictators into Gods" (*American Mercury*, March
    1939).
16. *Ibid.*; quoting from *The New York Times*, Feb. 11, 1937.
17. Mosse, *Nazi Culture*, p. 10; quoting from a speech in
    Munich, April 27, 1923.

18. Rauschning, *The Voice of Destruction*, p. 224. Lothar Gottlieb Tirala, *Rasse, Geist und Seele* (Munich, 1935), p. 220 (trans. G. Reisman).
19. Herman Finer, *Mussolini's Italy* (New York, Holt, 1935), p. 218; quoting a speech given in Naples, Oct. 24, 1922. *Cf.* Rader, *op. cit.*, p. 25.
20. *Essays in Pragmatism*, ed. A. Castell (New York, Hafner, 1952); "What Pragmatism Means" (Lecture II of *Pragmatism: A New Name for Some Old Ways of Thinking*), p. 150. *Ibid.*, "Pragmatism's Conception of Truth" (Lecture VI of *Pragmatism*), p. 170.
21. In his youth, Mussolini was personally acquainted with several Italian disciples of James, and published an occasional article in *La Voce*, a pragmatist journal of the period devoted to political and literary issues. Later, he made a point of giving James part of the credit for the development of Fascism. "The pragmatism of William James," he said in a 1926 interview, "was of great use to me in my political career. James taught me that an action should be judged rather by its results than by its doctrinary basis. I learnt of James that faith in action, that ardent will to live and fight, to which Fascism owes a great part of its success. . . . For me the essential was to act." *Cf.* Ralph Barton Perry, *The Thought and Character of William James* (2 vols., Boston, Little, Brown, 1935), II, 575; quoting the *Sunday Times*, London, April 11, 1926.
22. *Mein Kampf*, pp. 214-15.
23. Aurel Kolnai, *The War Against the West* (New York, Viking, 1938), p. 59. Rauschning, *The Voice of Destruction*, p. 223. Viereck, *op. cit.*, p. 314; quoting from *The Atlantic Monthly*, June 1940.
24. Rauschning, *The Voice of Destruction*, pp. 188-89. Goering quoted by Eugene Davidson, *The Trial of the Germans* (New York, Macmillan, 1966), pp. 237-38.
25. Rauschning, *The Voice of Destruction*, p. 189.
26. Gangulee, *op. cit.*, p. 123.
27. Kolnai, *op. cit.*, p. 29; quoting a statement made at Frankfurt a.M., Oct. 1935. Shirer, *op. cit.*, p. 662.
28. This widespread form of subjectivism is implicit in every variant of the theory. If a man's mental methods or contents are regarded as irreducible features of his con-

sciousness, as primaries not derived from an awareness of reality—if his ideas are claimed to have no source in the perception of *facts*—then, the inventions of certain philosophers notwithstanding, the source is his emotions, his arbitrary (and, to him, causeless) feelings.

29. *Mein Kampf*, p. 338. Kolnai, *op. cit.*, pp. 29-30; quoting a statement made by Goering in the spring of 1933. Mosse, *Nazi Culture*, p. xxxi; quoting from Benedikt Lochmüller, *Hans Schemm* (Bayreuth, 1935).

30. Kant does not repudiate the term "objective," and claims to oppose subjectivism. His method of opposition, however, is to redefine "objectivity," in accordance with his own presuppositions, in such a way as to make it a species of subjectivity. Hegel follows Kant's lead in this issue.

31. Kolnai, *op. cit.*, p. 61; quoting Franz Haiser. Rauschning, *The Voice of Destruction*, p. 223. *Cf.* the statement by the Nazi physicist Philipp Lenard, a 1905 Nobel Prize winner for his work on cathode rays, in his treatise entitled "German Physics": "Science, like every other human product, is racial and conditioned by the blood." (Quoted in Rader, *op. cit.*, p. 31.)

32. Rader, *op. cit.*, pp. 102-03; quoting *Nature*, Jan. 18, 1936.

33. Tirala, *op. cit.*, p. 190 (trans. G. Reisman).

34. *Ibid.*, p. 196.

35. *Mein Kampf*, p. 253. Rauschning, *The Voice of Destruction*, p. 97.

Chapter Four

1. *Mein Kampf*, pp. 404, 297. Jung quoted in Kolnai, *op. cit.*, p. 66; the last quoted sentence is Kolnai's summary of Jung's view.

2. *Ibid.*, p. 105, n. 3; quoting *Wille und Macht* (Munich, Dec. 1936).

3. *Mein Kampf*, p. 297.

4. *The Origins of Totalitarianism* (new ed., New York, Harcourt, Brace & World, 1966), pp. 348, 315-16.

5. *Ibid.*, p. 425, n. 98. Ziemer, *op. cit.*, p. 33. Hannah

Arendt, *Eichmann in Jerusalem* (New York, Viking, 1965), p. 42.

6. *Ethica Nicomachea* 1168b28-1169b2.
7. *Confessions*, trans. R.S. Pine-Coffin (Baltimore, Penguin, 1961), pp. 169, 93. *On Christian Doctrine*, trans. D.W. Robertson, Jr. (Indianapolis, Bobbs-Merrill, 1958), p. 19.
8. *Confessions*, p. 181. *Approaches to Ethics*, ed. W.T. Jones *et al.* (New York, McGraw-Hill, 1962), pp. 161-62; reprinted from *Meister Eckhart*, trans. R.B. Blakney (New York, 1957).
9. *Adam Smith's Moral and Political Philosophy*, ed. H.W. Schneider (New York, Harper & Row, 1970); *The Theory of Moral Sentiments*, pp. 39, 233-34, 249.
10. *Foundations of the Metaphysics of Morals*, ed. R.P. Wolff, trans. L.W. Beck (Indianapolis, Bobbs-Merrill, 1969), pp. 65, 14, 69.
11. *Religion Within the Limits of Reason Alone*, trans. T.M. Greene and H.H. Hudson (New York, Harper & Row, 1960), p. 41, n. *Foundations*, pp. 38, 6, 13, 49.
12. *Ibid.*, pp. 36, 49, 21 (n. 2), 14, 23.
13. *Ibid.*, pp. 27, 16-17.
14. *Ibid.*, p. 17.
15. *Ibid.*, p. 28.
16. *Ibid.*, pp. 79, 81, 83, 87, 82.
17. *Ibid.*, pp. 93-94.
18. *Ibid.*, pp. 23, 72.
19. *The Categorical Imperative* (4th ed., London, Hutchinson, 1963), pp. 50, 258.
20. *Foundations*, pp. 57-58. Kant grants that even the moral man requires an interest or incentive of some kind in order to act; the only interest Kant regards as moral, however, is the interest in acting from duty, i.e., an interest in action divorced from goals.
21. *Ibid.*, p. 35, n. 3.
22. *Ibid.*, p. 66. *Religion Within the Limits of Reason Alone*, p. 55. *Foundations*, pp. 35, 25, 19.
23. *Religion*, p. 31. *Foundations*, pp. 50 (n. 11), 21 (n. 2). *Religion*, p. 41, n. In this last note, Kant permits what he calls "moral self-love," described as "the inner principle of such a contentment as is possible to us" by reason of "unadulterated" obedience to duty. *Ibid.*, p. 41.

24. *Religion*, pp. 31-32.
25. *Ibid.*, p. 50. *Foundations*, pp. 27-28.
26. *Religion*, pp. 25, 28, 46, 38, 32, 28, 38.
27. *Ibid.*, p. 40.
28. *Ibid.*, pp. 44, 51 (n.).
29. *Ibid.*, p. 55.
30. *Ibid.*, pp. 55, 69.
31. *Ibid.*, pp. 55, 45.
32. New York, Random House, 1957; p. 1028.
33. *The Positive Philosophy of Auguste Comte*, trans. and condensed by Harriet Martineau (2nd ed., 2 vols., London, Trübner, 1875), II, 239.
34. Fichte, *The Characteristics of the Present Age*, pp. 33-34. Hegel, *The Phenomenology of Mind*, trans. J.B. Baillie (New York, Harper & Row, 1967), pp. 526-29. Schopenhauer, *On the Basis of Morality*, trans. E.F.J. Payne (Indianapolis, Bobbs-Merrill, 1965), pp. 165, 141-42, 139-40. Marx, *Economic and Philosophical Manuscripts*, p. 132. *The Communist Manifesto*, English trans. of 1888, ed. F. Engels; reprinted in Ebenstein, *Great Political Thinkers*, p. 670.
35. Nietzsche is an exception to the altruist trend. But he typically advocates the sacrifice of others to self. This viewpoint, though it is a form of egoism, leaves unchallenged the basic Kantian idea that man is an object of sacrifice. Nietzsche's view was easily adapted by the Nazis to suit their own purposes (*cf.* Ch. 2, above). A theory of egoism that does not accept the concept of sacrifice in any variant is indicated below (Ch. 16).
36. Kolnai, *op. cit.*, p. 89; the last sentence is a quote from Bergmann. Mosse, *Nazi Culture*, p. 223; quoting a lecture given by Gauger at Bad Neuheim, 1934. Murphy *et al.*, *op. cit.*, p. 68; quoting Beck, *Die Erziehung im dritten Reich* (Dortmund and Breslau, 1936). *Mein Kampf*, pp. 300, 298.
37. *Op. cit.*, p. 491.
38. *Philosophy of Right*, p. 109.
39. Kolnai, *op. cit.*, p. 54; quoting Wilhelm Stapel. Rosenberg quoted by Robert A. Brady, *The Spirit and Structure of German Fascism* (New York, Viking, 1937), p. 116.
40. Rauschning, *The Voice of Destruction*, p. 78.

41. *Communism, Fascism, and Democracy*, ed. C. Cohen (New York, Random House, 1962), pp. 406, 409; quoting speeches at Essen (Nov. 22, 1926) and at Chemnitz (April 2, 1928).
42. *Mein Kampf*, pp. 299, 138-39.
43. Quoted in Shirer, *op. cit.*, p. 982.
44. *Eichmann in Jerusalem*, pp. 137, 150.
45. Rauschning, *The Voice of Destruction*, p. 225.
46. A. James Gregor, *Contemporary Radical Ideologies* (New York, Random House, 1968), p. 214.

Chapter Five

1. Urian Oakes at Cambridge, in 1677; reprinted in *The American Puritans*, ed. P. Miller (Garden City, N.Y., Doubleday, 1956), p. 206. Cotton Mather, *Durable Riches* (Boston, 1695); in *Ideas in America*, ed. G.N. Grob and R.N. Beck (New York, Free Press, 1970), p. 49. Cotton Mather, *Essays to Do Good* (1710); Miller, *op. cit.*, p. 219.
2. *Writings*, ed. A.E. Bergh (20 vols., Washington, Jefferson Memorial Assoc., 1903), VI, 258.
3. *Principles of Nature* (New York, 1801); Grob and Beck, *op. cit.*, pp. 81, 83, 85, 84.
4. Charles Backus, *A Sermon Preached in Long-Meadow at the Publick Fast* (Springfield, 1788); Grob and Beck, *op. cit.*, pp. 133-34.
5. *Life and Works* (10 vols., New Rochelle, Thomas Paine National Historical Assoc., 1925), II, 179-80.
6. Joseph L. Blau, *Men and Movements in American Philosophy* (Englewood Cliffs, N.J., Prentice-Hall, 1952), p. 44; quoting the original provisional constitution of the State of New Hampshire (1766).
7. Adams, *Report of the Committee of Correspondence to the Boston Town Meeting* (Nov. 20, 1772); Grob and Beck, *op. cit.*, p. 107. Bernard Bailyn, *The Ideological Origins of the American Revolution* (Cambridge, Harvard U.P., 1967), p. 187; quoting Dickinson, *An Address to the Committee of Correspondence in Barbados* (Philadelphia, 1766).
8. Grob and Beck, *op. cit.*, p. 108.

9. *The Second Treatise of Government*, ed. T.P. Peardon (Indianapolis, Bobbs-Merrill, 1952), p. 15. This passage and others from Locke are quoted by Samuel Adams in *Report of the Committee.*

10. *Writings, op. cit.,* III, 318. *The Federalist Papers,* ed. C. Rossiter (New York, New American Library, 1961), No. 10, p. 81.

11. Robert C. Whittemore, *Makers of the American Mind* (New York, Morrow, 1964), pp. 131-32; quoting Adams, "Defence of the Constitution."

12. Quoted in Isabel Paterson, *The God of the Machine* (New York, Putnam's, 1943), p. 292.

13. *Lectures on Law* (1790-91); in *Documents in the History of American Philosophy,* ed. M. White (New York, Oxford U.P., 1972), pp. 93, 83, 92, 83.

14. Letters to Benjamin Rush (April 21, 1803) and Thomas Law (June 13, 1814); in *American Thought Before 1900,* ed. P. Kurtz (New York, Macmillan, 1966), pp. 157-58, 160-61.

15. Franklin quoted in Whittemore, *op. cit.,* p. 79.

16. *A History of American Philosophy* (2nd ed., New York, Columbia U.P., 1963), p. 30.

Chapter Six

1. George Ripley, book review in *The Christian Examiner* (Jan. 1833); White, *op. cit.,* pp. 137, 124. *The Philosophy of Loyalty* (New York, 1908); Kurtz, *op. cit.,* pp. 366, 373.

2. Blau, *op. cit.,* p. 123; quoting Emerson, "Politics," in *Essays, Second Series* (Boston, 1895). Royce quoted by Schneider, *op. cit.,* p. 423. Creighton, *Studies in Speculative Philosophy* (New York, Macmillan, 1925), pp. 49-50.

3. Schneider, *op. cit.,* pp. 380, 379; quoting Laurens Perseus Hickok, *Moral Science* (Schenectady, N.Y., 1853). *Ibid.,* p. 167; quoting Denton J. Snider, *Social Institutions* (St. Louis, 1901). Whittemore, *op. cit.,* pp. 281-82; quoting Snider, *The State, specially the American State, Psychologically Treated.* Edward R. Lewis, *A History of American Political Thought from the Civil War to the World*

War (New York, Macmillan, 1937), p. 187; quoting John W. Burgess.

4. *Mill's Ethical Writings*, ed. J.B. Schneewind (New York, Collier, 1965); *Utilitarianism*, pp. 291, 290.

5. Sidney Fine, *Laissez Faire and the General-Welfare State* (Ann Arbor, U. of Michigan P., 1964), p. 54. The economist quoted is Edward Atkinson, *The Industrial Progress of the Nation* (New York, 1890).

6. *The Principles of Ethics* (2 vols., New York, D. Appleton, 1893), II, 433.

7. *Ibid.*, I, 243, 256.

8. *Outlines of Cosmic Philosophy* (Cambridge, Riverside P., 1902); Kurtz, *op. cit.*, p. 390.

9. Fine, *op. cit.*, p. 88; quoting Sumner, "Laissez Faire," in *Essays*, ed. A.G. Keller and M.R. Davie (New Haven, 1934). *Folkways* (Ginn & Co., 1907); in *Problems of Ethics*, ed. R.E. Dewey *et al.* (New York, Macmillan, 1961), p. 31.

10. Fine, *op. cit.*, p. 44; quoting Edward Livingston Youmans speaking to Henry George.

11. Fine, *op. cit.*, p. 194; quoting George D. Herron, "The Message of Jesus to Men of Wealth" (*Christian Union*, Dec. 11, 1890). *Ibid.*, p. 173; quoting a letter from Josiah .Strong to Richard T. Ely (Aug. 8, 1889). *Ibid.*, p. 174; quoting Lyman Abbott, *Reminiscences* (Boston, 1915). *Ibid.*, p. 182; quoting Abbott, "Christianity versus Socialism" (*North American Review*, April 1889).

12. *The Quest for Certainty* (New York, Putnam's, 1960), pp. 44, 137.

13. *Ibid.*, p. 23, *passim. Cf.* Dewey, *Logic: The Theory of Inquiry* (New York, Holt, 1938), pp. 104ff.

14. The first and third quotes are from *Reconstruction in Philosophy*; quoted in Brand Blanshard, *The Nature of Thought* (2 vols., New York, Macmillan, 1939), I, 347. The second quote is from *Essays in Experimental Logic* (New York, Dover, n.d.), p. 310.

15. *The Quest for Certainty*, p. 276.

16. Castell, *op. cit.*, "The Moral Philosopher and the Moral Life," pp. 73, 77.

17. *Liberalism and Social Action* (New York, Capricorn, 1963), p. 12.

18. *Ibid.*, pp. 4-5, 32. *Philosophy and Civilization* (New

York, Minton, Balch, 1931), pp. 322f. "Authority and Social Change" (1936); in Ebenstein, *Modern Political Thought*, p. 649.

19. *Liberalism and Social Action*, pp. 65, 67. *Individualism Old and New* (New York, Capricorn, 1962), pp. 75, 119, 95, 119.

20. *The School and Society* (Chicago, U. of Chicago P., 1956), pp. 104, 101, 100.

21. *Ibid.*, pp. 99, 16, 91, 29. The second excerpt ("to share in the social consciousness") comes from *My Pedagogic Creed* (New York, 1897); quoted in Fine, *op cit.*, p. 288.

22. *The School and Society*, p. 15.

Chapter Seven

1. Pinson, *op. cit.*, p. 358; quoting a resolution passed by a workers' meeting called by the Bavarian Majority Socialists and the trade unions (Munich, Nov. 14, 1918).

2. *Ibid.*, pp. 201, 203; quoting an address by Lassalle to the court (April 12, 1862).

3. *Ibid.*, p. 458. *Seeds of Modern Drama*, ed. N. Houghton (3 vols., New York, Dell, 1963); *The Weavers*, trans. H. Frenz and M. Waggoner, III, 254, 281, 283-84, 320.

4. Pinson, *op. cit.*, p. 217; quoting Bebel, *Unsere Ziele* (10th ed., Berlin, 1893).

5. *Ibid.*, p. 359; quoting a program submitted by the new provisional government of Bavaria (Nov. 15, 1918).

6. Luther's statements are quoted by Walter Kaufmann, *The Faith of a Heretic* (Garden City, N.Y., Doubleday, 1963), p. 75.

7. Von Mises, *op. cit.*, p. 158. Gustav Stolper, *The German Economy*, trans. T. Stolper (New York, Harcourt, Brace & World, 1967), pp. 43-44.

8. Electoral figures for the Center party include the votes of the Bavarian People's party, a Catholic splinter group with views similar to those of the Center.

9. Rudolf Virchow, Jan. 17, 1873; quoted in Pinson, *op. cit.*, p. 193.

10. Erich Eyck, *A History of the Weimar Republic*, trans

H.P. Hanson and R.G.L. Waite (2 vols., Cambridge, Harvard U.P., 1967), II, 92.

11. *Ibid.*, I, 59; quoting Adolf Gröber (Feb. 13, 1919).
12. *Op. cit.*, p. 181.
13. *Cf. ibid.*, p. 184..
14. *Ibid.*, p. 182; quoting Bishop Wilhelm Emanuel von Ketteler, "The Great Social Questions of the Present Day" (sermons delivered in Frankfurt, 1848).
15. *Ibid.*, p. 394.
16. Quoted in Eyck, *op. cit.*, I, 76.
17. *The Abuse of Learning* (New York, Macmillan, 1948), p. 133.
18. *Ibid.*, pp. 137, 139.
19. Unless otherwise identified, translations of the Weimar Constitution are from Heinrich Oppenheimer, *The Constitution of the German Republic* (London, Stevens & Sons, 1923), Appendix. Articles 7, 9, 119, 144; pp. 220-22, 246, 251.
20. Articles 111, 117, 118, 120, 114; pp. 244-46.
21. Article 48, p. 230.
22. Article 151, p. 253.
23. Articles 153, 155, 156, 164, 162; pp. 253-56. The translation "in the interests of collectivism" is taken from S. William Halperin, *Germany Tried Democracy* (New York, Norton, 1965), p. 159.
24. Article 163, p. 256.
25. Pinson, *op. cit.*, p. 202; quoting a letter of Lassalle to Bismarck (June 8, 1863).
26. *Ibid.*, p. 379. The first and third quotes are from a statement to a Berlin meeting of the Independent Socialists (Dec. 1918). The second is from a statement of Nov. 20, 1918.
27. *Ibid.*, p. 370; quoting Philipp Scheidemann at the first congress of the Workers' and Soldiers' Councils (Dec. 1918).
28. *Ibid.*, p. 364; quoting from *Vorwärts*, Dec. 27, 1918.
29. *Cf. ibid.*, pp. 381-86.
30. Robert G.L. Waite, *Vanguard of Nazism* (New York, Norton, 1969), p. 269; quoting Ernst von Salomon, *Die Geächteten* (Berlin, 1930).
31. *Ibid.*, p. 164; quoting von Salomon, *Die Geächteten.*

Ibid., p. 56; quoting von Salomon, "Der verlorene Haufe."

32. *Ibid.*, pp. 42-43. The phrase "peace and money-grabbing" is taken from *ibid.*, p. 43; quoting Edgar Jung, "Die Tragik der Kriegsgeneration." *Ibid.*, p. 209; quoting Röhm, *Geschichte eines Hochverräters* (7th ed., Munich, 1934).
33. *Op. cit.*, p. 198.

Chapter Eight

1. Hilton Kramer, "E.L. Kirchner: Art vs. Life," *The New York Times*, April 6, 1969.
2. *Fifteen Famous European Plays*, ed. B.A. Cerf and V.H. Cartnell (New York, Random House, 1943); *From Morn to Midnight*, p. 506.
3. Pinson, *op. cit.*, p. 462; quoting *Preussentum und Sozialismus* (1920).
4. Shirer, *op. cit.*, p. 102.
5. This summary of Klages's views is by Frederick Wyatt and Hans Lukas Teuber, "German Psychology Under the Nazi System: 1933-1940," *Psychological Review*, Vol. LI (1944), pp. 230-31.
6. Kandinsky quoted in T.H. Robsjohn-Gibbings, *Mona Lisa's Mustache* (New York, Knopf, 1947), p. 168. Klee quoted in Laqueur, *op. cit.*, p. 174.
7. Harold C. Schonberg, *The Lives of the Great Composers* (New York, Norton, 1970), p. 568; quoting Schoenberg, *Style and Idea* (New York, 1950). Laqueur, *op. cit.*, p. 159; quoting a letter to Paul Bekker.
8. Quoted in Robsjohn-Gibbings, *op. cit.*, p. 160.
9. Pinson, *op. cit.*, p. 463; quoting *Preussentum und Sozialismus*.
10. Peter Gay, *Weimar Culture* (New York, Harper & Row, 1970), p. 86; quoting *Preussentum und Sozialismus*.
11. Walter Laqueur, *Young Germany* (New York, Basic Books, 1962); Introduction by R.H.S. Crossman, p. xviii. The views and slogans of the youth movement are presented in some detail in this book by Laqueur.
12. Waite, *op. cit.*, p. 20. The sentence Waite quotes is from

Howard Becker, *German Youth: Bond or Free* (London, 1946).

13. R.H. Samuel and R. Hinton Thomas, *Education and Society in Modern Germany* (London, Routledge & Kegan Paul, 1949), p. 141; quoting Robert von Erdberg, "Ten Commandments" for Folk high schools in Prussia (1919). Thomas Alexander and Beryl Parker, *The New Education in the German Republic* (New York, John Day, 1929), p. 172. Lichtwark quoted in *ibid.*, p. 102.

14. *Ibid.*, pp. 5, 133, 358.

15. *Ibid.*, p. 172. *Germany Puts the Clock Back* (New York, Morrow, 1933), p. 155.

16. *Gardner's Art Through the Ages*, rev. by H. de la Croix and R.G. Tansey (6th ed., 2 vols., New York, Harcourt Brace, 1975), II, 736. The statement about art is quoted in Laqueur, *Weimar: A Cultural History*, p. 119.

17. William Barrett, *Irrational Man* (Garden City, N.Y., Doubleday, 1958), p. 40.

18. Stolper, *op. cit.*, p. 85.

19. Laqueur, *Weimar: A Cultural History*, p. 68; referring to Gottfried Benn.

20. Otto Friedrich, *Before the Deluge* (New York, Harper & Row, 1972), p. 124.

21. Pinson, *op. cit.*, p. 447; quoting a statement made on June 29, 1927.

22. Friedrich, *op. cit.*, pp. 128-129; quoting Zweig, *The World of Yesterday* (Lincoln, Neb., 1943). *Ibid.*, p. 126; quoting Grosz, *A Little Yes and a Big No* (New York, 1946).

23. Halperin, *op cit.*, p. 267.

24. Quoted in Shirer, *op. cit.*, p. 62.

Chapter Nine

1. *Der Nationalsozialismus: Dokumente 1933-1945*, ed. W. Hofer (Frankfurt a.M., Fischer Bücherei, 1957); *Die 25 Punkte des Programms der NSDAP*. Unless otherwise identified, translations of the Points are from *Problems in Western Civilization*, ed. L.F. Schaefer *et al.* (2 vols., New York, Scribner's, 1968), II, 422-25.

2. Excerpt from Point 11 (trans. G. Reisman). *Händler und Helden* is the title of a book by Werner Sombart.
3. The last quote is from *Mein Kampf*, p. 34.
4. *Cf.* the following from Walter Laqueur: "[T]he sums paid to Hitler prior to 1933 were not only modest in absolute terms, they were small in comparison with what was given to other parties. German industrialists did not 'make' Hitler, they joined him only after his party had become a leading political force, and it is possible that Hitler would have come to power even if the Nazis had not received a single *pfennig* from the bankers and industrialists." "Fascism—The Second Coming," *Commentary*, Vol. 61, No. 2, Feb. 1976, p. 58.
5. Stolper, *op. cit.*, p. 47.
6. Alan Bullock, *Hitler: A Study in Tyranny* (rev. ed., New York, Harper & Row, 1964), p. 174. Shirer, *op. cit.*, p. 145.
7. Quoted in *ibid.*, p. 159.
8. Stolper, *op. cit.*, p. 128.
9. *The Voice of Destruction*, p. 186.
10. Waite, *op. cit.*, p. 268; quoting Friedrich Glombowski.

Chapter Ten

1. Laqueur, *Weimar: A Cultural History*, Preface, p. ix. Myers, "The Modern Artist in Germany," *The American-German Review*, Vol. XVI, No. 4, April 1940, pp. 16, 34. Gay, *op. cit.*, Preface, p. xiii.
2. *Ibid.*, p. 123. Pinson, *op. cit.*, p. 458.
3. *The Magic Mountain*, trans. H.T. Lowe-Porter (New York, Random House, 1969), pp. 55-56, 349, 348.
4. *Ibid.*, pp. 372, 85, 62, 246, 62, 61-62, 249, 100, 712.
5. *Ibid.*, p. 496. (The second quotation—"Man is master. . . ."—is taken from Gay, *op. cit.*, pp. 126-27.)
6. *Ibid.*, pp. 603, 496, 594, 583.
7. *Weimar: A Cultural History*, p. 123.
8. *Op. cit.*, p. 17.
9. Gay, *op. cit.*, p. 53. *Ibid.*, p. 54; quoting Zweig, "Abschied von Rilke."
10. *The Word and the World* (New York, Scribner's, 1931), p. 126.

11. "The Cry Was, 'Down With *Das System*,'" *The New York Times Magazine*, Aug. 16, 1970, p. 13.
12. Freud, "One of the Difficulties of Psycho-Analysis," (1917), trans. J. Riviere, in *On Creativity and the Unconscious*, ed. B. Nelson (New York, Harper & Row, 1958), p. 7.
13. *Ibid.*, pp. 4, 6, 9.
14. Pinson, *op. cit.*, p. 456.
15. Editorial Topic, Jan. 22, 1978.
16. Edna Heidbreder, *Seven Psychologies* (New York, Appleton-Century-Crofts, 1933), p. 393.
17. Quoted in Robsjohn-Gibbings, *op. cit.*, pp. 179, 104.
18. *The New Left: The Anti-Industrial Revolution* (rev. ed., New York, New American Library, 1975), "The Age of Envy," p. 153.
19. V.J. McGill, "Notes on Philosophy in Nazi Germany," *Science and Society: A Marxian Quarterly*, Vol. IV, No. 1, Winter 1940, p. 27.

Chapter Eleven

1. Quoted in Pinson, *op. cit.*, p. 452.
2. Franz Neumann, *Behemoth* (New York, Harper & Row, 1966), p. 31; quoting Fritz Tarnow (head of the Woodworker's Union), "Kapitalistische Wirtschaftsanarchie und Arbeiterklasse," in *Sozialdemokratischer Parteitag in Leipzig* (Berlin, 1931).
3. *Op. cit.*, pp. 123-24.
4. *Ibid.*
5. Laqueur, *Young Germany*, p. 191.
6. Gay, *op. cit.*, p. 143; quoting Ernst von Aster, "Metaphysik des Nationalismus" (1932).
7. *Cf.* Mosse, *Nazi Culture*, p. 346.
8. Eliot Barculo Wheaton, *Prelude to Calamity* (Garden City, N.Y., Doubleday, 1968), p. 412. Gay, *op. cit.*, p. 140.
9. Eyck, *op. cit.*, II, 211, 219. Hugenberg quoted in *ibid.*, II, 476. Mowrer, *op. cit.*, p. 203; quoting Pastor Mattiat of Kerstlingerode on the Prussian election of 1932, in the organ of the *Evangelische Bund*.
10. *The Voice of Destruction*, p. 131.

11. Quoted in Rudolf Morsey, "The Center Party between the Fronts," in *The Path to Dictatorship: 1918–1933*, intro. Fritz Stern, trans. J. Conway (Garden City, N.Y., Doubleday, 1966), pp. 74, 76, 73.
12. The Social Democrats did bring suit in the Supreme Court to protest the rape of Prussia, but the Court evaded the legal issues involved and essentially upheld the coup. Workers' signs mentioned in Eyck, *op. cit.*, II, 118.
13. Quoted in Halperin, *op. cit.*, p. 495.
14. Shirer, *op. cit.*, p. 179.
15. *The Voice of Destruction*, p. 75; quoting Puzzi Hanfstängel.
16. Susanne C. Engelmann, *German Education and Re-Education* (New York, International Universities Press, 1945), pp. 73-74.
17. George Murray, " 'New' radicals a 1930 rerun," *Chicago Today*, May 14, 1969.
18. Laqueur, *Weimar: A Cultural History*, p. 116; quoting a 1922 statement about "tragic youth."
19. Shirer, *op. cit.*, p. 165.
20. Halperin, *op. cit.*, p. 445.

Chapter Twelve

1. Quoted in Shirer, *op. cit.*, p. 194. The pretext for this decree was the Reichstag fire.
2. Davidson, *op. cit.*, p. 288.
3. Von Mises, *op. cit.*, p. 56. Von Mises describes the Nazi method of expropriating profits: "As all private consumption is strictly limited and controlled by the government, and as all unconsumed income must be invested, which means virtually lent to the government, high profits are nothing but a subtle method of taxation. The consumer has to pay high prices and business is nominally profitable. But the greater the profits are, the more the government funds are swelled. The government gets the money. . . ." (p. 226) Brady, *op. cit.*, p. 292; quoting Hjalmar Schacht at the opening of the National Labor and Economic Council in Nuremberg.
4. *The Voice of Destruction*, pp. 191-93.

5. Wheaton, *op. cit.*, p. 359; quoting Bishop Johannes Sproll of Rottenburg speaking to a gathering of Catholic clergy (Jan. 21, 1934). *Ibid.*, p. 319; the first part of this quotation is Wheaton's summary of the Pastoral's text. Two weeks after Hitler dissolved the Catholic Center party, the Vatican, in a move extremely important for the new German government's prestige, signed a concordat with the Nazis.
6. *Op. cit.*, p. 497.
7. *Ibid.*, p. 501; quoting a statement to American businessman S.R. Fuller (Sept. 23, 1935).
8. Quoted in Wheaton, *op. cit.*, p. 308.
9. *The Origins of Totalitarianism*, p. 315.

Chapter Thirteen

1. *The Informed Heart* (New York, Free Press, 1960), pp. 124-25.
2. Terrence Des Pres, *The Survivor* (New York, Pocket Books, 1977), pp. 223-24; quoting Alexander Donat, *The Holocaust Kingdom* (New York, 1965).
3. Quoted in Arendt, *The Origins of Totalitarianism*, p. 410, n. 62.
4. *Ibid.*, p. 424.
5. Primo Levi, *Survival in Auschwitz* (New York, Collier, 1961), p. 25.
6. Bettelheim, *op. cit.*, p. 214.
7. *Ibid.*, p. 150.
8. *Origins*, pp. 436-38, 455.
9. Bettelheim, *op. cit.*, pp. 110, 109. Des Pres, *op. cit.*, p. 191.
10. *Origins*, p. 454.
11. *Ibid.*, pp. 447-48, 451.
12. Rudolf Hoess, *Commandant of Auschwitz*, trans. C. FitzGibbon (New York, World, 1959), p. 80.
13. Arendt, *Origins*, p. 451, n. 151; quoting Himmler, "On Organizaton and Obligation of the SS and the Police" (1937).
14. *Ibid.*, p. 451. Bettelheim's observation (from "On Dachau and Buchenwald") is quoted in *ibid*, n. 151.
15. *Op. cit.*, p. 139.

16. *Ibid.*, pp. 210, 122.
17. Des Pres, *op. cit.*, p. 69; quoting Pelagia Lewinska, *Twenty Months at Auschwitz*, trans. A. Teichner (New York, 1968).
18. Levi, *op. cit.*, pp. 35-36.
19. *Origins*, pp. 451-53.
20. Bettelheim, *op. cit.*, pp. 153-54.
21. *Ibid.*, pp. 154-55.
22. *Ibid.*, p. 238.
23. *Origins*, pp. 443, 445. Eugen Kogon, *The Theory and Practice of Hell*, trans. H. Norden (New York, Berkley, 1958), p. 148. *Ibid.*, p. 191; quoting Hans Baermann, survivor of the Kaiserwald camp near Riga. *Ibid.*, p. 183; quoting Oskar Berger, survivor of Treblinka. Des Pres, *op. cit.*, p. 94; quoting Elie Wiesel, *Night*, trans. S. Rodway (New York, 1969). Private communication, 1968, from survivor of Auschwitz and Wüstegirsdorf; anonymity requested. Des Pres, *op. cit.*, p. 82; quoting Olga Lengyel, *Five Chimneys*, trans. P.P. Weiss (Chicago, 1947). Bettelheim, *op. cit.*, p. 127.
24. *Cf.* Jean-François Steiner, *Treblinka*, trans. H. Weaver (New York, Simon & Schuster, 1967), pp. 176-77.
25. *Origins*, p. 454, n. 159.
26. *Ibid.*, p. 445.
27. Des Pres, *op. cit.*, pp. 226ff. Bettelheim, *op. cit.*, p. 260.
28. *Origins*, pp. 457, 470, 473, 471, 351.

Chapter Fourteen

1. Arthur A. Ekirch, Jr., *Progressivism in America* (New York, Franklin Watts, 1974), p. 151; quoting Van Hise, *The Conservation of Natural Resources in the United States* (New York, 1910). Arthur A. Ekirch, Jr., *Ideologies and Utopias* (Chicago, Quadrangle, 1971), p. 116; quoting Tugwell, *The Battle for Democracy* (New York, 1935). Inaugural Address, Jan. 20, 1961. Rudd quoted in Roy Bongartz, "Three Meanies," *Esquire*, August 1970, p. 114. Kristol, *On the Democratic Idea in America* (New York, 1972), p. 27.
2. Fine, *op. cit.*, p. 173; quoting Charles Worcester Clark, "Applied Christianity: Who Shall Apply It First?" *Ando-*

ver Review (Jan. 1893). *Ibid.*, p. 205; this is Fine's summary of views held by Henry Carter Adams, George B. Newcomb, Richard Ely, and John R. Commons; *cf.* p. 205, n. 15.

3. *Ibid.*, p. 210; quoting Ely, "The Evolution of Industrial Society" (address to the Madison Literary Society, 1897).

4. *Ibid.*, p. 115; quoting Carnegie, "Wealth," *North American Review* (June 1889). *Ibid.*, n. 65; quoting a letter to William Gladstone (Nov. 24, 1890).

5. *Ibid.*, p. 341; quoting Lloyd, *Wealth against Commonwealth* (New York, 1894). *Ibid.*, p. 342; quoting Lloyd, "The New Conscience," *North American Review* (Sept. 1888). Ekirch, *Progressivism in America*, p. 23; quoting Ward, *Dynamic Sociology* (1883).

6. *Congressional Record*, 51st Cong., 1st sess. (March 21, 1890), p. 2460. Donald J. Dewey, "Antitrust Legislation," *International Encyclopedia of the Social Sciences*, ed. D.L. Sills (New York, Macmillan, 1968), p. 350.

7. Ekirch, *Progressivism in America*, pp. 158-59; quoting Croly, *The Promise of American Life* (New York, 1909). Comte, *The Catechism of Positive Religion*, trans. R. Congreve (London, John Chapman, 1858), pp. 332-33.

8. Ekirch, *Progressivism in America*, p. 170; quoting a 1912 campaign speech.

9. *Ibid.*, p. 110. *Ibid.*, quoting Frederic C. Howe, *Wisconsin: An Experiment in Democracy* (New York, 1912). *Ibid.*, p. 14; quoting Addams, *Newer Ideals of Peace* (New York, 1907).

10. *Ibid.*, p. 229; quoting Roosevelt, "Social and Industrial Justice," *Century*, Oct. 1913.

11. *Ideals and Self-Interest in America's Foreign Relations* (Chicago, U. of Chicago P., 1953), p. 47.

12. Ekirch, *Progressivism in America*, p. 266; quoting Croly, "The Effect on American Institutions of a Powerful Military and Naval Establishment," *Annals of the American Academy of Political and Social Science* (July 1916).

13. Quoted in Robsjohn-Gibbings, *op. cit.*, p. 241.

14. Quoted in Arthur A. Ekirch, Jr., *The Decline of American Liberalism* (New York, Atheneum, 1969), pp. 258-59.

15. Ekirch, *Ideologies and Utopias*, p. 46; quoting Lippmann, "The Permanent New Deal," *Yale Review* (June 1935).
16. *Ibid.*, p. 63; quoting Beard, "The Myth of Rugged American Individualism," *Harper's Magazine* (Dec. 1931). *Ibid.*, p. 35; quoting Wilson, "The Literary Consequences of the Crash" (1932).
17. *Ibid.*, p. 64; quoting Fairchild, "The Great Economic Paradox," *Harper's Magazine* (May 1932).
18. *Ibid.*, p. 57; quoting a special study commission of the Federal Council of the Churches of Christ in America (document to be read in the churches on Labor Day Sunday 1931). *Ibid.*, p. 134; quoting Arnold, *The Folklore of Capitalism* (New Haven, 1937). *Ibid.*, p. 133; quoting Arnold, *The Symbols of Government* (New Haven, 1935).
19. *Ibid.*, p. 68; quoting "The Principle of Planning and the Institution of Laissez Faire," *American Economic Review* (March 1932).
20. *Individualism Old and New*, p. 118.
21. Eric Goldman, *Rendezvous with Destiny* (New York, Knopf, 1952), p. 329. Carl N. Degler, *Out of Our Past* (New York, Harper & Row, 1962), p. 413; quoting Roosevelt, Commonwealth Club address (Sept. 1932). Ekirch, *Ideologies and Utopias*, p. 79; quoting a speech at Oglethorpe U. (May 22, 1932).
22. Degler, *op. cit.*, p. 415.
23. Ekirch, *Ideologies and Utopias*, p. 83; quoting Roosevelt, San Francisco speech (Sept. 1932). Chicago speech quoted in Degler, *op. cit.*, p. 412.
24. Mill, *Auguste Comte and Positivism* (Ann Arbor, U. of Michigan P., 1961), p. 148.
25. *The Roosevelt Myth* (Garden City, N.Y., Garden City Publishing, 1949), p. 303.

Chapter Fifteen

1. Rev. ed. (New York, Free Press, 1965), pp. 393, 402.
2. *Ibid.*, p. 16.
3. "Philosophical Implications of Physics," *Bulletin*, Vol. III, No. 5.
4. Richard Rorty, review of Ian Hacking, *Why Does Lan-*

guage Matter to Philosophy?, The Journal of Philosophy, Vol. LXXIV, No. 7, July 1977, p. 432.

5. Melvin Maddocks, Time, March 13, 1972, p. 51.

6. The Anxious Object (New York, Horizon, 1964), p. 41.

7. Donald Heiney and Lenthiel H. Downs, Recent American Literature after 1930; Vol. 4 of Essentials of Contemporary Literature of the Western World (Woodbury, N.Y., Barron's Educational Series, 1974), p. 271. Robert Brustein, "Drama in the Age of Einstein," The New York Times, Aug. 7, 1977, Sec. 2, p. 1.

8. Silberman quoted in "Back to Basics in the Schools," Newsweek, Oct. 21, 1974, p. 94B. For "Treasonable Activities" as a course, cf. The New York Times Magazine, Jan. 11, 1970, p. 62.

9. Theodore Roszak, The Making of a Counter Culture (Garden City, N.Y., Doubleday, 1969), p. 50. The course was "Physics for Poets," No. A85.0004, Spring 1973, Prof. Robert Schwartz. Interview by Bennett Kremen, "Unrequired Reading," The New York Times Book Review, Feb. 15, 1970, p. 5.

10. The New York Times Book Review, April 6, 1970, pp. 1-2.

11. Remark made in a debate with Gore Vidal; quoted in Sidney Hook, "Student Revolts Could Destroy Academic Freedom," The New York University Alumni News, May 1968, p. 3.

12. George Stade, review of Irving Howe, Decline of the New, The New York Times Book Review, April 12, 1970, p. 43.

13. Stephen Tonsor, "Science, Technology and the Cultural Revolution," The Intercollegiate Review, Vol. 8, No. 3, Winter 1972-73, p. 85.

14. Beck quoted in The New York Times Magazine, Oct. 13, 1968, p. 102. J. Edward Murray of the Arizona Republic, quoted in Martin Nolan, " 'A code word for playing it safe,' " The Village Voice, April 29, 1971. Roszak, op. cit., p. 55.

15. Kremen, op. cit., p. 24.

16. Robert Gorham Davis, "Rimbaud and Stavrogin in the Harvard Yard," Book Review, June 28, 1970, p. 2.

17. Quine, From a Logical Point of View (2nd ed., New

York, Harper & Row, 1963); "Two Dogmas of Empiricism," p. 44.

18. *The New Left*; "The Cashing-In: The Student Rebellion," p. 55.

19. *The New York Times*, May 12, 13, 21, 1970; quoting Peter J. Brennan, Leonard Lavoro, Walter Flynn, and Cliff Sloane.

20. *The Rise of the Unmeltable Ethnics* (New York, Macmillan, 1972); quoted by William V. Shannon, "The Need for Authority," *The New York Times*, Op-Ed page, July 30, 1972.

21. Keith Murray, "Four 'Changes,'" *The Environmental Handbook*, ed. G. De Bell (New York, Ballantine, 1970), p. 329. John B. Cobb, Jr., speech at a conference on the "theology of survival" at the School of Theology at Claremont; *The New York Times*, May 1, 1970. (The first phrase quoted is a summary by the *Times* writer, Edward B. Fiske, of the consensus of the conference.)

22. "National Humility," *A Treasury of Great American Speeches*, ed. C. Hurd (New York, Hawthorn, 1959), pp. 339-40.

23. "The Tragedy of the Commons," De Bell, *op. cit.*, p. 46. The Mobil ad appeared on the Op-Ed page, Sept. 7, 1972.

24. *A Theory of Justice* (Cambridge, Harvard U.P., 1971).

25. Louis Heren, deputy editor of *The Times* (London); quoted in *The New York Times*, March 23, 1975.

26. Israel Shenker, " 'Life of a Nation' Is Ponderous Event," Oct. 10, 1976; the professor quoted is Bruce Kuklick, U. of Pennsylvania.

Chapter Sixteen

1. For an example of the latter, *cf.* Garry Wills, *Inventing America* (Garden City, N.Y., Doubleday, 1978).

2. Quoted in Milton Mayer, *They Thought They Were Free* (Chicago, U. of Chicago P., 1966), pp. 169-70.

3. *Ibid.*, pp. 167-68.

4. Ayn Rand, *The Fountainhead* (25th anniv. ed., New York, Bobbs-Merrill, 1968), pp. 715, 717.

5. Ayn Rand, *Introduction to Objectivist Epistemology* (New York, New American Library: Mentor, 1979).

Ayn Rand, *The Virtue of Selfishness* (New York, New American Library, 1964). For the Objectivist politics, see Ayn Rand, *Capitalism: The Unknown Ideal* (New York, New American Library, 1966). For esthetics: Ayn Rand, *The Romantic Manifesto* (New York, World, 1969). For philosophy of history: Ayn Rand, *For the New Intellectual* (New York, Random House, 1961); title essay.

6. *Atlas Shrugged*, p. 1015.
7. *Ibid.*, p. 1016.
8. *The Virtue of Selfishness*; "The Objectivist Ethics," p. 13.
9. *Introduction to Objectivist Epistemology*, pp. 15 (statement italicized in original), 22.
10. *For the New Intellectual*; title essay, p. 33.
11. *The Virtue of Selfishness*; "The Objectivist Ethics," p. 16. *Atlas Shrugged*, pp. 1014, 1012.
12. *Ibid.*, p. 1014.
13. *Ibid.*, p. 1061.
14. Waite, *op. cit.*, Preface.
15. *Bartlett's Familiar Quotations* (15th ed., Boston, Little Brown, 1980), p. 348; quoting Benjamin Franklin.

Index